MW00809014

CrossCurrents

To Louise,
May God bless you!

Harry Tremosthe

CROSSCURRENTS

MAKING SENSE OF THE CHRISTIAN LIFE

HARRY JAMES FOX

FOXWARE PUBLISHING LLC

LAS CRUCES, NEW MEXICO

CrossCurrents: Making Sense of the Christian Life
Copyright © 2013 by Harry James Fox.

Published by Foxware Publishing LLC, 1156 Cave Springs Trail, Las Cruces, NM 88011.

All rights reserved, including the right to reproduce this book, or portions thereof, in any form. Except for brief quotations in books, articles, and critical reviews, no part of this text may be reproduced, transmitted, downloaded, decompiled, reverse engineered, or stored in or introduced into any information storage and retrieval system, in any form or by any means, whether electronic or mechanical, without the express written permission of the author, except as provided by USA copyright law. The scanning, uploading, and distribution of this book via the Internet or via any other means without the permission of the publisher is illegal and punishable by law. Please purchase only authorized electronic editions, and do not participate in or encourage electronic piracy of copyrighted materials. The publisher does not have any control over and does not assume any responsibility for author or third-party websites or their content.

Quotes from pp. viii, 58, 84, 89-90, 110 [420 words] from *Love Wins* by Rob Bell. Copyright © 2011 by Robert H. Bell Jr. Trust. Reprinted by permission of HarperCollins Publishers. Scripture quotations marked (HCSB) are taken from the Holman Christian Standard Bible ®, Copyright © 1999, 2000, 2002, 2003, 2009 by Holman Bible Publishers. Used by permission. Holman Christian Standard Bible ®, Holman CSB ®, and HCSB ® are federally registered trademarks of Holman Bible Publishers. Scripture quotations marked (NIV) are taken from the Holy Bible, New International Version®, NIV®. Copyright © 1973, 1978, 1984, 2011 by Biblica, Inc.™ Used by permission of Zondervan. All rights reserved worldwide. www.zondervan.com The "NIV" and "New International Version" are trade-marks registered in the United States Patent and Trademark Office by Biblica, Inc.™ Scripture references marked (KJV) are taken from *The Authorized, King James Version, The Holy Bible*. Quotations from *Salvation and Security: A Molinist Approach* Copyright © 2010 by Kenneth Keathley. Used by permission. Quotations from *Reasonable Faith* website are Copyright © William Lane Craig, used by permission.

Editing by Julie C. Belding www.simplyediting.net
Cover by Cal Sharp www.caligraphics.net Image © Gautier Willaume Dreamstime.com
Image Credit: James Overduin. Used courtesy of the Gravity Probe B Image and media archive, Stanford University, Stanford California, U.S.A.

Cataloging information
Dewey Decimal Classification 234
ISBN-13 978-1-62620-226-9
Library of Congress Control Number: 2012923449
Printed in the United States of America.
10 9 8 7 6 5 4 3 2 1

TO

BILL AND LYN HYDE

Turning and turning in the widening gyre
The falcon cannot hear the falconer;
Things fall apart; the centre cannot hold;
Mere anarchy is loosed upon the world,
The blood-dimmed tide is loosed, and everywhere
The ceremony of innocence is drowned;
The best lack all conviction, while the worst
Are full of passionate intensity.

— WILLIAM BUTLER YEATS

CONTENTS

Preface

This book is written to Christians. By "Christians" I mean more than those who simply give themselves that label. That might seem strange at first glance—even presumptuous. After all, if people say they are Christians, who am I to say they are not? That's a fair question, especially since I claim no ability to peer into the human soul. Furthermore, I have the impression that with most world religions, self-identification is enough. But my target audience are those who do more than intellectually agree with most (or even all) of the truth claims of Christianity. I identify as "Christians" those who have a living relationship with Jesus of Nazareth, the Son of the Living God, and who have accepted him as Savior and Lord. If you belong to that group, this book is for you.

For readers who do not fit that category, may I say that you too are welcome to read what I have written. I sincerely hope you will find it useful, although candidly, it may be tough-going in places. I have a mental picture of my readers as I write, and I may skip over certain details in the expectation that I can go directly to the heart of the matter and not always bother with tediously building from the fundamentals. I will offer suggestions for other reading if I think this would help. I'll introduce many an issue by naming a book that helped bring that issue to the attention of the Christian community. Most of these books would be available in any public library (possibly through inter-library loan), and it might be helpful to at least browse them to get a first-hand idea of what their authors are trying to say. For those who don't wish to take the time to do that, I will summarize their main points.

What I have written is not an apologetic. It doesn't try to prove the existence of God. It is not designed to show why Christianity is superior to other religions or to show where other religions or worldviews are inadequate. It certainly doesn't try to show why one Christian denomination is better than another. I assume my readers have already sorted through such issues and have been persuaded that the truths of Christianity are exactly that: truths. Excellent books are available that defend Christianity against other faiths, philosophies and world views and some of these are listed in the bibliography.

Having said what this work is not, perhaps I should say what it is and to do that requires some self-disclosure. I am an American, born in Colorado, and raised as a Baptist. My wife, Carroll, and I have been members of Baptist churches affiliated with the Southern Baptist Convention since 1974. I accept the label "born again," since I accepted Jesus Christ as my Savior when I was seven years old. Carroll and I were missionaries with the Southern Baptist Convention's Foreign Mission Board[1] for two and a half years in the Philippines and one year in Thailand. In 1998 I was ordained to the gospel ministry by Jerusalem Baptist Church of Fairfax Station, Virginia.

Over the years, we have observed the growth of crosscurrents within Western culture and within the Christian community that have torn at (and sometimes helped to shore up) the foundations of the Christian faith. We have been forced to deal with these as best we could. Some of them were in the form of popular books that challenged precious truths of Christianity. Others were novels that covertly sought to cast doubt on the credibility of beloved Christian teachings. Still others were new teachings, brought forward by popular pastors or church leaders, which threatened to water down Christianity and accommodate its teachings to an increasingly secular world. On the other hand, there have been positive influences on our Christian walk, and I shall also mention some of these.

In the following pages I will identify some fairly recent books, suggest why they may be significant, and provide a strategy that has helped Carroll and me (and Christians like us) to brave the contrary currents of this age. Although some of these books and their issues are no longer front-page news, they still merit close attention. Other issues (though the books may not be particularly recent) are just in the formative stages and thus not well known by most faithful Christians. They all have the potential to be a source of either support or confusion to believers of all denominations, their children and grandchildren.

---

[1] Now called "International Mission Board."

A final note. I am a Baptist and have remained one simply because I believe this denomination best reflects my understanding of the teachings found in God's Word, the Bible. There are many other worthy denominations, of course, as well as many splendid non-denominational churches. My vocabulary and worldview accord with those of the evangelical community. For those of you (such as Roman Catholic or Greek Orthodox) who do not fit that description, I do not think these discussions belabor the distinctive doctrinal differences that divide us. You need not fear that I want to seduce you into giving up the form of Christianity that is most pleasing to you. The dangers that concern me should also concern you. The threats to my faith are threats to yours too. Finally, I trust that my attempt to expose errors and present a correct Christian answer to them will be helpful to all true Christians, whatever their denominational label.

CHAPTER 1
†

Well-Meaning Error

Book: *When Bad Things Happen to Good People* by Harold S. Kushner.[2]

Issue: How can an all-powerful and all-loving God allow suffering?

In the late 1970s, my wife, Carroll, and I were the parents of two young sons, Tim and Mark, and were ourselves young in the Lord. We had been around long enough, though, that we were no longer starry-eyed novices. We realized that not every new book about God was necessarily based on the Bible nor did it always deepen our understanding of God or his plan and purpose for our lives.

1. CROSSCURRENTS MAKE US UNEASY!

Even our home church was not without strong currents that pulled us this way and that. Some of our friends went deep into Reformed theology and left our church because it did not adhere to the five points of Calvinism. A youth pastor caused us great concern because he believed a baby was not truly alive until it received "the breath of life" at birth. He was teaching that abortion was not necessarily wrong. This denial of the sanctity of unborn life caused a huge uproar. We sometimes felt that

---

[2] Kushner, Harold S. *When Bad Things Happen to Good People.* 2001. Schocken Books, New York.

holding on to the true faith was like a lumberjack balancing on a log in the millpond.

The federal government transferred us to Nevada in 1979, and we made the move across the country in the spring of that year. About one year later I joined a group of about fifteen federal employees of the Bureau of Land Management to float rafts down the East Fork of the Carson river. Tom, our district recreation specialist, had organized the outing. I was the senior person on the trip, but I left everything in Tom's hands since I had never before been on the river.

We had a wonderful time. The weather was perfect, and we put three rafts in at a point where we could experience some of the moderately difficult rapids and have an enjoyable trip. Tom gave a safety briefing which ended with an instruction about the take-out point. He said that in case the rafts got separated, we should all be on the lookout for a sign on the right bank that said: "Take-Out Point—1/4 Mile." At that point, we should head for the right bank and pull out at another sign that simply said, "Take Out."

We had fun learning how to steer the heavy rafts through white water without tipping over. Our raft stayed upright, but one other was not so fortunate. We all had some fun at our damp friends' expense, before stopping for lunch in a cove. Afterwards we walked up a side canyon where there was a hot spring which included a waterfall. We all enjoyed a natural hot shower under azure skies, against a background of russet-brown Ponderosa pines. Then we returned to the rafts to continue the trip. Now it was smoother—mostly a paddle and drift experience.

Our raft, for some reason, gained on the others, and we were probably six or seven hundred yards in the lead when we saw the sign we'd been looking for. Some of the people in our raft grumbled because they didn't want the trip to be over. I said we had to take out as we'd been told to do so. The other two rafts soon joined us, and we had them out of the water within minutes. Soon afterwards the trucks showed up. We loaded on the rafts and started the drive back to Carson City.

About a mile down from the take-out point, Tom flagged us all down near a forty-foot high waterfall created by the Ruhenstroth Dam. In his briefing he explained that once in a while, rafts went over the waterfall and the rafters drowned. The force of the plunging water held them under, despite their life jackets.

I almost fell over. Thinking that everyone knew about the waterfall, Tom had overlooked telling us why we shouldn't go past the take-out point, but none of us in my raft knew the waterfall was there. I had actually considered, for a brief moment, ignoring Tom's instructions. Even though I had been tempted, and even though I had not seen any strong reason to do what Tom had said, I had resisted the temptation to do as I pleased. It had been a good decision! It might have saved our lives.

Sometimes it's the crosscurrents of life that cause us problems. Some new way of thinking about God can arise and throw us altogether off course. It was a crosscurrent that overturned one raft in the white water. At least in white water the danger is obvious. But where the water is slow, a side current can nudge us into the wrong channel and cause big problems even when we sense no danger. Finally, we can sometimes drift into mortal danger by simply going with the flow. Just because the river current and everything floating on it are all going in the same direction, this doesn't mean it is safe. It could be leading us to a waterfall. Fortunately, God usually arranges circumstances so that we have some warning. If we heed the Holy Spirit, we can be sure of leaving the dangerous waters at the take-out point he has set up for that purpose.

2. WHY DOES GOD LET US HURT?

In 1978 a rabbi named Harold S. Kushner, from a small New England town, published a little book. It became a publishing sensation and went on to become an international best-seller and a classic. It has sold more than four million copies. Kushner was gut-wrenchingly honest in dealing with the pain caused by the death of his young son, Aaron. His search for meaning and answers reflects much of the human condition, and millions have found comfort in his message. Strangely, even though the answers Kushner gave revealed a God that was quite different from what most of learned from our religious teachers, people didn't seem to mind. In this account of a loving father's quest for meaning, they sensed their own search. The doubts and fears expressed in the book were doubts and fears they had felt also. The book was *authentic*, and it accurately showed why many conventional expressions of sympathy were anything but comforting.

Kushner was correct in saying that grieving people were often beset with well-intentioned but muddle-headed platitudes that did more harm than good. Imagine a young woman who has lost a child and is told, "God took the little one because he needed him to tend heaven's gardens." The grieving mother is going to hear "God took" as a selfish and cruel act. She might say, bitterly, "Why? Doesn't God have plenty of children up there already? Why couldn't he leave me mine?" The idea that God took someone because he needed him in heaven is neither comforting nor helpful. And it certainly is not scriptural.

Another unhelpful idea is the old saying, "Only the good die young." No parent is going to feel joy when someone suggests it is a wonderful thing that their child is now free from the pain and troubles of this life. One can imagine them thinking, "If you think it's so wonderful, it's a real pity it was not *your* child who died." Related to that is the comment: "Trials make you stronger. God sent this trial to deepen your faith." Anyone struggling with grief is likely to hear that as: "If only you had deeper faith or if you were stronger, your loved one would not have needed to die." Now guilt is added to their grief.

Perhaps the suggestion that offended Kushner most, however, was the one that the loved one was taken by God as punishment. Either way, whether the punishment was aimed at the dead or whether the person's death was a punishment to the living, it seemed an unlikely idea to Kushner and yet a common one. He mentioned cases where parents had neglected a religious tradition[3] and believed that the loss of a family member was because God was punishing them. He deplored this all-too-common view because, again, guilt was piled upon grief.[4]

In dealing with his own grief from the loss of his son and helping members of his congregation who were bereaved, Kushner began thinking about God and the problem of evil. He rejected the concept that suffering was always due to sin or to someone failing to do some religious duty. He could not accept that God killed people so they could go to a better place. Then he began to consider more involved explanations, all of which he found to be inadequate:

1. God has a hidden purpose in suffering, but we do not know enough to understand what it is.
2. God uses suffering to result in a greater good.
3. God has a comprehensive and perfect plan for the universe, even though it creates pain in the lives of people.
4. Suffering exists to teach a lesson, either to the sufferer or to observers or both.
5. Suffering is a test of our faith.[5]

Kushner was not interested in the idea that God will "wipe the tears from our eyes" in heaven, or that he will balance the cosmic scales of justice in another life. He was interested in a reasonable explanation in *this* life. He suspected that many of these explanations for the conditions we experienced were based more on a desire to defend God than anything else. He did not see that they were meant to help the sufferer.[6] Nevertheless, there is good reason to mount a defense of God since the

---

[3] He never explained what tradition was involved.

[4] In Luke 13:1–4 Jesus said that those suffering tragedies were not necessarily more sinful than those that were spared.

[5] Kushner, Harold S. *op. cit.,* See Chapter 1 for a discussion of all these explanations.

[6] *Ibid.,* p. 33.

presence of evil is often used to call his character into question. Such a defense is called a *theodicy*.

3. DEFENDING GOD: THEODICIES.

If a theodicy is a defense of God and tries to explain the existence of evil, what was wrong with the explanations Kushner rejected? To answer that, let us first look at the problem as it is usually presented. C. S. Lewis put the issue this way:

> "If God were good, He would wish to make his creatures perfectly happy, and if God were almighty, He would be able to do what He wished. But the creatures are not happy. Therefore God lacks either goodness or power, or both." This is the problem of pain, in its simplest form.[7]

C. S. Lewis presented a thoughtful and quite satisfactory answer to the pain problem in his classic book,[8] but Kushner did not want to follow his lead. The reason he went another way, it seems to me, had little to do with the fact that Lewis was a Christian and Kushner a Jew. Kushner did not discuss theology as a theologian might, with technical terms and legions of footnotes. Even so, many have concluded he was influenced by a philosophical/theological system called *process theology*. I will have more to say about process theology below,[9] and need not go into the matter now. Kushner was not inclined to believe God had a plan for the future, since process theology denies this as a possibility. Process theology does not see God as all-knowing (*omniscient*) or all-powerful (*omnipotent*) either.

---

[7] Lewis, C. S. *The Problem of Pain: The Intellectual Problem Raised by Human Suffering, Examined With Sympathy and Realism.* 1962. Macmillan,New York. p. 26.

[8] Lewis noted that not even God can do logically impossible things. It seems likely that to create creatures which are free, but which always choose good, is logically impossible. If so, then free creatures necessarily means the possibility of evil. So we might imagine a world without pain, but we can't be sure that it is logically possible. See *Ibid.*, Chapter 2.

[9] See Chapters 6 and 7.

Kushner finally concluded that one of these three things must be true about God: (1) he is not omnipotent, (2) he is not omniscient, or (3) he is not loving. He finally decided God was not all-powerful, since this was the least bad of the alternatives. He presented a *weakness of God* solution, presenting a God who was trying his best but could not prevent all evil from happening. He derived this idea from a sadly mistaken understanding of the book of Job, concluding the author was saying God was not all-powerful:

> Let me suggest that the author of the Book of Job takes the position which neither Job nor his friends take. He believes in God's goodness and in Job's goodness, and is prepared to give up his belief in proposition (A): that God is all-powerful.[10]

We read his book and immediately saw that Kushner was casting away one of God's precious attributes. Without God being all-powerful, how do we know he is really sovereign over the universe? How do we know good will triumph? How do we know God can keep his promises? Certainly, this idea removes any sense of purpose and nobility in suffering—it is all just a ghastly mistake—but we could not see how this book was at all encouraging. We were looking at the logical consequences of Kushner's ideas, not so much at how they were presented. Apparently a large number did not read the book that way.

Many people heard the emotional content of the book. Irrespective of the exact words, they heard such ideas as: "God is crazy about you. He hurts when you hurt. He is on your side. He is not trying to catch you doing something wrong so he can punish you. He did not want, nor did he cause, your loss. He cares. He offers sympathy. He feels your pain."[11] People connected—they understood this at a deep, emotional level. So what if some of his ideas about God sounded strange? So what if the readers tuned out some of the "why" explanations? Maybe the readers were less concerned about what the

---

[10] Kushner, Harold S. *op. cit.,* pp. 41–42.

[11] None of these impressions are quotations from the book.

book taught and more concerned about how the book made them feel. They felt comforted.

In the preface, Kushner mentioned his surprise when he learned of a Baptist pastor who gave copies of the book to his flock. He could not understand why, since he was sure his theology would be different from that of the pastor or the members of his church. He also mentioned a convent of Roman Catholic nuns who said they were not sure they agreed with his theology but gave out four or five copies of the book every week to help people "feel better."[12] I think we can understand Kushner's confusion. Why would people give out a book that had serious doctrinal errors, even if it were somehow comforting?

4. ANOTHER KIND OF COMFORT

When Carroll and I were missionaries in the Philippines, we lived quite near another missionary couple named Bill and Lyn Hyde. They were a remarkable team and were making a powerful impact for God's kingdom on the island of Mindanao. During our years there, I met with Bill on an average of once a week. He was a big, hearty, engaging fellow, with years of wisdom gained through service to his Lord. One of the things he told me, that I had never thought about before, was the impact of Christian music. "Nearly all the theology that average believers learn," he said, "they learn from the hymns they sing." This concept was difficult at first, but I finally concluded there was much wisdom in it.

Perhaps the thoughts Bill shared with me took on added significance when we learned to our sorrow that he had been martyred. We were serving in Thailand when we first heard on March 4, 2003, that Bill had been wounded by a Muslim terrorist bomb. Within minutes we learned from a second telephone call that he had died, and another friend, Barbara Stevens, and her two children were also wounded. Twenty more Filipinos died in the blast, which was at an

---

[12] Kushner, Harold S. *op. cit.,* Preface. pp. x–xi.

outdoor waiting area at the Davao City Airport.[13] Carroll and I had met flights there many times and knew it well. Our sense of grief and loss was profound.

I agree with part of the message of Kushner's book. I think God did love Bill and Lyn, but I disagree with Kushner's answer that God was not able to stop the tragedy, even though he was also grieved by it. I don't think the blast took God by surprise. I think God had known since before the foundation of the world what would happen that day. Just as God knew that Bill's Lord would be betrayed by Judas and sent to the cross, God knew the Muslim bomber would murder Bill and the others. So Bill was martyred as God had foreknown, and we who are left behind can know for certain he did not die in vain. "Precious in the sight of the Lord is the death of his saints."[14] Bill and the others did not die because God's arm was too weak, or his foresight failed. Bill went to be with the Lord that March day because it was part of God's perfect plan of the ages. Finally, we know that Bill was on the right side. God will ultimately defeat evil and will wipe the tears from every eye that sees heaven.[15]

Bill's words remind me it is not wise to hand out a book that teaches error about who God is, even if it makes people feel better. Many people wrongly think there will be no time in heaven. Wayne Grudem, in his book on systematic theology, had to carefully explain that there has to be time there, in the sense that we will experience one moment after another, but we will experience it forever.[16] Where do people get the false idea that heaven will be timeless? They get the idea, at least in part, from the beautiful hymn that says: "When the trumpet of the Lord shall sound, and time shall be no more ..."[17] We

---

[13] Accessed 20 August 2012, from http://bpnews.net/bpnews.asp?id=15357.

[14] Psalm 116:15 (KJV)

[15] See Revelation 20–22.

[16] Grudem, Wayne, *Systematic Theology: An Introduction to Biblical Doctrine,* 1994. Glossary, 2000. Zondervan, Grand Rapids, MI, p. 1162.

[17] The hymn is: *When the Roll is Called Up Yonder.* Words and music by James M. Black.

learn from these hymns, even if sometimes we seem to be singing them without appreciating their meaning. People who read Kushner's books would retain something of Kushner's theology. And that would be a bad thing.

FURTHER READING

Phillips, W. Gary and William E. Brown. *Making Sense of Your World from a Biblical Viewpoint.* Chicago: Moody Bible Institute. 1991.

Lewis, C. S. *The Problem of Pain: The Intellectual Problem Raised by Human Suffering, Examined With Sympathy and Realism.* New York: Macmillan. 1962.

DISCUSSION QUESTIONS

1. How do we account for the problem of evil in the world? Does Christianity have an answer?

2. Do you think we must conclude that God is not all-powerful?

3. Why do you think that Kushner's book was so powerful? Why was his solution so widely accepted?

4. What is your source of answers when you face life's difficult questions?

5. Do you see God's ultimate triumph over evil as a comfort in this lifetime?

CHAPTER 2
†

A Needed Correction
Decline of the West

Books: *How Should We Then Live?*[18] and *The Great Evangelical Disaster*[19]
  by Francis A. Schaeffer
Issue: Will Christians join Western culture in its decline?

Carroll and I, like most young Christians of our generation, were
tugged in various directions by conflicting voices in the public
square. Some books, and the philosophies they represented, were negative.
We have seen how the hugely popular book, *When Bad Things Happen
to Good People*, seemed to give comfort to many grieving people, at the
cost of offering them a diminished concept of God. Still, not all influences were negative.

1. THE WATERS BECOME MORE CHOPPY

Carroll and I attended a seminar put on by Bill Gothard, called *Basic Youth
Conflicts*.[20] We were challenged by the concepts he taught, but challenged

---

[18] Schaeffer, Francis A. *How Should We Then Live? The Rise and Decline of
Western Thought and Culture.* 1976. Fleming H. Revell, Old Tappan, New
Jersey.
[19] Schaeffer, Francis A. *The Great Evangelical Disaster.* 1984. Crossway Books.
Westchester, IL.
[20] See *Wikipedia, The Free Encyclopedia.* "Bill Gothard." From http://
en.wikipedia.org/wiki/Bill_Gothard.

even more by the vision that it was possible to live lives based on the principles set forth in the Bible. Not only was it possible, Gothard said, but this kind of life was the only one that had meaning and purpose. We had never before heard teaching like his that advocated home schooling of children. We were also confronted by the idea that American "dating" was a terrible system, which should be replaced by *courtship* where young couples respected the authority of their parents. Gothard has been criticized through the years, and perhaps some of the criticism is justified, but we found his ministry helpful at that time in our lives. A life verse we adopted was (and is): "All Scripture is given by inspiration of God, and is profitable for doctrine, for reproof, for correction, for instruction in righteousness: That the man of God may be perfect, thoroughly furnished to all good works."[21]

We also became more concerned about the growing wave of abortion that was sweeping the nation. When the Supreme Court Decision *Roe v. Wade*[22] was issued in January 1973, we didn't take much notice. We were dismayed, of course, but didn't foresee the full horror of the ruling; neither the implacable way in which it would be implemented nor the number of lives that would be lost.[23]

"It should be between a woman and her doctor," they said. At first I had naively believed this principle would afford protection for the unborn. Surely, I reasoned, no doctor who had taken the Hippocratic Oath could ever agree to an abortion except in the most extreme circumstance. As the years went by, however, it became obvious that my faith in the medical community had been misplaced. America had abortion, on demand, for any reason or for no reason at all. A live puppy had more protection

---

[21] 2 Timothy 3:16–17 (KJV) We believe the Bible is inerrant and God's Word to us.

[22] See 410 U.S. 113 (1973).

[23] Now nearly 55 million. See Christian Life Resources: U.S. Abortion Statistics By Year (1973–Current). Accessed 20 August 2012, from http://www.christianliferesources.com/article/u-s-abortion-statistics-by-year-1973-current-1042.

in our country than an unborn human baby did, if the baby's mother wanted him or her dead.

It became more and more clear that something was amiss in our culture. School prayer had been forbidden by the Supreme Court in 1962.[24] We were seeing an alienation of young people (only a few years younger than we were), with an explosion of drug abuse, promiscuous sex, disrespect for authority, and civil disobedience. The divorce rate skyrocketed, and more and more couples were moving in together without marriage. We could see a cheapening of values in the media, with films that would have been considered pornographic only a few years earlier, now being shown at our local movie theater. We discussed these problems with our Christian friends and occasionally heard a sermon that touched on them, but we did not seem to be able to articulate precisely what was wrong.

All that changed when in 1976 Francis A. Schaeffer published his insightful book, *How Should We Then Live?*[25] Schaeffer, in a mere 288 pages, swept across the entire field of Western civilization. He began with the Roman Empire (and the first Christians) and discussed the Middle Ages, the Renaissance, the Reformation, the Enlightenment, and the rise of modern science. Then he began to trace a long period of decline, discussing the breakdown in science, modern philosophy and theology, as well as modern art forms. Schaeffer's was a devastating assessment of contemporary society. He seemed to be saying we had gained an incomparable treasure in the Reformation by recovering much of the apostolic Christian faith of the early Church. That treasure had served the West well and was a major reason for its spectacular advance. He showed that the West had abandoned the Reformation base which had created its greatness and now had no firm base at all.

Finally, we had a coherent and well-articulated explanation of what we could see happening with our own eyes. Schaeffer had given a unified concept and a vocabulary to discuss it with. It was this book that helped

---

[24] *Wikipedia—The Free Encyclopedia.* "School Prayer." Accessed 20 August 2012, from http://en.wikipedia.org/wiki/School_prayer.
[25] Cited above.

me understand what a *worldview* was. I learned that our thought life, our presuppositions and our value system determined how we acted. That comprised our worldview, and the worldview of Americans[26] in the 1970s had been degraded and cheapened. He said we had only two impoverished values left: personal peace and affluence.[27] He went on to explain that *personal peace* meant to be left alone to control one's own destiny; while *affluence* meant to have ever-increasing prosperity, an abundance of material goods. We understood that we could no longer expect our culture to reinforce Christian values. We could even expect the culture to be hostile to us and our faith.

Schaeffer's book was accompanied by a film series, which had a great impact. It sold forty thousand copies in its first three months and in 1979 was still selling 1500 copies per month. No doubt its influence has been long-lasting. Some credit Schaeffer with galvanizing an effective opposition to abortion in the United States.[28] Schaeffer briefly mentioned theology and how theologians had been infected with humanism and existentialism. He was grieved that theological liberals had abandoned any belief in the supernatural, which left little, if any, belief in a "historical" Jesus. He said these liberal streams of theology were heading toward a dead end,[29] but he did not dwell on these points.

Schaeffer, with his comprehensive overview of Western culture and portrayal of its self-destruction, did not at first address issues related specifically to evangelical Christianity. He took on those issues in a subsequent book titled *The Great Evangelical Disaster*.[30] This book came out in 1984 and pointed out a disturbing trend. Evangelical Christians were also accommodating themselves to Western culture—the same culture that was deteriorating before their eyes.

---

[26] This is true of all Western culture, for that matter.

[27] Schaeffer, Francis A. *How Should We Then Live?* p. 205.

[28] Denis Haack, "Francis August Schaeffer, RIP," *National Review*, 15 June 1984, 20.

[29] Schaeffer, *How Should We Then Live? op. cit.*, pp. 174–181.

[30] Cited above.

The crucial issue facing evangelical Christians,[31] according to Schaeffer, was the issue of biblical inspiration and authority. He noted that until relatively recent times, a belief in the inerrancy of Scripture was part of the common faith of all Christians. He said:

> There are two reasons in our day for holding to a strong uncompromising view of Scripture. First and foremost, this is the only way to be faithful to what the Bible teaches about itself, to what Christ teaches about Scripture, and to what the church has consistently held through the ages. This should be reason enough in itself. But today there is a second reason why we should hold to a strong, uncompromising view of Scripture. There are hard days ahead of us—for ourselves and for our spiritual and physical children. And without a strong view of Scripture as a foundation, we will not be ready for the hard days to come. … Our spiritual and physical children will be left with the ground cut out from under them, with no foundation upon which to build their faith or their lives.[32]

2. SCHAEFFER'S WARNING COMES TRUE

Carroll and I had been blindsided by this very problem and had seen it attack our personal ministry. We were living in central Nevada, in a small mining town named Battle Mountain. Our church was also small and struggling, but the members had a robust faith that came from being Christian witnesses in a largely secular culture. The local people were hard-working, but many had no ties to the community. They were there to work a few years in the mine and then go back to wherever they came from with enough of a nest egg to make a new start. At least, that seemed to be a common plan. The town had two legal houses of prostitution,

---

[31] Schaeffer uses the term "evangelical Christian" to mean Bible-believing Christianity as opposed to the various kinds of liberal theology. It carries the idea of leading people to Christ, as well as engaging the culture. He did not say so, but, by implication, the term is restricted to Protestants. Roman Catholics, no matter how conservative they might be theologically, are not termed "evangelical," nor would they accept such identification. See Schaeffer, *The Great Evangelical Disaster. op. cit.*, pp. 96–97.

[32] *Ibid.*, pp. 46–47.

which did nothing to raise the spiritual tone. The pastors at our church (we had several during our time there) were all godly men who preached the word fearlessly, and the flock was certainly evangelical. We believed the Bible to be true, without error. But we needed all the help we could get.

One late summer day we received our order from the Sunday School Board of our denomination. The Fall Bible Study was to be on the book of Isaiah, and it turned out not to be helpful. When a couple of other teachers and I looked at the material, we noticed the introduction which said that Isaiah was not written by one person. It stated that part of the book (the part that prophesied the seventy-year captivity, the return to the land, and the name of King Cyrus) was written by someone else called Deutero-Isaiah. It strongly implied that the prophecies were not really prophecies at all. We were incensed. It wouldn't have been so bad had the study material said something like this, "Some scholars believe parts of the book were written by another whom they call Deutero-Isaiah." Unfortunately, this material did not use any such accommodating language. It was not given as a high probability or even a hypothetical possibility. Deutero-Isaiah was given as certain, and the tone was that the reader had better get used to the idea, because that was how it was.

We did not have to get used to the idea. We threw the entire lesson, all the copies for the entire church, into the trash can. Then we wrote to the Sunday School Board and said we never wanted to see anything like this liberal tract, ever again.[33] We never got a response, but this incident warned us that even in our conservative denomination, the Southern Baptist Convention (SBC), there were people who had been influenced by liberal views, and they were becoming bold enough to proclaim it and for us to notice it, even in far-off Nevada. Francis Schaeffer had predicted the problem, and it became more acute as the decade of the 1980s progressed.

I would like to clarify one thing before I discuss the upheaval faced by our denomination. While the controversy involved theological liberals, I realize that their numbers were relatively few. That term would not fit

---

[33] We mentioned John 12:37–39, which quotes from both "parts" of Isaiah and then says that the author of both parts was "Isaiah." We did not think the Apostle John had made a mistake.

the majority of those on either side of the controversy. It is also plain that the struggle was ugly: both sides had valid concerns, and both sides can justly be criticized. I mention the conflict only as an example of how a loss of focus on the inerrancy of Scripture can yield the most unfortunate results. Because this issue is so foundational, it strikes at the roots of every part of the Christian life, just as Schaeffer insisted. If Christians cannot agree that the Bible is totally trustworthy, then they have little basis for cooperation or fellowship.

We later learned that within the SBC, theological liberals had become influential within most of the seminaries and other institutions, without that fact becoming widely known by the Baptist churches that comprised the convention. Most members of these churches were, and are, theologically conservative. This fact opened the door to a simple but highly effective strategy. Conservatives simply used their numerical strength to elect presidents of the SBC, who used their power to appoint conservatives to leadership positions within SBC institutions. These new leaders then removed SBC seminary teachers and other employees who did not affirm a theologically conservative doctrinal position. The 1979 SBC meeting revealed that the major doctrinal controversy centered on the Scriptures: whether or not they were inerrant—true without any error. The new direction for SBC made it plain that denominational employees would no longer be welcome if they believed the Bible contained errors. Over time, the leaders and employees of the SBC became much more reflective of the conservative theology of the individual church members. The tilt toward liberal theology had been arrested.

It was nevertheless true that our church's concern (Sunday School literature that reflected theologically liberal views) was not immediately fixed. We did notice that teaching material gradually shifted to reflect conservative views. Ten years later, in 1991, Lloyd Elder, president of the Sunday School Board, resigned. About 159 other employees retired, some voluntarily, in November of that year. Since that time we have noted no further theological difficulties with Sunday School literature.

David Beale has written about the roots of the problem within the SBC and attributed it to the seminaries themselves. He quoted an MDiv thesis that studied Southern Baptist Theological Seminary students, the findings of which "generally indicate that Southern Seminary does not produce faith. It destroys it. A look at just the Master of Divinity students alone suggests the following: Nine percent lost their faith in the existence of God while in seminary; twenty-four percent lost their faith in Jesus as the divine Son of God." The study added that 47 percent of PhD and ThM students no longer believed in the afterlife by the time they obtained a degree.[34]

Admittedly, these newly-minted graduates were in a difficult position. Unless they adopted neo-orthodox, liberal views, they could be assured they had little chance of being selected to the faculty of a SBC seminary. On the other hand, they needed to keep these views to themselves if they wished to be called as pastors of SBC churches. C. S. Lewis spoke of this need to hide liberal views from the congregation. He advised liberal ministers:

> ... it would hardly do to tell them what you really believe. A theology which denies the historicity of nearly everything in the Gospels to which Christian life and affections and thought have been fastened for nearly two millennia ... if offered to the uneducated man it can produce only one or other of two effects. It will make him a Roman Catholic or an atheist. What you offer him he will not recognize as Christianity. If he holds to what he calls Christianity he will leave a church in which it is no longer taught and look for one where it is. If he agrees with your version he will no longer call himself a Christian and no longer come to church.[35]

After the turnaround in the SBC, the situation was at least consistent. Neo-orthodox, liberal views were not welcome in the SBC seminaries any more than they were in the congregations. Young

[34] Beale, David O. *S. B. C. House on the Sand?: Critical Issues for Southern Baptists*. 1985. BJU Press, Greenville, SC. p. 45.

[35] Lewis, C. S. *The Seeing Eye and Other Selected Essays From Christian Reflections*. 1967. Ballantine Books, New York. pp. 204–205.

seminary students were no longer under tremendous pressure to renounce their convictions. Sadly, though, not all was well, as we were to learn.

One characteristic of the federal Civil Service, as we experienced it, was frequent moves. In the early 1990s we found ourselves in northern Virginia and were worshiping in a small Baptist church in fellowship with the SBC. By that time, the problems of theological drift on the part of the SBC were well in hand. However, we quickly found out that the state convention, the Baptist General Association of Virginia (BGAV), had not reformed. We were told that the Baptist Theological Seminary at Richmond continued to harbor liberal professors that were the image of what C. S. Lewis mentioned above—denying the historicity of the Gospels in almost every conceivable way. The BGAV leadership, it seemed, was in profound opposition to the new direction of the SBC and, being independent, was free to chart its own course.

I attended the annual state convention of the BGAV as a messenger (or voting delegate) from our church. Once at the meeting, it became plain the gathering was formed into two camps: one liberal (they preferred to be called "moderate") and the other conservative. It also became plain that the moderates had the votes. Every issue put forward by the moderates was approved by a sixty-forty vote. Every issue put forward by the conservatives was defeated by a forty-sixty vote. The moderates were in control and uncompromising. I had attended with one simple idea and that was to have the BGAV put a Right-to-Life Sunday on the calendar for the next year—to call upon churches to pray against the deaths of the unborn and the pain that abortion causes. It was voted down, sixty-forty. No prayer against abortion.

To say I was surprised would be to put it mildly. I asked if it could be possible that 60 percent of Baptists in Virginia were opposed to prayer about the abortion issue. My friends told me, "No, of course not. Probably more than 90 percent of Baptists in the BGAV would support setting aside a Sunday to reflect upon the evils of abortion."

I asked how it could be voted down in the annual meeting if that were the case. They replied: "The congregations back home don't know what's going on here. Many of the pastors were trained in liberal seminaries like Richmond. They hand-pick messengers and when they get here they vote to support the liberal party line." I left the meeting discouraged and could see no spirit of compromise on the part of either the moderates or the conservatives. In 1996 a number of churches left the BGAV to form a new conservative SBC association in Virginia, called the "Southern Baptist Conservatives of Virginia."[36]

And what about the Baptist Theological Seminary at Richmond? Apparently it has continued its liberal drift from neo-orthodoxy to whatever theme seems trendy. A 2006 Baptist Press article quoted a dean of theology, Russell Moore, as saying that the seminary at Richmond, and a number of similar institutions, had a complete lack of accountability. He said: "The schools have become a haunt for every liberal fad imaginable: pluralism, inclusivism, feminism, process theology, liberation theologies and so forth."[37]

Francis Schaeffer's words were prophetic. If it had not been for the conservative resurgence, all SBC seminaries would now be slipping into liberalism. The warning to other evangelical Christians is clear. Christians must stand up for conservative theology, including a high view of Scripture. Without that, the churches will decline right along with the culture.

---

[36] Pinckney, T. C. "We Have a New State Convention!" *The Baptist Banner*, Vol. IX, No. 8, September 1996.

[37] Tomlin, Gregory. *SBC, CBF Seminaries Differ in Educational Approach, Profs Say*. Posted August 11, 2006. Baptist Press. Accessed 20 August 2012, from http://www.bpnews.net/bpnews.asp?id=23780. Also see Pinckney, T.C. "Seminary in Apostasy." *The Baptist Banner*, Vol. XIV, No. 4, April 2001.

FURTHER READING

Lindsell, Harold. *The Battle for the Bible*. Grand Rapids: Zondervan. 1976.

Lindsell, Harold. *The Bible in the Balance*. Grand Rapids: Zondervan. 1979.

Packer, J. I. *Beyond the Battle for the Bible*. Westchester: Cornerstone Books. 1980.

Geisler, Norman L. and Thomas A. Howe. *When Critics Ask: A Popular handbook on Bible Difficulties*. Wheaton: Victor Books. 1992.

DISCUSSION QUESTIONS

1. What did Schaeffer say was the cause of the deterioration of Western culture?

2. What is the pivotal danger facing evangelical Christianity, according to Schaeffer?

3. What is the responsibility of Christian churches in the face of cultural decline?

4. What is the responsibility of Christians to their society?

5. When someone says, "The Bible is full of errors," how do you respond?

CHAPTER 3
†

Conspiracy Theory

Book: *The Da Vinci Code, by Dan Brown.*
Issue: Can the Bible be trusted?

In Chapter Two, I mentioned Francis Schaeffer's observation that the arts in Western culture (including music, theater, cinema, painting, sculpture, and literature) had deteriorated and had become the enemy of common decency in general and Christianity in particular. Carroll and I now understood that no aspect of our culture could be trusted anymore and expected it would become more and more hostile to followers of Jesus Christ.

1. A PUBLIC SEDUCTION.

On October 4, 1997, I joined more than one million other men in Washington D.C. to attend a Promise Keepers rally called *Stand in the Gap: A Sacred Assembly of Men.* We spent the day in repentance and prayer for the nation. The American Bible Society gave out nearly one million New Testaments and encouraged all the men to form the habit of daily Bible study. It was a blessed time, and we all came away impressed (by the Holy Spirit) that our lives should revolve around the teachings of Scripture. It had a powerful impact for righteousness. But it did not take long for the culture to strike back.

No better example of a hostile attack can be found than the 2003 best-seller, *The Da Vinci Code*.[38] This book has reportedly sold more than 80 million copies, and that figure is several years old. It has been translated into at least forty languages. Since it mounts an anything-but-subtle attack on Christianity in general and on Catholicism in particular, it seems reasonable to take a careful look to see if any of the author's revisionist claims have a shred of merit. One thing is sure: though the book is cast in the form of an escapist adventure novel, many biblically-illiterate and historically-challenged readers are accepting the claims interwoven in the plot as factual, credible and reasonable.[39]

A reading of the novel suggests that the quality of the writing and the action-adventure plot are not adequate to explain its huge popularity. The opening chapters are well written, it must be conceded. The reader is quickly swept into a fast-paced (and far-fetched) plot and is enticed to feel sympathy for the hero and heroine, a professor of religious symbology and a female agent of the Judicial Police of Paris (who is also a cryptographer or code-breaker), respectively. The quality of the writing then deteriorates noticeably as the plot is reduced to a skeleton on which to hang a bizarre collection of feminist conspiracy theories. It then muddles on to an unbelievable and unsatisfying conclusion.

The most ludicrous of the theories is the claim that Jesus secretly married Mary Magdalene, that their descendants were secretly spirited off to France, and the Christian hierarchy had suppressed the truth to prop up the claim of Jesus' deity. This is bad enough, but it gets even more unbelievable. A secret society, "The Priory of Sion," had supposedly preserved the secret (and Mary's mummified body) all these years. Leonardo da Vinci was a member of the society and had hidden clues about these secrets in his paintings (thus the title). A second secret (Catholic) society called "Opus Dei" had supposedly been aware of all this and had been trying to kill the leadership of the Priory of Sion to obtain their secret documents.

---

[38] Brown, Dan. *The Da Vinci Code*. 2003. Anchor Books, New York.

[39] There is a movie by the same name, starring Tom Hanks.

Many novels of this kind are replete with secret societies and conspiracy theories. But perhaps the most outrageous marketing ploy of recent times was the author's claim to have had a factual basis for the book. This follows in the grand tradition of supermarket tabloids which always claim their outrageous stores of aliens and Elvises are completely true. Apparently this sort of thing can be quite profitable. Brown's claim was a bold attempt to seduce readers into viewing Jesus Christ as a mere man and the Bible as a deeply-flawed collection of fables. He said at the beginning of the book, "All descriptions of artwork, architecture, documents, and secret rituals in this novel are accurate." This was hardly the case.

2. CHRISTIANITY ON TRIAL

Unfortunately, the book has served to reinforce negative stereotypes against Christianity. This proves once again that Christians are the last minority group that can be attacked and ridiculed in mainstream publications and still be within the bounds of political correctness. Anti-Catholic bigotry is also still alive and well, which may account for part of the book's popularity. But there is another factor which may have sparked sales. Feminist writers have filled library shelves, with particular venom directed against Christianity. This has created a receptive audience for more of the same. Part of the allure of this book seems to be that it reinforces many of these preconceived feminist notions.

An example of a feminist writer is Naomi Goldenberg, whose 1980 work included the following admission: "The feminist movement in Western culture is engaged in the slow execution of Christ and Yahweh."[40] The hostility here is evident as it is also in an earlier book by Merlin Stone: *When God Was a Woman*.[41] Like Dan Brown's book, a recurrent theme in these two works is the revisionist idea that the primordial religion of the planet was goddess worship. Judaism

---

[40] Goldenberg, Naomi. *Changing of the Gods: Feminism and the End of Traditional Religions*. 1980. Boston, Beacon Press. p. 4.

[41] Stone, Merlin. *When God Was a Woman*. 1976. Harcourt Brace, New York.

and Christianity are interlopers, they insist. That this conflicts with the testimony of Scripture bothers them not at all.

Brown, however, seems to have drawn more heavily on two other books, *The Chalice and the Blade*, by Riane Eisler,[42] and *Holy Blood, Holy Grail*.[43] Eisler, another feminist author, considered the chalice as a symbol of the feminine principle and the sword the masculine. Brown converted the chalice image to that of the Holy Grail and to Mary Magdalene. The latter book (by Michael Baigent, Richard Leigh, and Henry Lincoln) was a conspiracy theory heavily mined by Brown; so much that in 2005 Baigent and Leigh unsuccessfully sued Random House, Brown's publisher, for plagiarism.

Even members of our own family who were reared in the Catholic faith seemed to find the novel persuasive. One said, "Most rabbis in Jesus' day were married. It seems to me to be highly likely that Jesus was married, too." Then, after being shown that she was, in fact, persuaded by the book, she asked why we were so concerned.

"After all," she said dismissively, "it's only a novel."

It seems this is part of the danger of Dan Brown and his ideas. By presenting them in an entertaining format that people will read, he can subtly influence them. It's like a torpedo bomber that slips in under the radar. The damage can be done before anyone realizes an attack is under way.

For example, Brown's main character, Leigh Teabing, sarcastically says that the Bible did not arrive by a fax from heavenly places nor did it fall "magically" from above. He insists that man, not God, produced the Bible. Any he also announces that, with all the revisions, translations, and edits, there is really no "definitive version" of Scripture. The implication is that the Scriptures cannot be considered divine in any sense of the word.[44]

---

[42] Eisler, Riane. *The Chalice and the Blade*. 1988. Beacon Press, Boston.

[43] Baigent, Michael, Richard Leigh, and Henry Lincoln. *Holy Blood, Holy Grail*. 1982. Jonathan Cape, London.

[44] Brown, Dan. *op. cit.*, Chapter 55. p. 231.

But he does not stop there. He mentions the Dead Sea Scrolls, and correctly notes that they were found in the 1950s in a cave near Qumran in the desert of Judea. He also mentions some "Coptic Scrolls" which were found in 1945 at Nag Hammadi. Then he makes two startling claims. He first states that these ancient documents tell the true story of the Holy Grail. Secondly, he claims they also reveal that Christ's ministry was merely a human one.[45]

This, of course, sounds very erudite. It is intended to make faithful believers seem ignorant and credulous. But it is essentially nonsense. The Dead Sea Scrolls had no New Testament literature at all (though there is some controversy over a few tiny fragments). On the other hand, the Nag Hammadi library codices (not scrolls) do discuss Christ, although Dan Brown obviously never read them. They say nothing about any grail legend, and they hardly speak of Christ's ministry "in human terms." In fact, these Gnostic texts did not doubt Jesus' deity in the least. What they doubted was his *humanity*. So not only did Dan Brown get it wrong, he got it backwards.

The reliability of the Gospel accounts of the life of Jesus, as well as the rest of the Scriptures, is based on strong evidence. No one has said they "fell magically from the clouds," but Christians do believe God inspired the writers of sacred Scripture so that the result can rightly be called the Word of God. For an excellent discussion of the Bible and why it can be trusted, see Josh McDowell's two-volume summary of the evidences for the Christian faith (details given below).

Is there any truth behind *The Da Vinci Code*? Precious little. The idea that Jesus was married is unsubstantiated. In the first place, if he were married we would all be well aware of that fact. Why conceal something that was not in the least shameful? In fact, the lack of a wife would not have been viewed in a positive light in the culture of the day. But a conclusive argument against the notion of Jesus' marriage is found in 1 Corinthians 9:5,[46] where Paul argues that he (Paul) had a right to have

---

[45] Brown, Dan. *op. cit.,* Chapter 55. p. 234.

[46] "Don't we have the right to be accompanied by a Christian wife like the other apostles, the Lord's brothers, and Cephas?" (HCSB)

a wife (even though he did not exercise that right). Paul mentions that Peter and others had wives, but he makes no mention of Jesus having one. Had Jesus been married, Paul would certainly have mentioned it since it would have settled the matter.

3. ATTACK ON THE DIVINITY OF JESUS

So the foundation of *The Da Vinci Code* conspiracy theory falls apart on even a casual examination of the facts. But an even more insidious idea, woven into the plot and reinforced many times, was that Jesus' divinity was an idea that gradually took form many years after Christ came. Brown even went so far as to say that Jesus' divinity was finally accepted as a Christian doctrine at the Council of Nicaea in AD 325. This was supposedly about the time Constantine arbitrarily selected which books would be part of the Bible (and suppressed others), according to the novel.

But a review of early church history shows these claims to be utterly twisted and deceptive. The early churches had no problem at all in accepting Jesus' divinity since he rose from the dead. But some people had problems accepting his humanity. The early heresies, such as Gnosticism, said Jesus was God but was not truly man. It was only after the issues of Jesus' humanity were settled that the Arian heresy arose, maintaining that Jesus was the first creation of God the Father. The Arians, by the way, did not deny Jesus was a co-creator of the universe nor that he had primacy over everything (all things that the novel denies). Arianism was shown to be a heresy and the Council of Nicaea made that official.

But to say that Christians did not accept Jesus as divine until a majority of bishops said so at Nicaea is a willful and perverse revision of history. Furthermore, there is no evidence that Constantine had anything to do with canonizing any book of the Bible. Westcott, in his classic book on the Canon of the New Testament, said of the Council of Nicaea: "Neither in this nor in the following Councils were the Scriptures themselves ever the subject of discussion." [47] Constantine did order some copies of the

---

[47] Westcott, Brooke Foss. *A General Survey of the History of the Canon of the New Testament* (6th ed). 1980 [1889] Baker, Grand Rapids, MI. p. 430.

Bible to be made at government expense, but the books of the canon were well settled by that time. In fact, the Muratorian Canon shows that most of the books of our New Testament were well accepted by 160 AD, if not before. And none of the spurious documents such as the *Gospel of Thomas* was included in this early list of received books.

So the theories of *The Da Vinci Code*, however effective they might be in selling books to this generation, are simply untrue. They are as worthy of belief as the conspiracy theories that say President Kennedy and Elvis are still alive or that the moon landings were faked on a sound stage in Hollywood. But can the book be recommended simply as "a good read" or a well-crafted escapist novel? Not really. The book loses its way in mid-course and drifts on to an unsatisfactory conclusion. It fails to maintain the "suspension of disbelief" and in almost every other respect fails as a novel. The only reason a thinking person might want to read the book would be to use it as a springboard to profitable conversations about Christ, the Bible and church history with those friends and family duped into believing the book was based on fact.

Fortunately, like the "Passover Plot" and other similar books of past years that have attacked Christ and the church, *The Da Vinci Code* is not likely to be more than a short-lived blip on the radar screen. That is not to say paperback copies will not sell. But the hard-back copies are already on the clearance table. And that is a good thing.

For those who want a profitable use of their time, I recommend instead the best-seller, *The Purpose Driven Life* by Rick Warren. In 2003, this book sold thirteen million copies (more than *The Da Vinci Code* and the Harry Potter series combined) and went on to become a classic. As of this writing, the book has sold an amazing thirty-two million copies. It remains popular and is being repackaged and released as a tenth-anniversary version by Zondervan.[48] Its message is that a meaningful life is found in serving God and others. Dale Buss, a reviewer for the *Wall Street Journal* noted: "*The Purpose Driven Life* accomplishes a great deal

---

[48] "Rick Warren's 'The Purpose Driven Life' Celebrates 10 Years of Transforming Lives." *PR Web*. Accessed 1 December 2012, from http://www.prweb.com/releases/Rick_Warren/The_Purpose_Driven_Life/prweb10020930.htm.

by simply bucking everything modern—by urging us to turn our focus above rather than within."[49]

FURTHER READING

Garlow, James L. and Peter Jones. *Cracking Da Vinci's Code: You've Read the Fiction, Now Read the Facts.* Colorado Springs: Victor. 2004.

McDowell, Josh. *Evidence that Demands a Verdict. Volume 1.* San Bernardino: Campus Crusade. 1972.

McDowell, Josh. *More Evidence that Demands a Verdict. Volume 2.* San Bernardino: Campus Crusade. 1975.

Warren, Rick. *The Purpose Driven Life.* Grand Rapids, Michigan: Zondervan. 2003.

DISCUSSION QUESTIONS

1. How do we account for the popularity of books that attack the Christian faith?

2. Do you think that the Gospels (Matthew, Mark, Luke and John) leave any doubt that Jesus was the Son of God?

3. Why did the early Church seem to have more problem accepting Jesus' humanity than his divinity?

4. Do you think books like *The Da Vinci Code* cause the public to doubt the reliability of the Bible?

---

[49] Buss, Dale. "Godliness—In 40 Days." *Wall Street Journal*. Wednesday, December 31, 2003. Accessed 1 December 2012, from http://online.wsj.com/article/0,,SB107283544792892400,00.html.

CHAPTER 4

†

A Wishful Deviation
Denial of Doctrine

Book: *Love Wins, by Rob Bell.*[50]
Issue: Does Hell exist? If so, who will go there?

Rob Bell was, until recently, the pastor of Mars Hill Bible Church in Grandville, Michigan. There have been reports that he will soon be writing and producing a television drama for ABC.[51] Bell has been a popular speaker and writer and plans to continue using a variety of media to communicate his message.

1. MEDIA-SAVVY WRITING

What is that message? That is confusing. The church that he founded seems to have a sound, scripturally-based theology. For example, Mars Hill has a web page in which they discuss their "Narrative Theology" or the doctrines in which they believe. Part of this page says:

> Jesus is our only hope for bringing peace and reconciliation between
> God and humans. Through Jesus we have been forgiven and brought

---

[50] Bell, Rob. *Love Wins: A Book About Heaven, Hell, and the Fate of Every Person Who Ever Lived.* 2011. Harper Collins, New York.

[51] Andreeva, Nellie. *ABC Buys Spiritual Drama From 'Lost' Exec Producer Carlton Cuse And Pastor Rob Bell.* September 29, 2011. Accessed 20 August 2012, from http://www.deadline.com/2011/09/abc-buys-spiritual-drama-from-lost-exec-producer-carlton-cuse-and-pastor-rob-bell/.

into right relationship with God. God is now reconciling us to each other, ourselves, and creation. The Spirit of God affirms as children of God all those who trust Jesus. [52]

I would find it difficult to argue with this statement. It seems clear and honest, and something evangelical Christians can accept. So why is Bell's latest book, *Love Wins*, causing a stir in evangelical circles? A columnist for the Boston Globe, Alex Beam, put the matter this way:

> Happily for Rob Bell's book sales, conservative divines across the country are denouncing him as a heretic for his core message: "Love Wins," also the title of his book. There is even a modestly populated Facebook site called "People against Rob Bell's (and Mars Hill's) heresy." "The purpose of this group is not to attack this man personally, but to attack his false teachings," we read.
>
> One big heresy that Bell has been blasting on YouTube and else-where is that non-Christians may not be condemned to burn in hell. "[Mahatma] Gandhi is in hell?" Bell asks. "He is? And someone knows this for sure? Will only a few religious people make it to heaven?" Ix-nay, quoth Bell, who must have the inside scoop on this. He is after all, the author of *Sex God*, another book with enviable sales figures.[53]

Alas, sales figures are part of the reason for considering Bell's mes-sage. Bell has a "rock star" popularity. He is using his former church as a springboard to expand his influence upon the larger culture. When he announced a pastor's conference at his church—with only word of mouth for advertising—thousands showed up to hear him speak for several days. David Crumm said: "Rob Bell is one of the hottest voices in American religion today."[54] But what if that message is unhealthy? What if Bell is

[52] See Mars Hill website. *Narrative Theology*. Accessed 20 August 2012, from http://marshill.org/believe/about/narrative-theology/.

[53] Beam, Alex. "A Heck of a Theological Debate." *Boston Globe*. Boston. com Website. March 18, 2011. Accessed 20 August 2012, from http://www.boston.com/lifestyle/articles/2011/03/18/alex_beam_provides_an_update_on_a_heck_of_a_theological_debate/.

[54] Crumm, David. "Conversation With Rob Bell, a Different Kind of Evangelist." September 30, 2008. *Read the Spirit Website*. Accessed 6 December 2012, from http://www.readthespirit.com/explore/2008/10/1/268-conversation-with-rob-bell-a-different-kind-of-evangelis.html.

leading Christians, particularly the youth, in the wrong direction? In that case his popularity, and the perception that he is an evangelical spokesman, could be a real danger.

So what is the problem with Bell's message? Why have his books drawn a hostile reaction? Part of the problem is his identification with the Emerging Church Movement. Candidly, this movement is difficult to categorize. Albert Mohler has said:

> The Emergent movement represents a significant challenge to biblical Christianity. Unwilling to affirm that the Bible contains propositional truths that form the framework for Christian belief, this movement argues that we can have Christian symbolism and substance without those thorny questions of truthfulness that have so vexed the modern mind. The worldview of postmodernism—complete with an epistemology that denies the possibility of or need for propositional truth—affords the movement an opportunity to hop, skip and jump throughout the Bible and the history of Christian thought in order to take whatever pieces they want from one theology and attach them, like doctrinal post-it notes, to whatever picture they would want to draw.[55]

To be fair to Bell, I must not paint him with a broad brush as simply a member of the Emergent movement. Truthfully, that movement has spawned a number of departures from the historic Christian faith—which sounds remarkably like old-fashioned liberalism. Matt Slick, a prominent Christian apologist, said:

> Even though there are some pastors in the Emerging Church Movement that are true to scripture, the movement as a whole needs to stick to the essentials of the Christian faith, otherwise, in spite of its proclamation to renew Christianity afresh, it will become stale and heretical. ... The Emerging Church movement has much good in it, but it also has a good bit of bad already within its doors.[56]

---

[55] Mohler, R. Albert, Jr. "First Person: Is a 'generous orthodoxy' truly orthodox?" March 8, 2005. *Baptist Press*. Accessed 6 December 2012, from http://www.sbcbaptistpress.org/printerfriendly.asp?ID=20305.

[56] Slick, Matt. *What is the Emerging Church?* Accessed 27 December 2012, from http://carm.org/what-emerging-church.

We see a skeptical treatment of the Scriptures, as Francis Schaeffer foretold. With the loss of an inerrant Bible, any hope of resisting the currently fashionable cultural opinions of the day is also lost. Some, such as John MacArthur,[57] have accused the Emergent movement of adopting the aims of the radical homosexual movement, radical feminism, pro-abortion lobby and all the rest. That may be where Bell ends up, but his book does not go there. Let us look at where his book does try to take us.

2. EMERGENT SPIRITUALITY

About six years ago, we had our introduction to what might be called "Emergent Spirituality" in our church in Las Cruces, New Mexico. (Yes, we had moved again.) Our Wednesday evening study group read and discussed a little book by Donald Miller: *Blue Like Jazz*.[58] Miller's book is difficult to describe, but it was a meandering tale of his spiritual journey. He seemed to speak with a voice that might relate well to young Christians. We found the book to have some useful insights. It helped us to see what might be stumbling blocks in our traditional churches. But we saw little that helped chart a path for young seekers to travel or to achieve authentic Christian sanctification.

All that has little to do with Rob Bell, except for one warning. It put us on guard against Emergent spirituality. The Emergent movement is postmodern and seems to delight in deconstructing traditional narratives that describe Christian thought and practice. Often described as *post-evangelical*, it seem to be suspicious of authority, even God's authority as expressed in the Bible. Admittedly, the movement is difficult to define precisely. Because it is not clear where the movement is going, it is not a train we wish to board.

I want to be clear on one point. I did not think *Blue Like Jazz* was a terrible book. Miller, when he told his story, reminded me of a sort of

---

[57] MacArthur, John. *The Truth War: Fighting for Certainty in an Age of Deception.* 2008. Thomas Nelson, Nashville, TN.

[58] Miller, Donald. *Blue Like Jazz: Nonreligious Thoughts on Christian Spirituality.* 2003. Thomas Nelson: Nashville, TN.

Christianized Holden Caulfield.[59] There was an adolescent innocence mingled with rebellion. Nevertheless, because of Miller, we became more aware of the growing Emergent Church movement. In 2005, we heard of Brian D. McLaren, a leading figure in the Emergent Church, with the publication of his book: *A Generous Orthodoxy*. The book appeared to us, from a cursory review, to confirm the criticism mentioned above by Albert Mohler.[60] The movement seemed to be spiritually unhealthy.

So when we heard of Bell's book *Love Wins*, we did not welcome it with open arms. In fact, we warned our fellow church members to be careful with any book coming out of the Emergent Church movement, even those that seemed to be relatively orthodox in their views. It was good that we raised the alarm. There is much about Bell's book to concern Christians. Not the least is a quotation on the back cover: "Rob Bell is a central figure for his generation and for the way that evangelicals are likely to do church in the next twenty years."[61] I devoutly hope this quotation is not literally true. Bell and his thinking represent a dangerous current, pulling us into troubled waters—maybe even towards a spiritual 40-foot waterfall.

3. WATERFALL AHEAD

When I was seven years old, my family was living on a cattle ranch in western Colorado, several miles from the small town of Burns. "Small" is putting the case mildly. Burns was a combination general store, filling station and post office. A few scattered houses sat nearby on a small shelf in a canyon bottom near the Colorado River. In the summer of that year, an evangelist from Denver, a Reverend Doll, arrived to put on a "tent revival." We called it that because he actually had his own circus tent, complete with benches, a stage and a pulpit, plus a piano. There was not

---

[59] A character in *Catcher in the Rye* by J. D. Salinger.

[60] For a criticism of this book by Albert Mohler see Mohler, Albert. *"A Generous Orthodoxy"–Is It Orthodox?* February 16, 2005. Accessed 6 December 2012, from http://www.albertmohler.com/2005/02/16/a-generous-orthodoxy-is-it-orthodox-2/.

[61] Attributed to Andy Crouch in the *New York Times*.

even enough room in the town of Burns to set up the tent, so he set it up in a small field a couple of miles downstream. My parents, my brother, two sisters, and I all went to the revival every night for several nights running.

It was there that I first heard and understood the gospel story: how I was separated from a loving God by sin, but that Christ had died on the cross for me. I understood that if I turned from my sins and accepted Christ as my Savior, my sins would be forgiven, and I would become a child of God. The afternoon before the last night of the revival I asked my parents if I could go forward and accept Jesus as my Savior. This request caused them some consternation. They did not think it likely that a seven-year-old could truly understand what all this preaching meant, and they did not want me to be "all mixed up." They asked me some questions and I answered them satisfactorily, so they finally gave their permission. To this day I am grateful to them and to Reverend Doll because when I walked that aisle and took the preacher by the hand, I believed then—and still believe—that I was saved and became a child of God.

The preacher, as the old saying goes, preached "hell hot." He made it clear that this was the hour of salvation and minced no words about it. When we left after one of his evangelistic messages, we clearly understood that if we died without confessing Christ as Savior we would go to hell and would be separated from God for eternity.

Rob Bell believes that Reverend Doll's message, the same words that led me to salvation, was "misguided and toxic."[62] I have a hard time believing that. For me, they were the words of life, but do they accurately summarize what the Scriptures teach? Could Bell be right and could Reverend Doll, Billy Graham, and all the previous generations of Christians have got it so utterly wrong?

Bell certainly thinks so. He scoffs at the idea that Mahatma Gandhi might be in hell, despite the there being no indication whatsoever that he ever accepted Christ as his Savior. He asks if there is any confirmation of this. Of course, he has a point. We do not know for sure whether or not Gandhi is saved, and we certainly are not Gandhi's judge. But

---

[62] Bell Rob. *op. cit.,* p. viii.

despite Bell's scoffing, we can say with great sorrow that there is no sound reason to suppose he will be in heaven, despite his reputation as a social reformer. Jesus' authority carries more weight that Bell's, and Jesus said, "No one comes to the Father except through me."[63] He expanded on this warning by saying: "Whoever acknowledges me before others, I will also acknowledge before my Father in heaven."[64] He also said: "Small is the gate and narrow the road that leads to life, and only a few find it."[65] Finally, in Revelation 20:15, we find these words: "All whose names were not found written in the book of life were thrown into the lake of fire."[66] This doctrine is no scoffing matter.

Bell's book is postmodern. Postmoderns like to deconstruct or tear down systems of thought, which they call "narratives." Bell begins by tearing at the heart of the evangelical understanding of the gospel:

> A staggering number of people have been taught that a select few Christians will spend forever in a peaceful, joyous place called heaven, while the rest of humanity spends forever in torment and punishment in hell with no chance for anything better. It's been clearly communicated to many that this belief is a central truth of the Christian faith and to reject it is to reject Jesus. This is misguided and toxic and ultimately subverts the contagious spread of Jesus' message of love, peace, forgiveness, and joy that our world desperately needs to hear.[67]

So Bell puts the reader on notice that he does not believe in hell; at least not as it is usually understood. He thinks this doctrine is keeping many from accepting the Christian faith. I understood him to be particularly referring to Bell's own generation and younger, whose worldview will not accept hell as literally true. He mentions the message of Jesus—nice things. For Bell, Jesus spoke only of "love, peace, forgiveness and joy." Bell does not mention sin, death, repentance, sacrifice, or sanctification, to say nothing of salvation from hell. And that is curious. Bell admits that

---

[63] John 14:6 (HCSB)
[64] Matthew 10:33 (NIV)
[65] Matthew 7:14 (NIV)
[66] (NIV)
[67] Bell Rob. *op. cit.,* p. viii.

most of the time the word "hell" is used in the New Testament, it is Jesus himself who uses the word.[68] Certainly, Jesus took hell seriously.

Bell's book, to put it mildly, is not straightforward (the above quotation is an exception—that is remarkably straightforward.). He does not usually say what he truly believes. He will ask leading questions; he will ridicule traditional beliefs; he will tell stories; he will lead the reader up to a point where some clear conclusion is called for, and then simply end with an enigmatic, noncommittal statement. Bell's defenders will say: "Rob Bell never said he did not believe in hell." That is quite true; he never does—quite.[69] People say: "Rob Bell never says he believes in universal salvation." Quite true, though he never says that he doesn't. It seems he wants to challenge orthodoxy but without any incriminating evidence. Suffice it to say, though, that any reader of the book will understand that conventional Christian views of heaven and hell are out of date—"misguided and toxic," in Bell's opinion.

4. THE DECONSTRUCTION OF THE FAITH.

The first idea that Bell intends to tear down or deconstruct is the concept of salvation. He questions all of our usual ways to express the acceptance of Christ as Savior. He asks if one has to say a certain prayer, or be baptized, or join a church. He asks if there is an age of accountability. He asks if getting to heaven is all that is necessary. He asks if there is "no hope" for a person who dies without Christ. He does agree "what matters is how you respond to Jesus."[70] He does not answer any of the other questions. That is not his purpose. He is tearing down.

He particularly wants to tear down the idea that a person must have a personal relationship with Jesus to be saved. He thinks most evangelical Christians would agree that without this personal relationship, "you will die apart from God and spend eternity in torment in hell."[71] Surprisingly, he says that the term "personal relationship" is not found in the Bible:

[68] Bell Rob. *op. cit.,* p. 67.

[69] He clearly believes in an earthly hell. See *Ibid.,* p. 71.

[70] *Ibid.,* p. 7.

[71] *Ibid.,* p. 10.

Old or New Testament. He wonders why it is not mentioned if it is so important. Why did no one use the phrase before the last century?

More deconstruction, but let's push back a bit. Bell makes a lofty point that the term "personal relationship" is not used in the Bible. Fine, let's agree with him, but so what? The words "Bible" or "Trinity" are not used in the Bible either. That does not mean that neither exists. The question is not whether the term "personal relationship" is found in Scripture. That is not decisive. The question is whether the concept is found there. Jesus said:

> I am the good shepherd. I know my own sheep and they know me, as the Father knows me and I know the Father. I lay down my life for the sheep.[72]

Does this promise sound like a personal relationship? I do not know what else it could be. Jesus said he and his sheep knew each other. There was a relationship, and it was like the relationship between two persons of the Trinity, the Father and the Son. What could be more personal than that? So the *concept* of the term "personal relationship" is found in the Scriptures, even if the words are not. Furthermore, this personal relationship defines which sheep are Christ's own. They are the ones who know him. Jesus also said his sheep knew his voice, and they followed him.[73] The phrase "personal relationship" was not used, but it is an apt term and easy to understand. Why does Bell not like it? He is tearing down what evangelical Christians believe about salvation. But Jesus is saying that if there is no personal relationship, the person is not one of his sheep.

Then Bell lifts up three verbs: accept, confess and believe. Evangelicals say these responses are necessary for salvation, but Bell asks if salvation is free in that case. He continues: "How is any of that grace? How is that a gift? How is that good news?" Since Christians say that an unbeliever does not have to do anything to be saved; that Jesus has done it all; then why all these verbs? Bell does not answer the question. He does not want an answer. He is trying to deconstruct our beliefs.

---

[72] John 10:14–15 (HCSB)
[73] John 10: 1–5

There is a perfectly correct answer, though. Salvation is by grace, which comes by faith. And even faith is a gift from God. "For you are saved by grace through faith this is not from yourselves: it is God's gift— not from works, so that no one can boast."[74] How does God nurture our faith? We learn that in the book of Romans: "So faith comes from what is heard, and what is heard comes through the message about Christ."[75] It is like the parable of the sower. The Word of God goes out, and it finds root in those with good, honest hearts, those with saving faith, and they bear fruit.[76] Do we have to believe? Yes. John 3:16 (perhaps the all-time favorite verse in the New Testament) says we have to believe, but belief comes through faith, which again, is a gift of God. Do we have to confess? Yes, Matthew 10:33 makes it clear that confession is vital, but confession also comes through faith. Saving faith is manifested in a number of ways, and some of those are verbs, just as Bell says. He asks if that is good news. I say it is the best news, but then, I am not deconstructed.

Then Bell mentions the Roman centurion whose servant is healed in Luke 7, the tax collector who went to the temple to pray and had his sins forgiven in Luke 18, and the "thief" on the cross who is promised a place in paradise in Luke 23.[77] Bell seems to be saying that all of these stories are telling about how to be saved. First, he notes that Jesus not only expresses acceptance and approval—he is amazed at the centurion. Then, Bell implies that the tax collector's words put him in better standing with God than the people of God. Third, Jesus promised the criminal that he would be in paradise that very day. Bell asks if salvation might be dependent on certain words that we say and implies that these three incidents are examples of this principle. [78]

Bell is attempting to argue that the evangelical Christian understanding of salvation is incorrect. He apparently mentions these three cases to show that salvation is more complicated than simple formulas like:

[74] Ephesians 2:8–9 (HCSB)
[75] Romans 10:17 (HCSB)
[76] See Luke 8:4–15.
[77] Bell Rob. *op. cit.,* p. 12.
[78] *Ibid.,* p. 12–13.

"salvation is by grace through faith." These examples, however, show no such thing. All three men mentioned are shown as having strong faith. In the first case, the centurion is mentioned as having such faith that it put Israel to shame; but the story is not talking about salvation. The faith mentioned is faith that Jesus can perform a miracle. I can answer Bell in the negative. This teaching does not imply that saying certain things saves you.

The second case, despite what Bell says, has nothing to do with saying certain words nor is it about a Gentile with greater faith than God's own people. The two men praying at the temple are both sons of Israel, and the issue is not salvation, but the forgiveness of sins. In an example that echoes 1 John 1:9, the man who confessed his sin and asked for forgiveness, in faith believing, was forgiven of his sins. So this case does not exactly concern salvation, though it is certainly related. Once again, to answer Bell's question, it does not imply that saying certain words is what saves you.

The third case, however, is talking about salvation. Bell is correct about that. Although the man did ask for salvation,[79] it is clear that it was not the exact words that were pivotal. The man showed great faith; beyond great faith: incredible faith. It is a perfect example of salvation by grace through faith. How can Bell or anyone else cheapen this marvelous leap of faith, which he displayed in spite of our Lord being humiliated and nailed to a cross, by saying that it was intended to show that what we say saves us? Bell has gone too far here. He has gone beyond deconstruction to something worse. There is a mocking tone which is most unsettling. There is no legitimate reason for him to take this attitude. Does he seriously think his careless misuse of these verses will convince anyone that the plan of salvation, as found in the Gospels, is confusing and contradictory?

Whatever he intends, he continues, mentioning John 3 and the famous story about Nicodemus and being "born again." He brings up

---

[79] He said: "Jesus, remember me when you come into your kingdom." Luke 23:42b (NIV)

Luke 20, where Jesus mentions "those who are counted worthy to take part in that age,"[80] and implies these two passages are saying something different. Bell asks if salvation comes by what you say, by being born again, or by being counted worthy.[81] He is simply being unfair. He plods on with his argument with no real concern for what is truly being said. What is being said is not complicated. The new birth is a wonderful analogy for our salvation which comes by grace through faith. Therefore, those who are "worthy" are those who have received salvation by grace through faith. There is only one way to be saved, but Bell seems determined to confuse the issue.

There seems to be little point in ploughing through all of Bell's taunting. He does not want a reasoned response. He wants to leave the reader deconstructed and feeling confused. Then he goes on to an actual conversion story, that of Paul in Acts 22. He implies that Paul was converted because he is asked a question by Jesus and then asks a question in return. But this inference makes no sense. Clearly, the narrative is not intended to explain exactly how Paul was saved. The point of the narrative seems to be the extraordinary lengths God employed to turn Paul from his wicked ways and bring him to salvation. Luke had described salvation experiences before this one and apparently expected his reader to realize subsequent incidents would follow the same pattern.[82] So he did not repeat all the details in the case of Paul.

Bell sums up his deconstruction of the doctrine of salvation by the words in the title of the first chapter of his book: "What about the flat tire?" He quotes a passage from Romans 10: "How can they hear without someone preaching to them?"[83] And then he asks, what happens if Christians don't bear the message? "What if the missionary gets a flat tire?"[84] This is a fair question since it does remind us we have a responsibility to share the gospel. However, the fate of a lost person does not seem to

---

[80] Luke 20:35. (HCSB)

[81] Bell Rob. *op. cit.* p. 13.

[82] See Acts: 2:38–47, 8:36–40.

[83] Bell Rob. *op. cit.* p. 9.

[84] *Ibid.*

be improved by Bell's contention that the gospel is hopelessly muddled. The answer, it seems to me, is that Christians should pray for salvation as though it all depended on God and offer ourselves as witnesses as though it all depended on us. But this answer is much too traditional for Bell.

5. BELL PLAYS THE GREEK CARD

His next line of argument seems to be aimed at denying that "eternal life" means anything like the conventional understanding of the term. He initially makes a valid point in insisting that Jesus did not come so that we can simply go to heaven when we die. Eternal life begins on this earth, on the very day of our salvation. Had Bell confined himself to this truth, all would have been well. However, it is here that he goes wrong. He implies that the word *aion* has two meanings in Greek but that *it does not mean "forever" as we think of forever.*[85] He goes on to explain that *aion* sometimes means an "age" or a period of time with a beginning and an end. Sometimes *aion* means a particularly intense experience of time, a kind of "timelessness," which is the second (and he says the only other) meaning. Then he sums up:

> *Aion* is often translated as "eternal" in English which is an altogether different word from "forever." Let me be clear: heaven is not forever in the way that we think of forever, as a uniform measurement of time, like days and years, marching endlessly into the future. That's not a category or concept that we find in the Bible. This is why a lot of translators choose to translate *aion* as "eternal." By this they don't mean the literal passing of time; they mean transcending time, belonging to another realm altogether. [86]

Bell is correct in saying that *aion* can mean an age of time, and he is also correct that eternal life is often used to refer to the quality of life in the age to come. To refer again to John 3:16, "whoever believes in him shall not perish but have everlasting life."[87] There is a sense that "everlasting" or *aionios* implies both quality *and* duration, since even the unrighteous

[85] Bell Rob. *op. cit.,* p. 31.

[86] *Ibid.,* p. 59.

[87] (NIV)

dead will have eternal life in hell, if duration is the only concept in view. In John 10:10 Jesus promised abundant life, which underlines the idea of quality. The idea that God in his essential being is timeless, transcending time, is also scriptural.[88] So part of what Bell is saying is correct.

There is a problem with the rest of his discussion, however. As an explanation of the meaning of a Greek word as it is used in the Scriptures to apply to God's creatures, it is completely wrong. One wonders if Bell stayed awake during his *Koine* Greek class. This is wrong because:

1. *Aion* does carry the meaning "forever" as we think of forever.

2. Heaven is seen as "forever" in the way we think of as forever—days marching endlessly into the future.

3. The concept of "forever" is found in the Bible, in both Old and New Testaments.

4. There is not a significant difference in the Scriptures between the meanings of "eternal" and "forever."

Almost everything in the previous quotation from Bell is wrong. It is not just a little wrong but almost 100 percent, 180-degrees-out-of-kilter wrong. What he said is almost the exact opposite of the truth.[89] Why he would say this is puzzling. It is not clear why he would maintain that eternal life in heaven is not everlasting, but the facts are otherwise. First, let us consider the meaning of the Greek word *aion* and the less commonly used word *aionios*. To do this, we need to look at some Greek dictionaries, called *lexicons*.

---

[88] See Romans 16:26.

[89] Bell's point, that *aion or αιων* does not refer to the endless passing of time, but of a timeless eternity on the part of God, is found in the Scriptures and in the thought of Plato, particularly in his *Timaeus*. But this idea is not expressed in the New Testament to mean eternal life for God's creatures. See Sasse, Hermann, Erlangen, "Aion" In the *Theological Dictionary of the New Testament,* edited by Gerhard Kittel, translated by Geoffrey W. Bromiley. 1964. Eerdmans,Grand Rapids, MI. Vol. 1, pp. 197–198.

A short lexicon is found with the Greek New Testament. It defines the primary meaning of *aion* as "*age; world order; eternity.*" The same dictionary defines *aionios* as: "*eternal* (of quality rather than of time); *unending, everlasting, for all time.*"[90] This definition shows Bell is wrong to say the concept of "forever" is not part of the meaning of those words which are used to describe heaven. Is this short lexicon the most authoritative reference work? The answer is "No."

The most authoritative lexicon is the work of Walter Bauer, since published in various revisions and translations. A review of the 1957 translation shows much agreement with the short dictionary. Bauer shows *aion* to mean: 1. *very long time, eternity.* 2. a segment of time or *age.* 3. the world. 4. the *Aeon* as a person. He defines *aionios* as: 1. without beginning. 2. without beginning or end. 3. without end.[91] We should note that the last meaning can include the idea of eternal quality.[92] Again, this summary conclusively shows the word can mean *eternity* or *time without end.* So despite what Bell says, this is a concept clearly (and frequently) found in the Bible.

Let us look at some texts found in the Bible that use the words *aion* and *aionios*:

Galatians 1:5 "To whom be the glory forever and ever."[93]

1 Peter 1:25 "But the word of the Lord endures forever."[94]

1 John 2:17 "The world and its desires pass away, but whoever does the

---

[90] *The Greek New Testament.* Kurt Aland, *et al.*, eds. Second Edition. United Bible Societies. Stuttgart. 1968. Including: *A Concise Greek-English Dictionary of the New Testament.* Barclay M. Newman, Jr. 1971. United Bible Societies, London. "αιων." pp. 5–6. "αιωνιος." p.6.

[91] Bauer, Walter. *A Greek-English Lexicon of the New Testament and Other Early Christian Literature.* William F. Arndt and F. Wilbur Gingrich, eds. 1957. University of Chicago Press. Chicago, Illinois. αιων. pp. 26–27. αιωνιος. pp. 27–28.

[92] See 2 Timothy 2:10. The *eternal glory* mentioned (*aionios*) is clearly a reference to quality of our salvation and not simply eternal duration.

[93] (HCSB) Note that this is a reference to God.

[94] (HCSB)

will of God lives forever."[95]

John 14:16 "And I will pray the Father, and he shall give you another Comforter, that he may abide with you forever."[96]

Luke 1:33 "He will reign over the house of Jacob forever, and his kingdom will have no end."[97]

So the idea of everlasting duration is found in the Bible, but does heaven mean endless time, an endless sequence of one moment after another, or *timelessness*? Clearly, timelessness has meaning with respect to the Lord God Almighty in his essential being. Conversely, it has no meaning whatsoever for any created being, whether angelic, human, or animal. Creatures are not timeless. We absolutely need time for our existence, whether in this life or the life to come. This idea will be discussed below in some depth. The definitive work on the theological meaning of New Testament words is the *Theological Dictionary of the New Testament* (TDNT). It is a massive work, in ten volumes. What does the TDNT have to say?

In the first place, it confirms that *aion* and *aionios* can mean "eternal," and that endless time and eternity mean exactly the same.[98] However, when referring to God there is also the thought of timelessness.[99] Even in rabbinic teachings, the idea of heaven was present. Ladd writes: "It was commonplace in rabbinic teachings that the study of the Torah would lead to 'Life in the Age to Come.'"[100] This life in heaven will consist of a

---

[95] (NIV)

[96] (KJV)

[97] (HCSB) Note that this refers to 2 Samuel 7:13,16. The Hebrew word translated "forever" is *owlam* which means *eternity, everlasting duration*. See Davidson, Benjamin. *Analytical Hebrew and Chaldee Lexicon*. 1970. Zondervan. Grand Rapids, Michigan. "Owlam." p. 601.

[98] Sasse, Hermann, Erlangen. "Aion." In *Theological Dictionary of the New Testament, op. cit.,* pp. 200–201.

[99] Sasse. "Aion." TDNT. *op. cit.,* p.203.

[100] Ladd, George, *A Theology of the New Testament.* 1993. Eerdmans, Grand Rapids, MI. p. 292.

succession of moments, one after another, as we can see from Revelation Chapters 4–6; particularly Revelation 6:9–11.[101] Wayne Grudem, as mentioned above, was careful to emphasize that heaven is not timeless.[102]

6. A KINDER, GENTLER HELL!

So Bell's assertions about heaven are deeply flawed, but it is not clear why he maintains such ideas as the timelessness of heaven or denies that heaven will offer eternal life in the sense of infinite duration. What is clear is that we cannot expect him to be careful with the facts. If he is careless with heaven, which he must like, what can we expect of his discussion of hell, which he doesn't like?

We need to realize that for people like Bell with a postmodern mindset, it seems perfectly reasonable to refuse to believe things they do not like. It is the smorgasbord theology idea, again. One of our dear family members, in discussing hell, said: "The God that I believe in would not send anyone to hell." That made me stop and think, long and hard. Did she think there was a selection of gods out there, like kitchen appliances from some big-box department store? Did she see God as a kind of consumer item? Did she realize there was only one God, and while we may not choose to worship him, we do not have the choice to redefine him? Or was she saying she thought hell was incompatible with a God of love? I am not sure. Maybe it was all of these.

Bell shadow-boxes with our concept of hell through twenty pages or so. He implies there are not many verses relating to hell and explains that the word "Gehenna" or "hell" was the city dump for Jerusalem. He believes hell is on earth when people commit wickedness. He says Jesus often used hyperbole or exaggeration. He hints that some of Jesus' warnings about the coming wrath were political: more to do with the Roman Empire than

---

[101] See verse 11: "So a white robe was given to each of them, and they were told to rest a little while longer until the number would be completed of their fellow slaves and their brothers, who were going to be killed just as they had been." (HCSB)

[102] Grudem, Wayne, *Systematic Theology: An Introduction to Biblical Doctrine, op. cit.*. 1162.

with God's judgment. We see, though, that in all of this tapestry of words Bell does not deny the reality of hell. He just downplays it.[103]

Then he twists a little-known passage from the prophet Ezekiel to try to show that Jesus did not mean what he said about hell. In Ezekiel God promises a restoration to "Sodom and her daughters."[104] Bell reminds us God had destroyed Sodom and Gomorrah. Then he says:

> Restore the fortunes of Sodom? The story isn't over for Sodom and Gomorrah? What appeared to be a final, *forever*, soldering, smoking verdict regarding their destiny … wasn't? What appeared to be over, isn't. Ezekiel says that where there was destruction there will be restoration.[105]

Bell then recounts the story of how God punished his people by sending them into exile, but though he banished them in his wrath, he brought them back to the land of promise when they had learned their lesson. This summary is well and good. It is true God will judge a people, with the intent that they will learn and repent from their evil ways. This is often his way, too, in the case of an individual person. Then Bell implies that the people of Sodom and Gomorrah, who were destroyed when the Lord rained brimstone and fire from heaven, will get another chance. But this is not at all what Ezekiel was saying. The cities may be restored but not the wicked inhabitants. The Bible provides no hint of a second chance after death. In fact, in a crystal clear way, it says there is none. Hebrews explains: "Just as people are destined to die once, and after that to face judgment …"[106] Peter states that the inhabitants of Sodom and Gomorrah are examples of how God will "keep the unrighteous under punishment until the day of judgment, especially those who follow the polluting desires of the flesh and despise authority."[107]

So Bell is wrong when he implies there are second chances for the inhabitants of Sodom and Gomorrah who died in their sins. Then he

---

[103] Bell Rob. *op. cit.*, pp. 63–83.

[104] Ezekiel 16:55 (KJV)

[105] Bell Rob. *op. cit.*, p. 84.

[106] Hebrews 9:27 (NIV)

[107] 2 Peter 2:9b–10 (HCSB)

builds on this error and reveals where he is going with a brief discussion of Matthew 25. Jesus tells us he will come in his glory and separate the sheep from the goats. The goats are the unrighteous. Jesus says: "And they will go away into eternal punishment, but the righteous into eternal life."[108] This verse poses a problem for Bell. He tries to escape from the plain meaning by going back to his attempted deconstruction of the Greek word *aion*. He is determined to foist his flawed understanding of the word on the unwary:

> The goats are sent, in the Greek language to an *aion* of *kolazo*. *Aion*, we know, has several meanings. One is "age" or "period of time"; another refers to intensity of experience. The word *kolazo* is a term from horticulture. It refers to the pruning and trimming of the branches of a plant so it can flourish.
>
> An *aion* of *kolazo*. Depending on how you translate *aion* and *kolazo*, then, the phrase can mean "a period of pruning" or "a time of trimming," or an intense experience of correction.
>
> In a good number of English translations of the Bible, the phrase "*aion* of *kolazo*" gets translated as "eternal punishment," which many read to mean "punishment forever," as in never going to end. But "forever" is not really a category the biblical writers used.[109]

Bell is incorrect when he says the Bible writers did not use "forever." They did, and it is a common theme. The most respected authorities all agree on this. So using the word *aion* to mean "forever" or "eternal" almost certainly is the correct translation, especially since the word here is the adjective *aionion*. We certainly hope and trust it means "eternal" when Jesus promises eternal life (using the same word for *eternal*) to the righteous.[110] What about *kolazo* or, more correctly, *kolasis*? Bell used a classical Greek lexicon, which is the wrong one.

Bell says the word is from horticulture, and it refers to the pruning and cutting of a plant so it can flourish. It seems to be true that in ancient

---

[108] Matthew 25:46 (HCSB)

[109] Bell Rob. *op. cit.*, pp. 89–90.

[110] The same word (*aionion*) is used to refer to eternal punishment and eternal life.

Attic[111] Greek, long before New Testament days, the root meaning of the word was "to lop off," "dock," "prune," or "cut off."[112] It was often used to refer to animals, as the cutting of wings off a bird. It was not necessarily tied to horticulture, and the cutting or chopping off did not necessarily have anything to do with improving the plant or animal. Thayer says the word probably derived from the word *kolos* or "lopped." He gives the older use of the word as: "Properly to lop, prune, as trees, wings." Thayer goes on to say that in the New Testament the word means to "chastise, correct, punish."[113] The definitive modern lexicon, abbreviated BADG,[114] gives dozens of examples from New Testament times and concludes that all mean "punish." An earlier edition of Walter Bauer's work lists Matthew 25:46 and says *kolasin aionion* means "eternal damnation."[115] So we have to conclude that while in classical Greek the word could mean "cutting off," in Koine Greek the word means "punishment."

Bell seems to be trying to show that hell is not forever. He suggests it is a place much like the Roman Catholic idea of purgatory where sins can be purged. He likes the idea that hell is temporary, that it is redemptive, but Matthew 25:46 is saying the opposite. The goats are being sent to eternal punishment, and *eternal* means forever, time without end. Is this a pleasant idea? No, it is not. C. S. Lewis said this:

And here is the real problem: so much mercy, yet still there is hell. I am

---

[111] Attic is one dialect of classical Greek.

[112] The Liddell-Scott lexicon, however, notes that even in classical times the word could also mean "punish." They add this definition: "*to chastise, punish*, Sophocles, Euripides, etc.:—Med. *to get* a person *punished*, Aristophanes, Plato:—Pass. *to be punished*, Xenophon." Liddell, H.G. and Scott, R. 1998. *An Intermediate Greek-English Lexicon*. Electronic STEP Files. Cedar Rapids, IA: Parsons Technology.

[113] Thayer, Joseph H. *Thayer's Greek-English Lexicon of the New Testament*. 1975. Zondervan,Grand Rapids, MI. p. 353.

[114] Bauer, Walter; Danker, Frederick; Arndt, William; Gingrich, F. Wilbur. 2000. *A Greek-English Lexicon of the New Testament and Other Early Christian Literature*. Third Edition. The University of Chicago Press, Chicago, IL. (BDAG).

[115] Bauer, Walter. *A Greek-English Lexicon of the New Testament and Other Early Christian Literature*. William F. Arndt and F. Wilbur Gingrich, eds. 1957. University of Chicago Press. Chicago, IL. "κόλασις." p. 441.

not going to try to prove the doctrine tolerable. Let us make no mistake;
it is *not* tolerable. But I think the doctrine can be shown to be moral. ...[116]

Bell is not interested in this old story, though. At this point he has
deconstructed the biblical narrative of hell, and now he wants to construct
his own story based on what he wants to believe. Bell hangs this story
on a line in 1 Corinthians 13:8, "Love never fails." He likes this narrative
better, explaining:

> ... some stories are better than others. Telling a story in which billions
> of people spend forever somewhere in the universe trapped in a black
> hole of endless torment and misery with no way out isn't a very good
> story. Telling a story about a God who inflicts unrelenting punishment
> on people because they didn't do or say or believe the correct things in
> a brief window of time called life isn't a very good story.[117]

Now I want to ask few questions. Does Bell think Christians believe
in hell because they *like* the story? Is the important thing about a story
that it be sweet and friendly with all the rough edges sanded off? Did
Jesus spend all that time warning about the dangers of hell because he
liked the thought? Who inflicts the "unrelenting punishment," anyway?
If one has an untamed, rebel heart that will not submit to God or anyone
else, whose bloated pride is all-consuming, would not heaven be the
most noxious place imaginable? Perhaps for these blighted souls, hell is
as much a refuge as it is a place of punishment: a place where one can
feed one's ego forever.

In 2004 Mel Gibson released his film *The Passion of The Christ*, which
was a violent, graphic portrayal of the last twelve hours of Jesus' life. The
film had an "R" rating for violence, and many reviewers said it was the
most violent movie they had ever seen.[118] Carroll and I certainly found

---

[116] Lewis, C. S. *The Problem of Pain. op. cit.,* p. 120.

[117] Bell Rob. *op. cit.,* p. 110.

[118] Roger Ebert said: " The movie is 126 minutes long, and I would guess that
at least 100 of those minutes ... [concern] the torture and death of Jesus.
This is the most violent film I have ever seen." Ebert, Roger, "The Passion of
the Christ." February 24, 2004. *Chicago Sun-Times.* rogerebert.com Movie
Review.

it so. It was excruciating just to *watch* the flogging of Jesus. I thought the sadistic ripping of his flesh was never going to end. Then the soldiers released one hand from the manacle, and I thought, *Finally. It's over*. But I was wrong. They simply exposed the front of his body to the clawed tips of the lash. When it was over, Jesus' body was a ragged mass of bloody flesh: hardly human. This was not a film for young children.

Yes, I got it. The cruelty of the flogging and the crucifixion itself was not just gratuitous violence. It was not gore as entertainment. The point was to show how terribly Christ had suffered for us; the price he paid so that our sins could be forgiven. We can see the passion, the agony, he suffered to save us from the agony of hell. No human, no rational being, would allow their son to go through that suffering unless there were no alternative. God allowed his own dear Son to drink that cup but only because the alternative, his human children going to hell, was even worse. Sin is shown as the monstrous evil that it is. Hell must be a terrible danger, otherwise the Son of God would have never willingly borne the physical suffering. Yet we believe his spiritual suffering was even worse. All the sins of the world were poured out on the Sinless One. In that moment, he was separated from the Father. Spiritual agony at its most excruciating. God suffering on the tree so that we would not have to suffer hell.

Bell tells us not to worry. Maybe hell is not that bad. Bell has a new story, and in that story, hell is a much kinder and gentler place. In the new story, the goats do not go to eternal punishment; they go for some "intense correction." They get a little pruning; their "goatiness" is lopped off, and then they go to heaven. Hell is just a bit of a detour, apparently, and the gates of the heavenly city are left open. It does sound nice. It's a plot that might sell better, particularly in a made-for-TV movie. The only question is this: Is it true?

After seeing *The Passion of The Christ* and gaining some understanding of the price Christ paid, my heart tells me Bell's "better story" is not true. Why not? Because God would never have allowed his Son to suffer so excruciatingly to spare people from a detour in hell. If the worst the wicked denizens of Sodom and Gomorrah would suffer was a long therapeutic rest cure, what's the big deal? Why would Jesus say it would be better to tie a millstone around your neck and throw yourself into the sea,[119] than to cause a little one who believes in Jesus to sin? Jesus says sin is a monstrous evil. Bell's book does not worry much about sin. That is understandable. If hell is reformative and if we have unlimited chances, then sin is not so bad. If hell is forever, if a loving God suffered and died for us, then our refusal to follow him becomes even more perverse —and damnable. Let us not forget the words of Daniel: "Multitudes who sleep in the dust of the earth will awake: some to everlasting life, others to shame and everlasting contempt."[120]

Bell's book goes on for a few more chapters, but we will not go there. Bell tries hard to tear down our evangelical Christianity and replace it with a postmodern narrative. He gives us a poisonous dish of reckless distortion of the Scriptures, basted with clumsy translation, seasoned heavily with skepticism, and frosted over with old-fashioned liberalism. It is the gospel without real sin, God stripped of real justice, rebellion without repentance. The problem is, as liberal churches have learned, this theology is self-defeating. People quickly figure out that if what Bell says is true, they don't need Rob Bell, they don't need his church, and they don't need his Jesus. If what he says is true, and we all get to the same place eventually, then "don't worry—be happy." We end up with watered-down pap that is to the gospel of Jesus Christ as fool's gold is to the real thing. The danger is that the unwary may stumble into a trap and neglect the salvation that is freely offered. The gospel is "by grace you are saved," and not simply "love wins."

FURTHER READING

Veith, Gene Edward, Jr. *Postmodern Times: A Christian Guide to Contemporary Thought and Culture.* Wheaton, Illinois: Crossway. 1994.

DeYoung, Kevin and Ted Kluck. *Why We're Not Emergent: By Two Guys Who Should Be.* Chicago: Moody. 2008.

---

[119] See Mark 9:42.
[120] Daniel 12:2 (NIV)

DISCUSSION QUESTIONS

1. Why does Rob Bell try to so confuse the plan of salvation?

2. Jesus talked more often about hell than he did about heaven. Why do you think this is so?

3. Does the horrible nature of Christ's sacrifice provide convincing evidence of the seriousness of sin and hell?

4. What is more important: telling a good story or telling the truth? What does Rob Bell mean when he says that hell is not a good story?

5. Does Rob Bell's mishandling of New Testament Greek weaken his argument?

6. Why is it so hard to believe unpleasant truths?

CHAPTER 5

†

A Great Gulf
Calvinism vs. Arminianism

Book: *Calvinism: A Southern Baptist Dialogue,* edited by E. Ray Clendenen and Brad J. Waggoner.[121]

Issue: Can the divide between Calvinism and Arminianism be bridged?

C hristians in the evangelical community cannot escape the fact that we tend to be divided along the lines of an ancient theological argument between Reformation scholars. One side is often termed *Calvinist* or *Reformed* and the opposite side *Arminian.*

1. WHAT IS THE GREAT GULF?

The essence of the great gulf is the difficulty in comprehending how God can be sovereign in his decrees and yet allow human beings to have freedom and responsibility for their actions. No less an expositor than Charles Haddon Spurgeon believed the two could not be reconciled, even though he believed both to be true. Spurgeon said:

> That God predestines, and yet that man is responsible, are two facts that few can see clearly. They are believed to be inconsistent and contradictory to each other. If, then, I find taught in one part of the Bible that everything is foreordained, that is true; and if I find, in another Scripture, that man is responsible for all his actions, that is true; and it is only my folly that leads me to imagine that these two truths can ever

[121] *Calvinism: A Southern Baptist Dialogue,* ed. E. Ray Clendenen and Brad J. Waggoner. 2008. B & H Publishing Group, Nashville, TN.

contradict each other. I do not believe they can ever be welded into one upon any earthly anvil, but they certainly shall be one in eternity. They are two lines that are so nearly parallel that the human mind which pursues them farthest will never discover that they converge, but they do converge, and they will meet somewhere in eternity, close to the throne of God, whence all truth doth spring.

Of course, as we shall soon see, there is more between Calvinists and Arminians than this one point, but this point is certainly a key. What Spurgeon called "parallel lines that never meet this side of eternity," I am calling a great gulf, but the idea is the same.[122] I am not as pessimistic as Spurgeon. Before we reach the end of this book, we shall have considered, not one, but two models which can at least throw a slender bridge across the gulf and perhaps bring Christians to see how God's sovereignty and human accountability can be harmonized.[123]

2. PERSONAL EXPERIENCE

I first became aware of a great gulf or abyss between Christians when we were living in Battle Mountain, Nevada. I am not talking about the split between Protestants and Catholics. I knew about that, of course. I am not really talking about the distinctive differences between denominations, either. I knew about some of those. This gulf is part of the reason for different Protestant denominations, to be sure, but it is a more fundamental divide than the name on the front of a church building.

It was in the early 1980s and our small church was in the process of calling a new pastor. It was a struggle, as it always is when a church is using

---

[122] Christian apologist Don Matzat insists that Martin Luther's view was the same as we have seen expressed by Spurgeon. Luther recognized the tension between God's sovereignty and free will but never tried to harmonize the two. See Matzat, Don. "Martin Luther and the Doctrine of Predestination," *Issues, Etc. Journal*. vol 1, no. 8 (October 1996) [online]. Accessed 11 October 2012, from http://www.issuesetcarchive.org/issues_site/resource/journals/v1n8.htm.

[123] The two models are: Molinism, ably presented by Kenneth Keathley, and my own proposal, called the "Chosen Contingency Model." See Chapters Nine and Ten.

a different supply preacher each Sunday. Our attendance was dwindling, and Carroll and I were among a few families which were trying to give leadership to fill in the gap until a new pastor could arrive on the field. It was at that time that a couple from one of our most active families came for a visit and said that they had been having a home Bible study with a retired minister, and he had introduced them to a theological system called "Calvinism." The young man and his wife were excited and asked if we would be willing to have this material taught to our church. I had heard of Calvinism, of course, but was not overly familiar with the details. So our friends provided us with some study materials.

When we reviewed the materials, we could see immediately that much in the doctrine was sound. But there also seemed to be much that conflicted with our understanding of what the Scriptures taught. So when we met with our friends again, we discussed our misgivings. We met several times and even met briefly with the retired minister. We could never feel comfortable with allowing the material to be taught in our church in any official way, and in the end, the young couple left the church to join with the retired minister in a home church which taught a rigorous version of Calvinism or Reformed theology. It was a great loss to our small church, but we parted on good terms.

A few years later we learned another couple had made the same decision. They were dear friends of ours who were living in Virginia. We had attended a Baptist church with them, but they too had begun studying Calvinism and decided to move their membership to a small Sovereign Grace Baptist Church. We recognized their strong commitment to the Lord through all this searching. Our friend Chris was an engineer, and he said that Calvinism seemed so reasonable and logical that he simply could not attend a church that did not teach this view. His wife Pam was perfectly agreeable, and they are happy in that church to this day.

Now, I do not want to say I know better than these two couples, or that they made a wrong decision about their church home. I am content to let that decision be between them and the Lord. Still, our conversations with them opened my eyes to a divide in Christian theology that is difficult to reconcile. It forced me to take a careful look at my own beliefs to see whether Calvinism, Arminianism, middle-of-the-road Baptist theology, or something else had the most scriptural support. Accordingly, let us back up for a moment and review how we got to this divide.

3. A FEW WORDS ON CHURCH HISTORY

Reformed theology, or Calvinism, came about from another great divide that took place in the 16th century. Most people have heard of Martin Luther who in 1517 nailed a document to a church door in Wittenberg, Germany. Thus began a split in the Christian church of Europe. When the dust settled, most of northern Europe was Protestant and the rest remained Catholic. The movement was called the Reformation because the initial idea was to reform the Roman Catholic Church rather than splitting off from it

Strangely enough, what we call Reformed theology owes more to a French lawyer named John Calvin and Ulrich Zwingli of Switzerland than it does to Martin Luther. Their ideas became well known due to the recently invented printing press, and their theology, which became known as Calvinism, also spread to the British Isles. John Knox had much to do with this theology being adopted in the Presbyterian church in Scotland. To this day, Reformed and Presbyterian churches follow various forms of Calvinism as do many Baptist churches.

What I call the great gulf is not the Protestant Reformation, itself, but a divide between the teachings of Zwingli, Calvin and Knox (Calvinism), on the one hand, and the teachings associated with Jacobus Arminius (Arminianism), on the other. Arminius was a Dutch theologian who differed in several important respects[124] from the Calvinists. Churches today that are strongly influenced by Arminius would include some Baptists, as well as Methodist, Pentecostal and Holiness churches.

The points of strongest disagreement between Calvinists and Arminians center on predestination and the nature of Christ's atonement for

---

[124] We must not lose sight of the fact that he also agreed with Calvin in many important respects.

sin. In debates in the early seventeenth century, though, followers of Arminius expressed their objections to Calvinism in a list of five points. Calvinists responded with five points of their own, which were called by the acronym TULIP. These points were affirmed by the Synod of Dort in 1618 and still capture much of the essence of Calvinist theology.

4. A TULIP THAT IS NOT A FLOWER

The Arminian position does not seem to have a handy acronym, so it is convenient to frame the discussion after the Calvinist model. The meaning of the TULIP acronym of Calvinism is commonly summarized as follows:

T = Total depravity

U = Unconditional election

L = Limited atonement

I = Irresistible grace

P = Perseverance of the saints

Of course, these five points are only a small part of Calvinist theology, but they do capture the points of greatest conflict on the issue of salvation. There are other differences, but the others seem to have potential for resolution or at least a live-and-let-live attitude. These points are difficult to resolve, and as we have seen, some say that they are irreconcilable. Let's take a look at what each of these concepts mean:

Total depravity means that every aspect of our being (body, soul, spirit, mind, will and emotions) is fallen. We are incapable of saving ourselves or even wishing for salvation. Arminians say people are incapable of gaining salvation by their own efforts. So the differences here are not great.

Unconditional election means God chose whom he would save, but this choice was not based on any merit or good works done by the persons concerned. God simply chose to save some and not to save others because of his sovereign will. Calvinists deny that God looked into the future to see who would choose him and then elected (chose) them for salvation. Arminians agree that works or human effort are not a basis for salvation. Arminians also agree that salvation is based on God's grace alone, but Arminians insist that salvation is conditioned on faith in Jesus. Arminians also say, in contrast to Calvinists, that God's election is based on his foreknowledge of those who would freely choose to accept Jesus as Savior. This difference is perhaps the primary point of contention.

Limited atonement is a doctrine which holds Christ's atonement to be effective only for the elect. In that sense, Christ did not die for all, even though it would have been sufficient for all. Arminians say that Christ's atonement is unlimited in its benefits and so is potentially for all people. Calvinists say that Christ paid the penalty for our sins, while Arminians have the concept that "Christ suffered for us." The end result of Christ's atonement is the same, but the two views comprise a difference of understanding about the mechanism of the atonement.

Irresistible grace means the elect cannot resist God's call to salvation. Arminians are diametrically opposed, holding grace to be resistible. This means God allows his grace to be resisted by all who refuse to believe in Christ. There is no room for compromise on this point.

Perseverance of the saints means a believer cannot lose his salvation. Salvation is seen as a work of God, from start to finish and those who are saved are eternally secure. Arminianism teaches that salvation can be lost, since salvation continually requires faith. Again, the two sides simply teach the exact opposite of the other.

What causes Christians to be drawn to Calvinism? For one thing, I think people are impressed by the commitment of Calvinists to uphold the sovereignty of God. Calvinists also seem to have had an abundance of able defenders over the years. We can think of such people as Charles Haddon Spurgeon, J. I. Packer, John Piper, R. C. Sproul, and Albert Mohler. Many excellent books have persuasively argued the Calvinist position. Furthermore, the Calvinist position is logical, with each point following and building from the one before. Arminians seem to have more difficulty in explaining their views, and I find their model to be untidy,[125] but these are superficial considerations. The real question is, "What do the Scriptures say?"

5. AN OVERVIEW OF SCRIPTURE.

The Scriptures are not kind to either of these two views. However, aspects of both Arminianism and Calvinism do have strong scriptural support. In an apparent effort to harmonize seemingly contradictory passages into a coherent model, however, both views are guilty of distorting the plain meaning. Christians who let these passages speak for themselves will find themselves uncomfortable in either camp and will be left without a coherent model that explains God's plan of salvation. It is frustrating to admit that the more one looks into the situation, the more confusing it gets.

For example, the Scriptures teach that God elects individuals as an act of his sovereign will, yet they also teach that it is God's desire to save everyone. Calvinism has not given a satisfactory way to resolve this conflict. Calvinism holds that God determines the future, and this concept has strong scriptural support. Even so, Calvinism has trouble explaining how their view does not make God the author of sin. Calvinism says that the atonement is limited, but 1 John 2:2 clearly says that Jesus is a propitiation for the sins of the whole world. Finally, the Scriptures make plain that the gospel is genuinely offered to everyone, yet Calvinism seems to teach the opposite.

On the other hand, the most distinctive teaching of Arminius is that God elects those people whom he foresees will freely choose him. Yet Arminians insist that because God can foresee the future does not mean the future is foreordained by God. A pithy phrase to express this idea is "foreknowledge does not imply foreordination." However, if the future is not foreordained by God, what causes it? Is the future caused by fate? Are we in a clockwork universe of impersonal determination generated by cause and effect? Or is the future caused by human choices?

---

[125]But Arminians do not lack able defenders. See Olson, Roger E. *Against Calvinism*. 2011. Zondervan, Grand Rapids, MI.

Arminianism and Scripture both agree that we humans were created with the ability to make free choices, and we are held accountable for those choices. Calvinists have to use much creative interpretation to explain away many passages that teach human freedom. Alternatively, they simply say that human freedom is a mystery; and is true, even though it seemingly contradicts the concept of divine foreordination.

We will go into more detail on specific passages of Scripture in further discussions below. Note that the views of salvation seem to be arranged on a continuum with hyper-Calvinists on the hard right and ultra-Arminians in the form of "Open Theists" on the far left, as follows:

| Open Theists | Arminians | | Calvinists | Hyper-Calvinists |

\ /

\ /

Great Gulf

6. CALVINISM IS COOL

For a system that seems synonymous with a 400-year-old argument among theologians, an argument that is often seen as simply irreconcilable, Calvinism would seem likely to be a focus of discussion in seminaries but not in other places. We would not expect to see these fine points of doctrine being discussed in the average pulpit or worship service, but we would be wrong. Timothy George, in a recent article in *Christianity Today*, put the issue in perspective:

> Calvinism is making a comeback. This past year has seen numerous conferences, lectures, and publications evaluating Calvin and his role as one of the most consequential thinkers of the last millennium. A few months ago, *Time* magazine published a story on the top ten forces that are currently changing the world. In addition to expected trends like the increasing role of the Internet and the global financial crisis, the renais-

sance of Calvinism in America came in as number three on the list. The evangelical blogs are abuzz, and Twitter is atweet, with comments on free will and predestination, original sin and sovereign grace.[126]

It is not only the blogosphere that is abuzz with Calvinism. The new, cool and post-emergent church of Mark Driscoll is Calvinist. He is controversial, popular with the young, and his sermons are racy with a sort of macho predestination.[127] He is not alone. Being young and Calvinist seem to go together, these days.

The book that I have chosen to illustrate the issue is *Calvinism: A Southern Baptist Dialogue.* In that book, the first section, "Calvinism, The Current Climate," began with a paper by Ed Stetzer entitled "Calvinism, Evangelism, and SBC Leadership." Stetzer highlighted studies showing that Mark Driscoll is not the only young evangelical pastor embracing Calvinism. In the SBC[128] about ten percent of church leaders call themselves five-point Calvinists, but among the set of young graduates about thirty percent accept the five-point label. Clearly, the number of Calvinists within the SBC is growing.[129] This point is reinforced by a 2007 study by the SBC's North American Mission Board that showed the number was closer to 35 percent.[130]

Some in the non-Calvinist element of the SBC chose, on 30 May 2012, to issue a document opposing these trends toward Calvinism and to encourage young, non-Calvinist pastors. The document, "A Statement

[126] George, Timothy, "John Calvin: Comeback Kid," *Christianity Today.* vol 53, no. 9 (September 2009) [online]. Accessed 11 October 2012, from http://www.christianitytoday.com/ct/2009/september/14.27.html.

[127] Worthen, Molly. "Who Would Jesus Smack Down?" *The New York Times.* 6 January 2009. [online] Accessed 11 October 2012, from http://www.nytimes.com/2009/01/11/magazine/11punk-t.html.

[128] Southern Baptist Convention.

[129] Stetzer, Ed. "Calvinism, Evangelism, and SBC Leadership." pp. 13–16. *Calvinism: A Southern Baptist Dialogue,* edited by E. Ray Clendenen and Brad J. Waggoner. *op. cit.*

[130] Gentry, Weston. "As Baptists Prepare to Meet, Calvinism Debate Shifts to Heresy Accusation." *Christianity Today.* 18 June 2012. [online] Accessed 12 October 2012, from http://www.christianitytoday.com/ct/2012/junewebonly/baptists-calvinism-heresy.html?start=2.

of the Traditional Southern Baptist Understanding of God's Plan of Salvation," has been signed by at least 650 Southern Baptists, many in leadership positions. The statement has been criticized for being needlessly confrontational, and it is certainly not kind to Calvinist views.[131] The fact that such a statement was issued is evidence of the growing influence of Calvinism and not just among Southern Baptists. This trend is generally found all across North America.

7. HOW CAN THE GAP BE BRIDGED?

We have seen that the divide between Calvinists and Arminians is real. It is not just an historical controversy that we can relegate to the realm of a curious, past unpleasantness. Calvinism is growing in influence, and there are fears adherents may be less willing to sit quietly in the same place with Arminian brethren. This trend is worrisome, and it is clear that now would be a good time to try to resolve these differences, if that is possible.

Have there been any attempts to find a middle road? The answer is "yes." One of these attempts has been put forward by Professor Kenneth Keathley and will be discussed in a subsequent chapter. I have also tried to articulate a model that steers a middle path, which I call the Chosen Contingency Model. The third approach is to articulate a Baptist vision for soteriology,[132] which does not depend on either Calvinism or Arminianism. The statement of May 2012, mentioned above, is one attempt to articulate God's plan of salvation. Another recent paper by a Baptist pastor (which seems to be consistent with the above statement), deliberately sets out to define and defend a Baptist position that is neither Calvinist nor Arminian.

This attempt at reconciliation, authored by Eric Hankins,[133] is based on four presuppositions. The first is that both Calvin and Arminius were

---

[131] *Ibid.*

[132] The term "soteriology" means the study of the doctrine of salvation: what it is and how we get it.

[133] Hankins, Eric. "Beyond Calvinism and Arminianism: Toward a Baptist Soteriology." *Journal For Baptist Theology and Ministry.* Vol. 8, no. 1 (Spring 2011). pp. 87–100. [online] Accessed 12 October 2012, from: http://baptist-

wrong in interpreting such passages as Romans 8:29–30 and 9:11 to be referring to individual election. Hankins argues that they refer, instead, to *corporate* election. In other words, he maintains these verses merely say that God predestined a body of people to be saved. People become members of the group because of faith in Jesus Christ.

The second presupposition of Hankins deals with the problem of *determinism* and *free will*. He says: "God has made a free and sovereign decision to have a universe in which human free will plays a decisive role. Human agency is one force among many that God has created to accomplish his cosmic purposes." In other words, Hankins rejects absolute causal determinism and calls it "untenable."[134] That is, he does not believe God has preordained all things.

As for the third presupposition, Hankins addresses the issue of what is known as *federal theology*. This doctrine involves the idea that when Adam fell into sin, he did so in such a way as to make all of his descendants guilty of sin and "depraved" or unable to do other than commit more sins. Hankins rejects this concept, believing that God enables all who put their faith in Christ to be saved. He apparently does not believe we are guilty through Adam's sin but only our own. He dismisses much of the standard doctrines relating to the state of fallen man as theological "fudge factors."[135]

Hankins then (as the fourth and last presupposition) takes on the doctrine of *total depravity*. This doctrine was discussed above as the "T" in TULIP. Since there is much agreement on this point between Calvinists and Arminians, there would seem to be little to reconcile. Hankins admits there is little debate in evangelical theology about the plight of sinful human beings. What he does think is debatable is the ability of a sinner to respond to God's offer of salvation. Hankins insists that with God's revelation through Christ and the work of the Holy Spirit, a sinner

---

center.com/Documents/Journals/JBTM%208-1%20Spring11.pdf Internet.
[134] *Ibid.,* p. 89.
[135] *Ibid.,* pp. 91–93.

does have the capacity to respond in faith, even though he lacks the ability to save himself.

With these four presuppositions in effect, Baptists, according to Hankins, can reject both Calvinism and Arminianism. The Baptist view of salvation refuses to speculate and go beyond what is clearly taught in Scripture. He concludes:

> Baptist soteriology (specifically including the doctrines of the sovereign, elective purposes of God, the sinfulness of all humans, the substitutionary atonement of Christ, salvation by grace alone through faith alone, and the security of the believer) is not in jeopardy and does not need to be reinforced by Calvinism or Arminianism. It can be successfully taught, maintained, and defended without resorting to either system.[136]

Hankins' proposal has merit, and it accurately reflects a theological position actually held by many Baptists. It certainly has the virtue of simplicity, and it deals with the relevant Scriptures at least as well as the complicated systems of Calvinism and Arminianism. However, there are two problems. The first deals with God's election of individuals. Even if the favorite Calvinist proof-texts are all viewed as simply dealing with corporate election (and this is certainly a possibility)[137] we are not completely home free. This analysis still leaves the tension between God's desire that all come to salvation, God's foreknowledge that many will not accept salvation, and God's omnipotence. We still have such verses as Acts 13:48, "When the Gentiles heard this, they rejoiced and glorified the message of the Lord, and all who had been appointed to eternal life believed."[138]

Some would insist Acts 13:48 is also concerned with corporate election. It is true that a group of people are being discussed. Proponents of the concept of corporate election simply say God appointed a group of Gentiles to be saved and those that believed joined that group. This view

---

[136] *Ibid.,* p. 96.

[137] Abasciano, Brian J. "Corporate Election in Romans 9: A reply to Thomas Schreiner." *Journal of the Evangelical Theological Society (JETS)* 49/2 (June 2006) 351–71.

[138] (HCSB)

holds that God did not preordain the *individuals* to be saved in eternity past, but there is a problem. The verse does not say that. It says that all (every person) who had been appointed[139] (by God) to receive eternal live did believe. Only by a strained interpretation, based on a presupposition of corporate election, could we ever imagine individuals are not the focus. If individuals are the focus, the group is simply the aggregate of the individuals. So I believe individual election is being discussed here. Corporate election is not clearly taught in this instance and if Baptists are not to go beyond what is clearly taught, then a doctrine of corporate election (as the *only* form of election) cannot be sustained.

If individual election cannot be eliminated as a scriptural position, then Hankins' first presupposition must fail. Furthermore, I think his second presupposition, however accurate it might be with respect to human free will, does not accurately reflect God's predetermination of the future as taught in Scripture. So the second problem is this: there is a thread running through Scripture that the future is determined by God, and it will not do to simply say this is not true, even if it complicates our theology. Consider Job 14:5: "A person's days are determined; you have decreed the number of his months and have set limits he cannot exceed."[140] So, however much I might accept Hankins' other points, and I think they have much merit, we cannot agree that this attempt to bridge the gulf is entirely successful. It is not so much that I doubt what he affirms; rather, I affirm what he doubts.

There is one final point concerning Hankins' view that God has universally given sinners the grace to overcome the impediment of their

---

[139] A contrary view by Dr. Brian Abasciano lists a number of alternate possible translations but all seem forced and less persuasive that the obvious interpretation. It is not likely that the point would simply be that those individuals who were predisposed (in the normal way) believed. Clearly, a work of God is in view, and that work must involve individual election. But see Abasciano, Brian. "Dr. Brian Abasciano Responds To Dr. Dan Wallace On The Issue Of Corporate Election." Submitted by Martin Glynn on Fri., 10/22/2010 - 12:45pm. *Society of Evangelical Arminians.* Accessed 12 October 2012, from: http://evangelicalarminians.org/glynn. Dr Brian-Abasciano-Responds-To-Dr Dan-Wallace-On-The-Issue-Of-Corporate-Election.

[140] (NIV)

lostness, of being "dead in sins."[141] This kind of grace is sometimes called *prevenient grace*. Calvinists think this concept of universal grace does not do justice to verses in the Scriptures that describe sinners as remaining in a state of spiritual blindness as in 2 Corinthians 4:4.[142] So if the Scriptures show this blindness as continuing for sinners, how can Hankins say God has completely removed this overwhelming obstacle to salvation? I must agree that the state of the lost without Christ is hopeless. The many verses that speak of sinners loving darkness, being blinded, hard-hearted, and of the devil clearly make this point. Yet this hopeless position of the lost does not prove God's prevenient grace is only for the elect. I agree Hankins' position on this matter is reasonable and is at least as well-supported from the Scriptures as is the Calvinist view.

Although I can agree with Hankins in part, I also see significant weaknesses. So I must conclude that Hankins' idea for a synthesis, a Baptist position, attractive though it seems, is not likely to be the bridge across the gulf. Fortunately there is another position, called *Molinism*, which may bring us closer to this goal. We shall consider this idea in a following chapter, but first, we need to look at the difficult concept of *time*.

FURTHER READING

Allen, David L. and Steve W. Lemke, Eds. *Whosoever Will: A Biblical-Theological Critique of Five-Point Calvinism*. Nashville: B & H Publishing Group. 2010.

Geisler, Norman L. *Chosen But Free: A Balanced View of God's Sovereignty and Free Will*. Bloomington, Minnesota: Bethany House. 2010.

Sproul, R. C. *What is Reformed Theology?: Understanding the Basics*.

---

[141] See Ephesians 2:5.

[142] See Wills, Gregory A. "Whosoever Will: A Review Essay." *The Journal For Baptist Theology & Ministry*. Vol. 7, No. 1. (Spring 2010) p. 12. Wills lists in a footnote these additional verses that make the same point: Matthew 11:20–27, 13:11–15; John 3:19, 6:37–39, 44–45, 65, 7:17, 8:43–47, 9:39, 10:25–28; Ephesians 5:8; 1 Peter 2:9; I John 2:9–11.

Grand Rapids: Baker. 1997.

DISCUSSION QUESTIONS

1. What do you see as the greatest strength and weakness in the Calvinist position?

2. What is the greatest strength and weakness in the Arminian position?

3. What are the strengths and weaknesses of the attempt at reconciliation authored by Eric Hankins?

4. Do you see a possible reconciliation between Calvinism and Arminianism?

CHAPTER 6

†

What is Time and Why Does it Matter?

Chronology is the science of ordering events in time. But what is time? This is a simple question, and it seems to merit a simple answer. Unfortunately, the answer is not simple, and in recent years it has become a theological controversy.

1. HOW DO WE KNOW WHAT TIME IS?

Chapter Seven will deal with a new theology called the openness of God, or open theism, which tries to explain how God interacts with his creation. Before we go into detail, it would be helpful to consider the ways we learn truth about any subject. We can add to our store of knowledge in three main ways: observation, human reason, and authority. Some might say scientific study is another way, but it is better to think of scientific study as a systematized form of observation, as informed by human reason. Revelation is the highest form of authority, consisting of truths revealed directly by God, primarily in his holy Word—the Bible.

Let us consider how observation and human reason can contribute to one foundational concept—time. This concept is mysterious—physicists admit the current state of knowledge is limited. Yet we can deal with time as it is commonly experienced. In one sense we are all experts, because we interact with time every day.

First, we understand the past to be fixed. In the Rubaiyat of Omar Khayyam we find these lines:

> The Moving Finger writes: and, having writ,
> Moves on: nor all thy Piety nor Wit
> Shall lure it back to cancel half a Line,
> Nor all thy tears wash out a Word of it.[143]

So we generally believe our actions can affect the future, but we never think our actions can affect the past. We see the past as fixed and unchangeable.

Secondly, we perceive the present to consist of a brief instant, caught on the edge of past and future. We see the present as the kind of time that we can affect by our volition. Present time, to us, seems like a wave moving at a steady rate of speed in the direction away from the past towards the future.

Thirdly, we see the future as open but unknowable by humans. It is potential reality which is affected by our present actions. These perceptions are common to humankind, and yet, experimental science has contributed little to confirm or deny them.[144] Time remains a mystery in many ways. David Hume put it this way:

> When two people meet, they unconsciously affect one another in ways the mind cannot even begin to comprehend. The meeting may be brief and uneventful with nothing fruitful happening as a result of it. But the die is cast and the wheels of time have turned. The present as we know it is now the past and the future is always just beyond reach. Looking backwards, we see the roads we travelled and everything is fated. Looking forward, we see nothing but mist and mazes. Nothing

---

[143] *The Rubaiyat of Omar Khayyam*, translated by Edward FitzGerald, quatrain LI in his 1st edition. [online] Accessed 12 October 2012, from http://www.library.cornell.edu/colldev/mideast/okhym.htm Internet.

[144] Philosophers call this idea, that the present is the prime reality, as "A-theory" time. This terminology was proposed by John M. E. McTaggart, in his work: *The Nature of Existence*, published in two parts: 1921 and 1927. But also see McTaggart, John McTaggart Ellis. *The Unreality of Time. Mind: A Quarterly Review of Psychology and Philosophy* 17 (1908): 456–473. Accessed 30 Aug. 2012, from http://www.ditext.com/mctaggart/time.html.

happens out of mere coincidence and randomness. No effect is without a cause just as no cause is without an effect. For every action there is a reaction and we find that events of the past are necessary and certain. Our meeting today is inevitable.[145]

However much we might agree that time is mysterious, there has always been a sharp difference of opinion on one point and that concerns the beginning of time. Some religions, cultures and philosophers have maintained that time has no beginning. Usually this view is taken to mean that the universe as a whole had no beginning but has existed from all eternity. Others disagree, insisting the universe and time itself did have a beginning. One thing is sure. One, and only one, of these ideas can be true. Either time and the universe had a beginning or they did not.

What does reason tell us? One general principle we can derive by logical deduction is that to arrive at the end of an infinite sequence is impossible. In other words, if time always existed, then it existed from a period infinitely long ago. To put it another way, there would have had to be an infinite number of seconds (minutes, hours or other time periods) before the present time. It would mean the present time is an infinite total formed by the successive addition of finite units of time, which is impossible. So, if the universe is infinitely old, this present time cannot exist because one can never reach an infinite number by the addition of finite units. Clearly, though, the present has arrived, so it must have arrived by the addition of a finite number of time units. Therefore, time had a beginning.[146]

The concept is difficult because we are used to the idea from our study of math that infinity (or an infinite set of numbers) exists. This is true, from a mathematical viewpoint. The problem is when we assume that an infinite number of *real* things can exist. There is really no evidence for

---

[145] Hume, David. 1748. *Enquiry Concerning Human Understanding.* "Meditation XXIII."

[146] As philosopher David Hume admitted, "An infinite number of real parts of time passing in succession ... appears so evident a contradiction that no man whose judgment is not corrupted ... would ever be able to admit of it." Hume, David Hume. *Enquiry.* xii. II 125.

the latter. Logically, we can't have an infinite number of apples, because we could always add one more to the pile.

Process theologians, whom I will discuss in more detail below, insist they do not say that the past is infinitely long; they say the past has no beginning. But that does not help. If the past had no beginning, there still would be a time that had an infinitely long interval before a subsequent time.[147] So the deductive argument remains valid. If time is finite, it must have had a finite beginning.

It might be well to mention in passing that there are good reasons for saying that not only is time not infinite, but nothing in the created universe is infinite either. Of course, we understand angels and humans will have an infinitely long future, but that should be regarded as a special case, since those life spans are not infinitely long at this point.[148] David Hilbert, a distinguished mathematician, has written, "The infinite is nowhere to be found in reality. It neither exists in nature nor provides a legitimate basis for rational thought. The role that remains for the infinite ... is solely that of an idea. ..."[149]

Current scientific theories seem to bear this out. When the universe and its rate of expansion is considered, everything seems to have originated from a single point at a finite time in the past. That means the universe had a beginning, which is sometimes called the "Big Bang."[150] Modern physics suggests that matter, energy, space and time all originated at a finite time in the past. This suggestion agrees with what reason says. Time has not existed forever. It, along with everything else, had a definite

---

[147] See Craig, William Lane. "The Kalam Cosmological Argument." *Library of Philosophy and Religion Series*, ed. John Hick. 1979. Barnes and Noble, New York.

[148] Actually, these life spans will never be of infinite duration, since they all had a beginning.

[149] Hilbert, David. "On the Infinite", in *Philosophy of Mathematics*, With an Intro. by Paul Benacerraf and Hilary Putnam. 1964. Prentice-Hall, Englewood Cliffs, NJ. p. 151.

[150] This is not to suggest agreement with any sort of atheist explanation for the big bang or to suggest the creation story in Genesis should be reinterpreted to fit current models of the big bang.

beginning. Science has no real answer as to what happened before the Big Bang nor is there a scientific explanation as to how something arose from nothing.[151]

What does the Bible say about this idea? God wanted to clarify this point before any other revelation. The first verse in the Bible, Genesis 1:1, begins with the sentence: "In the beginning, God created the heavens and the earth."[152] From God's revelation, we see there was a beginning when God created all things, which we now understand to mean matter, energy, space and time.

So if reason, science, and revelation all generally agree that the universe and time itself had a beginning, we have a happy case of general accord. Revelation alone would have been sufficient, but we do expect that most of the time reason, observation and revelation should agree. Therefore, we must believe that since God created all things from nothing, he must have created time also. This conclusion follows because time is an integral part of the universe which God created. God created time and he did it in the beginning. This answer is also the only one that sufficiently explains the origin of the universe. It did not spontaneously arise from nothing. It was created by the all-powerful, eternal God revealed in the Bible.

So if God created time when he created the universe, then prior to the creation he must have existed outside of time, a state often referred to as *timelessness*. He not only did not need time for his existence, but he did not need space, matter, or energy, either. He transcends all these things, and since he created them, they are subject to his power. God did not need the

---

[151] Not all physicists agree time started at the big bang. Some believe that this universe may have arisen from an unlikely fluctuation of a previous universe. But that does not explain the origin of the previous universe. It reminds one of ancient cosmologies that saw the world sitting on a turtle, who was sitting on the back of an even bigger turtle and so on to infinity. See the discussion of "baby universes" in: Carroll, Sean, *From Eternity to Here*. 2010. Dutton, New York, NY. p. 357.

[152] (KJV)

universe for his existence, but the universe, which means everything that is not God,[153] absolutely requires God and his creative power in order to exist.

God is not part of the universe, though he manifests his presence within it. He is not confined to any particular place but is fully present in all places. The same is true with time. God does not need time for his existence, but he can manifest himself within time. He is not confined to a particular time but is fully present in all times.[154] If he wishes, he can join with his creatures in experiencing the flow of time, in the succession of events. In his essential nature, since he transcends all time, he can view time as a unit, with past, present, and future being all one. To God, time is like the view that an observer from a high hill might have of a caravan stretched out on a road below. He can see time in its totality.[155] In other words, we can deduce, simply from knowing that God created time, that time has no mastery over him.

Deductions, however logical they may seem to us, need to be put to the test of revelation. What do the Scriptures say about God and his relationship to time? We see in 2 Peter 3:8: "Dear friends, don't let this one thing escape you: With the Lord one day is like a thousand years and a thousand years like one day."[156] Psalm 90:4 says much the same thing, "For in your sight a thousand years are like yesterday that passes by, like a few hours of the night."[157] Clearly, God views time differently from the way humans do. Revelation 1:8 emphasizes the essential timelessness of God:

"I am the Alpha and the Omega," says the Lord God, "the One who is, who was, and who is coming, the Almighty."[158] Isaiah is even more specific: "This

---

[153] God also created heaven, which may not be part of this universe.

[154] This idea, that past, present and future are all equally real, is called B-theory time by philosophers. See McTaggart, John McTaggart Ellis. *The Unreality of Time. op. cit.*

[155] Stanley Grenz put it this way in his classic text on systematic theology: "The divine mind perceives the entire temporal sequence – all events – simultaneously in one act of cognition." Stanley Grenz, *Theology for the Community of God* (Nashville: Broadman & Holman, 1994), pp. 120–21.

[156] (HCSB)

[157] *Ibid.*

[158] (HCSB)

is what the Lord, the King of Israel and its Redeemer, the Lord of Hosts, says: 'I am the first and I am the last. There is no God but Me. Who, like Me, can announce the future?'"[159]

Many more verses could be mentioned, but these are enough to show God is not limited to experiencing time as we do. He was before all time and even if time ended, he would still be. He knows the future as well as the past—which is an important point. If past, present and future are all one to God, then past, present and future are all equally real. So if the past is fixed, then the future must in some sense be fixed as well. If the future is contingent and subject to change, then the past would be contingent, also. I will discuss this surprising concept in more detail below.

Does God's timelessness mean our common perception of time is wrong? It might seem so, but it is better to think of our perception of time as valid but incomplete. Psalm 90:4 (quoted above) speaks of a thousand years as like yesterday that "passes by." We notice the reference to God's perception of time as being quite different from ours, yet it also says that yesterday passes by. The Scripture validates our human perception of time, as well as telling us that it is incomplete.

Why have I spent so much time discussing the concept of time and God's timelessness? Simply because time is a critical feature of the new *openness of God* theology. So we need to understand what the Scriptures teach about time in reference to God. To summarize:

A. God existed before[160] he created the universe, which we understand to consist of matter, energy, space and time.[161]

B. God does not need time to exist, and he is timeless in his essential character.

C. God created time and is master over time. He may experience time as a

---

[159] Isaiah 44:6–7a (HCSB)

[160] Some might object to the use of the term "before" to discuss something that happened when time was uncreated, but the term is used here to describe a logical sequence and not a temporal sequence.

[161] Titus 1:2, speaks of a promise "before time began." (HCSB) Also 2 Timothy 1:9.

succession of events but need not. He is fully present in each particular time and in all time.[162]

D. Because God can experience the past, present and future as he chooses, we can see there is no essential difference between past, present and future. All time is one to him, which means that fundamentally, all time is one. Yet our experience of time also has validity.

E. Because God created time and can experience all time, he naturally knows every detail of all times.[163] He knows the future quite as well as the past. That is why he can "announce the future."

2. A CHALLENGE FROM PHILOSOPHICAL THEOLOGY

At this point, we must discuss a possible problem with our analysis of time. Most evangelical theologians agree that God stands above time, can see all times equally vividly and is timeless in his own being.[164] But philosophical theologians such as William Lane Craig sharply disagree with this idea, finding it incoherent. Craig puts it like this:

> At issue here is God's relationship to time: Does God exist temporally or atemporally? God exists temporally if and only if He exists in time, that is to say, if and only if His duration has phases which are related to each other as earlier and later. In that case, God, as a personal being, has experientially a past, a present, and a future. No matter what moment in time we pick, given God's permanence, the assertion, "God exists now," were we to make it, would be literally true.
>
> By contrast, God exists atemporally if and only if He is not temporal. This definition makes it evident that temporality and timelessness are contradictories: an entity must exist one way or the other and cannot

---

[162] To put it another way, in his transcendence God experiences time as B-theory time; but in his immanence he can choose to experience time as A-theory time.

[163] At this point, it does not matter whether the future is determined or contingent. These statements remain true.

[164] Grudem, Wayne. *Systematic Theology. op. cit.*, pp. 169–173.

exist both ways at once. If, then, God exists atemporally, He has no past, present, and future. At any moment in time it would be true to assert, "God exists," in the tenseless sense of "exists," as when one says, "The natural numbers exist," but not true to assert, "God exists now."[165]

Clearly, Craig has defined the terms to show that God must either be temporal or atemporal. He insists God cannot be both at the same time, but is this viewpoint actually true? We have seen that theologians who draw their beliefs about God primarily from Scripture, with less reliance on the conventions of contemporary philosophy, have come to the opposite conclusion—although it must also be said that philosophical theologians are divided on the issue. Rather than consider the wide variety of opinions, however, it may be sufficient to consider Craig's arguments as representative of the contention that God is clearly limited with respect to time. Craig has arrived at the conclusion that God is atemporal before the creation but is now (subsequent to the creation) temporal. To strengthen his point he says:

> Now clearly, both of these views cannot be right because they are contradictory to one another. To say that God is timeless is simply to say that He is not temporal. So one is the negation, or denial, of the other. If God is timeless, He is not temporal; if He is temporal, then by definition He is not timeless. Very often, lay people will say, "Well, why can't God be both? Why can't He be both temporal and atemporal?" Well, the problem with that answer is that unless you can provide a model that makes sense of that claim, it is flatly self-contradictory and therefore cannot be true. It's like saying that something is both black and not black. That is logically impossible, unless you can provide some sort of model that would provide a distinction that would make it possible. For example, something might be black on one side and not black on the other side. Or it might be black at one time but later be non-black at another time. So if you're going to maintain that God is both temporal and atemporal, you need to provide some sort of a model that would make sense of that. But obviously, in this case neither of these

---

[165] Craig, William Lane. "Divine Eternity." In *The Oxford Handbook of Philosophical Theology*, 2009, eds. Thomas Flint and Michael Rea. Oxford University Press, Oxford. pp. 145–66. Accessed 17 September 2012, from http://www.reasonablefaith.org/divine-eternity#ixzz26kdpoZRj.

two alternatives would do. One part of God can't be temporal and the other part atemporal, because as an immaterial being God doesn't have separable parts. He's not made up of parts. Neither can you say coherently that God is atemporal at one time and temporal at another time because it's flatly self-contradictory to say that He's non-temporal at a certain time. That's a contradiction in terms. So both of these views of divine eternity cannot be right. We have to decide whether God is timeless or temporal.[166]

Craig's points should be considered, since he is saying it is impossible for God to be both timeless and immanent. First, we need to look at several implicit and explicit assumptions or premises upon which he seems to base his conclusion:

- God is a monad with respect to time.
- All time is A-theory time. In other words, past, present and future are not equally real.
- There is a kind of absolute time called "cosmic time."[167] This statement is true, even if there is more than one universe.
- God cannot be atemporal at one time and temporal at another time.
- God is temporal if he has any relation to a temporal creation.
- God is not simple[168] or immutable.[169]

Are these assumptions reasonable? Craig says that an immaterial being does not have separable parts, so he cannot be partly in time and partly outside of time. This idea can be described as that of a monad, but we know God is not a monad; he is a Trinity. Yet he is One in essence. We know that God in his essence is Spirit, yet we

[166] Craig, William Lane. *God, Time and Eternity.* Oxbridge Conference. July 23, 2002. Accessed 17 September 2012, from http://www.reasonablefaith.org/god-time-and-eternity.

[167] Craig, William Lane. *Divine Eternity. op. cit.,* pp. 145–66.

[168]"Simple" means God is a unity, a complete and integrated whole.

[169] "Immutable" means that God is unchangeable in his essential being (see Psalm 102:25–27), but that is not to say he does not feel emotions, or that he does not have genuine relations with his creatures.

also know that the Son, being incarnate, is fully God and fully man. Using this divine relationship as an analogy, there seems to be no reason to doubt that God in his essence is timeless, yet God, in his immanence, is temporal. It is probably not exactly correct to see God the Father as timeless—yet see God the Holy Spirit and God the Son as temporal—but at the same time this idea may have a grain of truth. So the Trinity seems to be an adequate model to explain how God can be both atemporal and temporal. At the very least, the doctrine of the Trinity forces us to reject a concept that God is a monad in any way.

John M. E. McTaggart (1866–1925) proposed, early in the 20th century, the distinction between A and B theories of time. There has been much debate about whether one or the other of these theories accurately reflect reality and if so, which one.[170] The A-series theory largely reflects what we perceive. The theory sees time as something like a river which flows, consisting of a series of events. The future is seen as contingent if it exists at all. The present is real and the place where we exercise volition. The past is fixed and its reality is debatable.

McTaggart saw B-series time as being fixed. It is common to describe it as a four-dimensional block of spacetime, though McTaggart did not use those terms. Under this theory, past, present and future are all equally real. The future is as fixed as the past, since there is actually no difference between them. This view seems contrary to common sense, but it seems demanded by the idea that God, being timeless, can view all time simultaneously. The theory of relatively, as proposed by Albert Einstein, supports B-series time, as well. Einstein summed the situation with respect to time in this way: "People like us, who believe in physics, know that the distinction between past, present, and future is only a stubbornly persistent illusion."[171]

---

[170] McTaggart, John M. Ellis. *The Unreality of Time. op. cit.*

[171] Letter from Einstein to the family of his lifelong friend Michele Besso, (March 1955) as quoted in *Science and the Search for God: Disturbing the*

However, even though there are devotees to both systems of time, McTaggart, himself, saw both theories as inadequate. He even proposed a "C-series," but that was simply an ordering of events and not actually temporal since it involved no concept of change. So C-series time is not a resolution of the problem.

Therefore, the idea that all time is A-theory time was rejected by the originator of the concept.[172] McTaggart believed the concept of A-theory time had fatal weaknesses, mainly that it was incoherent. Of course, he also said A-theory time was needed to allow for change and to explain how events could be caused by previous events.[173] Without going into detail, the idea that only A-theory time exists is dubious.[174] It is much better to see both A-theory time and B-theory time as containing parts of the truth.[175] B-theory time very well describes the underlying reality of the universe and helps us to understand God's perspective (from a timeless view), being separate from the spacetime universe. A-theory time is how we, and any intelligent creature, experience time. We must see the block of B-theory spacetime[176] as infused with A-theory time and understand that God created both aspects of time and can experience both at his pleasure.

Universe (1979) by Freeman Dyson, Ch. 17, "A Distant Mirror," London: Pan Books.

[172] McTaggart, John McTaggart Ellis. *The Unreality of Time. op. cit.*

[173] We should remember that the Scriptures speak of time passing, of the past, present, and future as real things. See Grudem, Wayne. "The Nature of Divine Eternity: A Response to William Craig." *Philosophia Christi*. 20:1 (Spring, 1997) 55–70. p. 65.

[174] Scripture speaks of the future as having real existence, which fits B-theory time better than A-theory time. See Genesis 41:26–41.

[175] Also we note that Craig can visualize God as relating to the universe in the context of B-series time without being Himself temporal. See Craig, William Lane. "Timelessness and Omnitemporality." *Philosophia Christi*, Series 2, Vol. 2, No. 1, 2000, pp. 29–33. See online: < http://www.reasonablefaith.org/timelessness-and-omnitemporality>. Accessed 17 September 2012.

[176] The concept of "spacetime" will be discussed in more detail below.

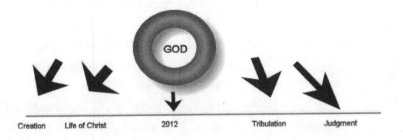

Figure 1: God's Perspective of Time

The idea of "cosmic time" as advocated by Craig, was denied by Einstein. Craig says Einstein was wrong, and cosmic time would be possible in the General Theory of Relativity, which would allow an absolute time for God. Yet as we shall see below, this idea does not explain the fact that the speed of an object in space plus its speed through time must equal the speed of light. This finding is based on experimental data, does not lie in the realm of speculative philosophy and suggests absolute time may not exist—in other words, that time is relative. Relative time is deadly for A-theory time, if one wishes it to exist as the sole category of time. Craig's explanation as to the possibility of absolute time is on shaky ground. The idea that God can have an accurate understanding of time, even when experiencing it in an A-theory way, seems reasonable. Craig went further and said there must be a common time even if there was more than one universe. This comment seems to be off-topic, though it might be relevant if heaven is considered to be separate from our universe. However, since there is no evidence for a trans-universal global time, we must consider that concept born more of speculation than logical analysis or the study of Scripture. So I deny the concept of trans-universe common time, in the absence of proof to the contrary. The idea of heaven also takes away from the idea that God is trapped in our temporal existence, which is possibly why Craig raised the topic in the first place.

Craig says God cannot be temporal at one time and atemporal at another. We might wonder at this assertion, because Craig himself says exactly that. He says God was atemporal before the universe was created and temporal since then. Apparently he assumes the truth of that concept in arguing that God cannot change from temporal to atemporal. We understand that becoming atemporal at a moment in time seems to be a contradiction. If becoming atemporal means God ceases to have any further relationship with the universe, we would find that inconceivable. So we must agree that since the creation God has been involved with the universe, and his involvement has occurred in a temporal way. I deny that God is forced to continue this temporal relationship, and in that sense, God would have the power to terminate any form of A-theory temporality.

Craig's final point is that God is temporal if he has any relationship with the creation which is temporal. Of course, Craig is operating under the assumption that A-theory time is the only time that exists. I deny this but admit that God has a relationship with his creation. I will discuss below what that might mean and what it does not mean, but it definitely does not mean he is "trapped in time."

We should expand on this argument by using another attribute of God: his omnipresence. The omnipresence of God is well established in Scripture.[177] 1 Kings 8:27 says: "But will God indeed live on earth? Even heaven, the highest heaven, cannot contain you, much less this temple I have built."[178] In other words, God has no spatial limitations whatsoever. God cannot be contained within the entire universe. This absence of spatial limits is important because there is not a clean division between space and time. If the universe cannot contain God spatially, then it cannot contain him temporally, either. God is simply greater than the universe in every way. So whatever God "being temporal after the creation" might mean, it certainly must mean the universe cannot contain him in a temporal sense.

Craig denies God's *simplicity* and his *immutability*, but he takes these doctrines in a most extreme fashion, as held by Aquinas, for example.[179] I take it to mean that God does not change in his essential being, which

---

[177] See 1 Kings 8:27; Jeremiah 23:23, 24; Psalm 139:7–10; 1 Kings 8:27; Proverbs 15:3; Acts 17:27–28.

[178] (HCSB)

[179] Craig, William Lane. *Divine Eternity. op. cit.*

means he remains timeless in his essential being even after the creation. I agree he is engaged in creation in a relational way. I agree the classic definitions of simplicity and immutability are too restrictive, and to this extent, I agree with Craig, but this agreement does not help Craig's case.

To sum up, I agree with Craig that in some sense of the word, God has been temporal since the creation, but I agree in a rather weak sense. I deny that God is restricted to A-theory time. I deny that A-theory time is a complete description of time and how it works in our universe. I deny that God cannot both be temporal and atemporal. I deny that God is a monad with respect to time and insist that his triune nature is the key to understanding how he can be above time and engaged in time as his plan for the universe unfolds. I deny God is trapped in time. I see no reason to believe time in heaven is the same as time on earth and deny there is a trans-universe common time. I am not wedded to theories advanced by science, such as special or general relativity, but our discussion must take account of experimental data. Experimental data suggest time and space are related. So omnipresence suggests omnitemporality. To conclude, I deny that philosophical theologians such as Craig have demonstrated God is not timeless in his essential character after creation. To the contrary, I assert there is good reason to believe God is timeless in his essential nature, even though he is involved with his creation, in time, in a loving way.

3. A CHALLENGE FROM OPEN THEISTS

We will take a long, hard look at open theism in Chapter Six. The important thing to realize, at this point, is that open theists say the future does not exist. In order to look at the open theists' view of time, we have to discuss their theological presuppositions.

John Sanders, a proponent of the open view, said this about God as timeless:

> The problem is that a timeless being is strongly impassible ... and it is impossible for an atemporal being to experience grief or any changing emotional state since changing states require a before and an after —

something an atemporal being simply does not have.[180]

We see a failure of the imagination and a denial of the capacity of an omnipotent God. This denial is disturbing, since it has more than a hint of condescension towards the Almighty. I see no particular problem with affirming God's timelessness as *essential*, while at the same time affirming that God has the capacity to enter into time if it is his good pleasure to do so. It is as if Sanders would view God like a man who built a swimming pool and then was condemned to jump into the pool and never come out. From then on the pool owner would have to experience life as aquatic. But this perception is not true. A man can build a pool which gives him convenient access to water, but he is perfectly able to take a dip and then climb out if he wishes.

Sanders says it is impossible for an atemporal being to experience grief. Yet God is seen as atemporal in Psalm 90:2, "from eternity to eternity You are God."[181] Psalm 95:10 shows God saying: "Forty years long was I grieved with this generation ..."[182] So it seems a timeless God can experience time as well as grief. Grudem says it well: "God can act in time *because* he is Lord of time."[183] If he wants to experience time, he can do so. Sanders glibly pontificates on what is impossible for a timeless God. He is quick to declare, "God cannot do this" or "God cannot do that," but it is madness to define God by our ignorance. We cannot put God in a box. We should simply admit we rarely know enough to put limits on God and be careful about opining about what he cannot do. We know as much about timelessness as a pig does about Christmas.

Open theism's fundamental point of departure from classical Christian teaching is the idea that *the future does not exist*, not even in the mind of God. Yet contrary to every reasonable expectation, the proponents of

---

[180] Sanders, John. "Divine Relationality and Theodicy in The Shack." Presented at the American Academy of Religion in Montreal, Canada, November 7, 2009. Accessed 17 December 2012, from http://www.opentheism.info/pdf/ sanders/ divine_relationality_the_shack.pdf.

[181] (HCSB)

[182] (KJV)

[183] Grudem, Wayne, *Systematic Theology. op. cit.*, p. 172.

open theism make no effort to prove this assumption. It is simply stated as a self-evidently true. It is often expressed like this: "The future does not exist because it hasn't happened yet." Even though that sounds almost reasonable from our perspective, it is not really an argument. Of course the future "hasn't happened yet." That is why we call it the future. One might as well say the past does not exist, either, because it has already happened. Or we might as well say the present doesn't exist, either, because it occupies only an infinitely small fraction of time. These three thoughts, taken together, would prove time didn't exist at all, but it still seems to be progressing as I type this line. Time is mysterious, to be sure, but an assumption like this one requires some kind of proof, and this has not been seriously attempted.

Some might disagree. Saint Augustine, in Book XI of his *Confessions*, said this:

> What is by now evident and clear is that neither future nor past exists, and it is inexact language to speak of three times—past, present and future. Perhaps it would be exact to say: there are three times, a present of things past, a present of things present, a present of things to come. In the soul there are these three aspects of time, and I do not see them anywhere else. The present considering the past is memory, the present considering the present is immediate awareness, the present considering the future is expectation.[184]

Augustine may have doubted that past and future time had earthly reality outside of the consciousness of those who participated in it, but he certainly did not doubt God's omniscience. He may have been a "presentist,"[185] but that did not affect his understanding of God's attributes. And even Augustine made no real effort to prove that only the present existed. He simply presented it as a metaphysical idea. It is important to note, though, that he apparently saw no conflict with this idea and the idea of a future foreordained in the mind of God. He

---

[184] Augustine, *Confessions*. Translated by H. Chadwick. 1998. Oxford University Press, Oxford. p. 235.

[185] That is, one who believes that only the present is real.

understood that God knew all times—past, present and future—and said of God:

> For He does not pass from this to that by transition of thought, but beholds all things with absolute unchangeableness; so that of those things which emerge in time, the things of the future, indeed, are not yet, and the present are now, and the past no longer are; but all of these are by Him comprehended in His stable and eternal presence.... For as without any movement that time can measure, He Himself moves all temporal things, so He knows all times with a knowledge that time cannot measure.[186]

Another train of thought which might have validity is this: If the future does not exist, what is it that we move into an instant from now? Where does it come from? Is it created just in time for us to move into, in a temporal way? If so, who creates it? If God creates it, then he must know what it is going to be. How could he create it otherwise? And if he creates it, how could parts of it take him by surprise? Or do we create it by our actions? And if we create the future in whole or in part, are we not co-creators with God, like demi-gods? And what about the past? Does it immediately de-materialize? All these questions are designed to show that the idea that "the future doesn't exist because it hasn't happened yet" is a more difficult concept than it first seems. There are good reasons why theoretical physicists like Brian Greene (professor of physics and mathematics, Columbia University) are convinced both past and future are equally real.[187] This is why McTaggart considered A-theory time to be incoherent, standing alone.

Sean Carroll, a theoretical physicist at the California Institute of Technology, had this to say about the question of time: "To a physicist there seems to be no contradiction between stepping outside the universe and thinking of all spacetime as one, and admitting that from the point

---

[186] Saint Augustine. "On the Two Cities: Selections from The City of God." *Milestones of Thought*. F. W. Strothmann, ed. 1957. Frederick Ungar: New York, N.Y. p. 39.

[187] See Greene, Brian R., *The Fabric of the Cosmos: Space, Time, and the Texture of Reality.* 2004, Vintage Books (Random House), New York.

of view of any individual inside the universe, time seems to flow."[188] Carroll's statement is amazingly close to what a classical theologian would say about the matter, but it is diametrically opposed to the view of openness theologians. He goes on to say:

> "That distinction between the fixedness of the past and the malleability of the future is nowhere to be found in the known laws of physics. The deep-down microscopic rules of nature run equally well forward or backward in time from any given situation. If you know the exact state of the universe, and all the laws of physics, the future as well as the past is rigidly determined beyond John Calvin's wildest dreams of predestination."

Nothing here gives much hope to the view of openness theology.[189] Open theists do realize that the idea of a nonexistent future will not stand scrutiny if God is truly timeless. If God created all things, including time, then he must be timeless. And if he is timeless, he is not bound to time as we are, This means he must be able to see time from the outside—past, present and future—just as Sean Carroll said. So past, present and future must all have reality; they must be ontologically real. God's timelessness destroys the idea of a nonexistent future.[190] Yet open theists (to their credit) are reluctant to give up the idea that God created all things.

A possible way to avoid this trap might be to say that somehow time existed before the creation. Of course that would mean creation would not really be creation from nothing, and open theists say they do believe in creation *ex nihilo*.[191] So the only other possibility would be to believe God

---

[188] Carroll, Sean. *From Eternity to Here*. 2010. Dutton, New York, NY. p. 386. Footnote 17.

[189] We must say that just because the mathematical model of the universe works just as well in reverse, does not necessarily mean that the actual universe could run backwards in time.

[190] It does not necessarily destroy the idea of a contingent future, but it eliminates the notion of a future that is mostly unpredictable, even by God.

[191] This would again bring up the problem of infinite time. If God existed for an infinite time before creation, the creation would never happen because one can never come to the end of an infinite series. This is why classic theology views God as timeless in his essential being.

existed outside of time until the creation and then was somehow "sucked in" to the universe and forced to experience time in the same way as his creatures. It sounds as if God were forced to give up his foreknowledge and became half blind.[192] In other words, open theists suggest God was caught in time, in the machine that he created, like Johnny Rebeck in the children's song:

> Johnny Rebeck, oh, Johnny Rebeck,
> How could you be so mean?
> We told you you'd be sorry
> For inventing that machine
> Now all the neighbors' cats and dogs
> Will never more be seen
> For they've been ground to sausage
> In Johnny Rebeck's machine
> One night the thing got busted,
> It just wouldn't go
> So Johnny Rebeck climbed inside
> To see what made it so.
> His wife she had a nightmare
> She was walking in her sleep
> She gave the crank a terrible yank
> And Johnny Rebeck was meat.

This concept of a God who is helplessly gobbled up by his own creation is pitiful and ridiculous. How could God have been trapped? It seems open theists either must embrace the premises of process theology and deny creation *ex nihilo* or they must abandon the idea that God is trapped in time (is not timeless in his eternal nature). As it is, they remain on the horns of a dilemma.

Still, it is clear that open theists have been so entranced by the idea of an "open" God that is vulnerable, who interacts, who co-creates, who

---

[192] It reminds one of Oedipus, the king of Thebes who blinded himself.

changes, who risks, who dialogues with his creatures, like some all-wise, caring professor in the faculty lounge, that they cannot give it up. They simply like a touchy-feely God. They think God's timelessness interferes with this vision, so they simply maintain (with no proof) that God cannot be timeless. They admit they adopted this view because that they did not see how God could interact with his creatures (as he is seen doing in the Scriptures) if he were essentially timeless. That inability to see how both aspects of God could be true is apparently the main reason they reject God's timelessness. But the lack of imagination or understanding on the part of open theists is no proof that their beliefs are true.

4. MORE PROBLEMS WITH OPEN THEISM

There is a further problem with the open theism viewpoint that says the future does not exist. For this idea to be true, other ideas must also be true. Note that classical Christian theology need not assume the truth or falsity of any of these, but open theism would fall if any of these are false:

1. Present time must be absolute in nature. Simultaneity must be ontologically real. However, the special theory of relativity casts serious doubt on this whole concept. For example, according to this theory, if a car crash happens in New York and another in London, it is impossible to say whether or not they happened at the same time. So the question of whether events are simultaneous is relative, not absolute.[193]

2. The timeline which separates past from future must also be absolute. All over the universe, future must be turning into present simultaneously. That is, there must be an absolute timeline for the open theism position to be true. According to special relativity, the timeline seems to be inextricably linked to an observer, and there seems to be no reason why it must be universal.

3. Whether the timeline is truly universal or not, every human being or observer must have an absolute experience of the temporal present. However, there seems to be no known principle to show this universal

---

[193] See http://en.wikipedia.org/wiki/Relativity_of_simultaneity.

timeline exists. We simply have no way to tell if "now" for one person is "now" for someone else (this idea will be expanded on below).

4. Time must absolutely and always go in one direction, from past to future. This assumption may not seem to be difficult to verify. As far as we know, it has always been unidirectional, except possibly in the case of Hezekiah, where the shadow on the sundial went backward ten degrees.[194] In the view of modern physics, there seems to be no demonstrable reason why time could not go backward. Time does seem to go in the direction of less entropy to greater entropy, which would logically be from past to future. Significantly, though, the equations will work the same if time goes backwards. If so, then there is no essential difference between past and future.

Einstein summed the situation with respect to time in this way: "People like us, who believe in physics, know that the distinction between past, present, and future is only a stubbornly persistent illusion."[195] There are no clear statements in Scripture that can be taken as proof that the future does not exist. Traditional, orthodox Christian beliefs about God are not threatened by Einstein's comments, but they are fatal, if true, for the openness-of-God theology. Similarly, none of the above four points would threaten orthodox Christian beliefs in any way, whether absolutely true or not. The assumptions would *all* have to be true for openness theology to be true.

Heaven seems to be a problem for open theists. Some have protested this is not true, citing scriptural proof that there is time in heaven.[196] We must admit the open theists are perfectly correct in one respect. There is time in heaven, and there will be time in the new heavens and the new earth. No problem with this idea, but there is some question as to whether time in heaven is synchronized with earth. In *The Chronicles of Narnia*, by C. S. Lewis, Narnian time did not match time in England.

---

[194] 2 Kings 20:9–11

[195] Letter from Einstein to the family of his lifelong friend Michele Besso, cited above.

[196] Verses usually cited are Revelation 8:1, 6:9, 11:17–18; Hebrews 10:12–13.

Several months in England could equate to centuries in Narnia. Eustace Scrubb said to Jill Pole,

> "I didn't tell you that this world has a different time from ours."
> "How do you mean?"
> "The time you spend here doesn't take up any of our time. Do you see?"[197]

Of course, we don't know that heaven will be like Narnia, but it is clearly something "other." It has often been suggested that heaven is not part of this universe, properly speaking. Perhaps it is another universe or perhaps another dimension. We do not know. The book of Revelation shows a different sort of time than earth time. Saints in heaven remember things of earth, they know what the future holds, but they do not know how long they must wait.[198] The only reason to mention this reference is simply to point out the brittle nature of open theism. Their rigid view of time depends on a lockstep time linkage between heaven and earth. If not, then God could escape from being locked into earth time when he is in heaven. To the extent that there is any doubt about heavenly time being the same as earth time, open theism is weakened. Of course, for classical theology the question is not significant, even though it may perhaps be of interest.

The main arguments I have given above should be sufficient to show that the open theism statement about the future seems to have been based on a sudden leap, if not of faith, at least of fondness, toward an idea of process theism. It will not do to simply accept beliefs as one selects garbanzo beans from a salad bar. Most fundamental concepts come with a substructure of preconditions which must be valid if the doctrine is to make any sense. It seems obvious to me, at least, that this idea of a nonexistent future has not been thought through. It was simply accepted. It seems to be based largely on ideas current in the scientific community toward the end of the nineteenth century, which would make sense if it was drawn from process theism.

---

[197] Lewis, C. S. *The Chronicles of Narnia: The Silver Chair.* 2000. First Harper Trophy Edition. Harper Collins. New York. pp. 44–45.
[198] Revelation 6:9–10

Modern physics is vastly different from the consensus held in those days. I agree theology must hold the hand of physics with a gentle grip. Theories of physics that seem to be supportive of scriptural teachings today might change tomorrow. And I fear this change is what has happened to process theism, as well as open theism. Science has changed dramatically in the last hundred years, and yet, these theologians are holding onto previous models of physics with a death grip. We Christians who remain committed to classical, orthodox Christianity (this may seem surprising) are seeing our conceptions of God, if not confirmed, at least not threatened in any significant way by modern ideas such as the theory of relativity. However, these ideas, if true, would mean the death of the basic assumption of openness theology.

5. IS TIME A DIMENSION?

One might argue that what open theists are really saying is that the future is not a thing but a dimension. If this is so, then the future is more a concept or an idea than it is a reality with actual existence. In answer to that, we might well agree that the future is more like a dimension than a material object. But that is not the same as saying the future has no reality.

Let us consider a spatial dimension such as *distance*. We can visualize a road, with different parts of the road at different distances from an observer. We can walk along the road for some distance, but we never arrive at a place called "distance." This limitation does not mean distance has no reality. It is a measure of the spatial location of the road, and it is certainly real, even though we cannot touch it or arrive at it. Accordingly, even if the future can best be described as a dimension, that does not prove it has no reality. To the contrary, it proves it is real.

Open theism's challenge to the idea of a real future is simply not well substantiated. Proponents do not seem to have derived this idea from the Bible. Indeed, the very concept of prophecy and God's foreknowledge suggests the existence of a future in some sense of the word.

So nothing in the new theology of open theism contributes usefully to a discussion of time and what it is.

FURTHER READING

Carroll, Sean. *From Eternity to Here: The Quest for the Ultimate Theory of Time*. New York: Dutton. 2010.

DISCUSSION QUESTIONS

1. How would you describe time?

2. Does the Bible describe God as limited in space or time?

3. When did time begin?

4. Where did time come from?

5. What evidence does the Bible give concerning time in heaven?

6. Do you think the future exists in some way?

CHAPTER 7
†

Cutting-Edge Heresy?
The "Openness" of God

Book: *God of the Possible: A Biblical Introduction to the Open View of God*
       by Gregory A. Boyd[199]
Issue: Can God know the future?

In the past few years, a new doctrine has appeared that undermines belief in foundational attributes of God. Despite many doctrinal differences between churches and denominations, Christians have agreed that God knows the future. Now, even that has been called into question. Open theism is a theological model that redefines our understanding of God in a radical new way.

1. WHAT IS A "HERESY" ANYWAY?

In every age of the Christian Church, believers have had to confront what have come to be called "heresies." *Heresy* comes from a Greek word that originally meant "choice." However, it came to mean a doctrine proposed by some (from within Christendom) that contradicted a fundamental principle of the Christian faith. The Gnostics were probably the first to be labeled as heretics, but there were many others. Not every idea contrary to traditionally accepted Christian beliefs can or should be considered

---

[199] Boyd, Gregory A., *God of the Possible: A Biblical Introduction to the Open View of God*, 2000, Baker Books, Grand Rapids, MI.

heretical. A heresy is a deliberate denial of a revealed truth taught in the Bible. Furthermore, it should be foundational, dealing with a core truth of Christianity. For example, the Scriptures clearly declare that Jesus Christ was born of a virgin. To declare otherwise would be a heresy. On the other hand, most Christians believe that John Mark, the companion of Paul and Barnabas, wrote the Gospel of Mark. To deny this belief is not a heresy, though, because the authorship of this book (the Gospel of Mark does not say who wrote it) is not a core truth of the Christian faith.

With depressing regularity, however, prominent teachers and theologians rise up and expound new and novel teachings that affect core truths as taught in the Scriptures. Some might protest, "What does it matter? I don't care what some theologian somewhere teaches." But it does matter to some Christians, and it might matter to you. Suppose you are grieved and confused about some depraved act of monstrous evil, such as the 9/11 attack on the Twin Towers, the Columbine school shooting, or the more recent massacre in the movie theater in Aurora, Colorado. Finally, you go to your pastor for some words of comfort and for some answers. You are concerned about why God could allow such a thing to happen.

Your pastor explains that God was as surprised as you were by these wicked events. He says, "God cannot know the future, because the future does not exist. God has given people free will, and he expects them to use that gift wisely. He hopes for the best, but sometimes bad people do bad things."

You say, "That's your answer? God knows no more than we do? He hopes for the best? What kind of God is that?" You go home even more depressed. You feel cheated and betrayed. It is almost if you caught a man whom you loved and respected reading a dirty magazine, only a thousand times worse. You begin to wonder if your faith is even meaningful.

That is how bad theology can affect the average Christian in the pew. Unfortunately, the normal church-going believer is not isolated from these consequences. Ideas don't just stay locked away in dusty theology books. They rise up and bite us. In fact, that is the story of the twentieth century. Philosophical ideas of the nineteenth century did not stay in philosophy classrooms or in the reading rooms of libraries. They found their way into the streets and, like vicious predators, slew innocents by the millions. Ideas like eugenics, the survival of the fittest, communism, and the thoughts of philosophers like Friedrich Nietzsche (e.g. the "death of god," the *Ubermensch* or "superman," and opposition to Christianity, which were later closely associated with Adolf Hitler and Nazi Germany) were put into practice pitilessly and, carried to their logical conclusion, resulted in the deaths of millions. Ideas have a life of their own.

Ideas have consequences, and ungodly philosophies can lead to demonic abominations in real life. Are Bible-believing pastors saying such things as: "God does not completely know the future"? Unfortunately, pastors who do claim to believe the Bible are indeed saying such things. In fact there is a movement, growing in popularity, called the "openness of God" theology, and it says exactly that. It is highly dangerous to Christians because it is an internal threat. It is coming from Christian teachers and church leaders whom we have every right to trust, which makes it even more treacherous. That is why heresies, in general, are dangerous.

Why are internal threats more dangerous than external ones? Precisely because we Christians are less on guard from those in our midst. If a philosopher claims to be an enemy of Christianity and attacks precious articles of faith, we have a tendency to consider the source and reject his ideas out of hand. Such ideas can infect the culture at large and eventually affect Christians, since we are part of the culture, but they can almost never come in the front door of Christian belief. A wolf in wolves' clothing is not likely to get into the sheepfold and mingle quietly with the sheep, for the sheep instantly recognize a wolf for the deadly enemy he is. But if a sheep secretly slips poison into the feed of the other sheep, he may indeed do harm before any of the flock becomes aware of the danger.

Some readers may think calling this new theology a heresy is needlessly harsh. I agree. It does sound like name-calling, but it is also accurate to think of the term "heresy" as a technical term with a well-accepted definition. Of course, the proponents object to the use of the term, mostly because they believe themselves to be correct. But if they can be shown to be incorrect, then they can hardly object to the term since they acknowledge it is not a trivial matter. Clark H. Pinnock, in the introduction to a book on the "openness" of God, said this:

> First, no doctrine is more central than the nature of God. It deeply affects our understanding of the incarnation, grace, creation, election, sovereignty and salvation. Moreover, the doctrine of God is full of implications for daily living. One's view of God has a direct impact on practices such as prayer, evangelism, seeking divine guidance and responding to suffering.[200]

Since the doctrine is so central, then, proponents of the new theism can hardly complain if their theology is called a heresy.[201] The only defense against heresy would not be that the matter is trivial but that their view is true. So, logically, the teaching is either true or it is heretical. It is not inconsequential. Nevertheless, we should be cautious about calling anyone a heretic. Perhaps it is sufficient to simply label open theism as an extreme form of Arminianism and a serious error and leave it at that.

2. WHAT IS "OPENNESS OF GOD THEOLOGY" OR "OPEN THEISM"?

The book I have chosen to illustrate this new teaching is mentioned above (*God of the Possible: A Biblical Introduction to the Open View of God* by Gregory A. Boyd).[202] It is more current than some of the other works, and

---

[200] Pinnock, Clark H., *et al., The Openness of God: A Biblical Challenge to the Traditional Understanding of God*, 1994, Intervarsity Press, Downers Grove, IL, p. 8.

[201] They do complain, nonetheless. One proponent of open theism, John Sanders, has said: "Some have criticized openness for departing from 'the' tradition and a few even called it 'heresy.' ... Finally, regarding the charge of heresy it should be noted that no ecumenical council discussed this issue and a theory of omniscience has never been a test of orthodoxy." Sanders, John. *The Early Church Fathers on Hellenism and Impassibility*, p. 2. Accessed 17 December 2012, from http://www.opentheism.info/pdf/sanders/early_church_impassibility.pdf.

[202] An earlier work (cited above) that was perhaps more foundational: Pinnock, Clark H. *et al., The Openness of God: A Biblical Challenge to the Traditional Understanding of God.*

it shows some fine-tuning of the theology to make it a bit more reasonable. Generally, open theists admit that the foundational belief driving their theology is the question as to whether God is affected by what human beings do and whether he responds in any way to his creatures as time unfolds.[203] To put it another way, open theists seem to be saying that orthodox believers view God as cold and unresponsive to his creatures and that this novel theology is necessary to correct that error.

A. PROCESS THEISM

There may be validity to the notion that open theism developed to correct a supposedly false view of God's unresponsiveness, even though it sounds unlikely at first glance. If so, it is a gross over-reaction. Theologians have had different views on the attribute of God called "impassibility."[204] Open theists could have interjected an understanding of God as somehow having feelings without disparaging his omniscience.[205] Yet, unlikely as it sounds, if one assumes that open theism is a spin-off from an earlier trend in theology called "process theology" or "process theism," then questions of impassibility may actually have been the core motive.

Process theism is best thought of as a philosophical understanding of the nature of God. The primary proponents were Alfred North Whitehead and Charles Hartshorne. The term "process" is based on their idea that

---

[203] Sanders, John, home page, "Our rejection of divine timelessness and our affirmation of dynamic omniscience are the most controversial elements in our proposal and the view of foreknowledge receives the most attention. However, the *watershed issue* in the debate is not whether God has exhaustive definite foreknowledge (EDF) but whether God is ever affected by and responds to what we do. This is the same watershed that divides Calvinism from Arminianism." (emphasis in the original). Accessed 17 December 2012, from http://www.opentheism.info/.

[204] "Impassibility" is the idea that God, in his essence, does not experience pain nor can he be affected emotionally by anything in creation.

[205] Wayne Grudem in his *Systematic Theology* said this about impassibility: "The doctrine, often based on a misunderstanding of Acts 14:15, that God does not have passions or emotions. Scripture instead teaches that God does have emotions but he does not have sinful passions or emotions." Grudem, Wayne, *Systematic Theology: An Introduction to Biblical Doctrine*, 1994. Glossary, 2000. Zondervan, Grand Rapids, MI, p. 1244.

God is fully involved with his creatures in time (moment-by-moment time) and is affected by what happens in time. It is important to note two things: First, Whitehead, Hartshorne and nearly all of their followers rejected the notion of God's creation of the universe from nothing,[206] and they deny the universe had a first instant. In this denial they were no doubt influenced by the dominant view of science at the time, which also rejected the idea that the universe had a beginning. Secondly, we must understand that these philosophers did not consider the Scriptures to be inspired or infallible writings. In their opinion, they were no different from any other ancient writings which speculated on the nature of God. Process theists believed that not even God could fully know the future because the future did not yet exist (in their view), and they concluded it was not possible to predict the actions of creatures that had the ability of choice.[207]

So is open theism a direct descendant of process theism?[208] Proponents of open theism generally say "No." It is easy to understand why. If proponents admitted they derived their ideas from secular philosophy, it would destroy much of the force of their argument that orthodox views of God were derived from Greek philosophy (more on this argument below). Still, it is hard to avoid the notion that open theism proponents were captivated by the idea of an "open" God who evolves and interacts with his creatures as time unfolds into an open future. This idea is in tune with the spirit of the modern age. One of the leading voices of open theism, William Hasker, freely admits it was the thoughts of Nelson Pike

---

[206] *Creatio ex nihilo* is the technical term, meaning a creation from nothing that pre-existed.

[207] For further information on process theism, see Viney, Donald, "Process Theism", *The Stanford Encyclopedia of Philosophy (Winter 2008 Edition)*, Edward N. Zalta (ed.), Accessed 17 December 2012, from http://plato.stanford.edu/archives/win2008/entries/process-theism/.

[208] Clark H. Pinnock, a prominent open theism spokesman, said: "Process thought is an impressive modern conceptuality with a lot to offer." See Pinnock, Clark H. *Most Moved Mover: A Theology of God's Openness (Didsbury Lectures)*. 2001. Baker Book House. Grand Rapids, MI. p. 141.

(a prominent voice of process theism) that impelled him (Hasker) toward open theism.[209]

Donald Viney's encyclopedia article puts it this way:"To speak of open theism as a school of thought distinct from process theism is ironic since God's openness to creaturely influence is precisely the shared content of their views."[210] Viney goes on to cite a number of specific points where process theism and open theism are identical. This is not to say the two are identical in every respect.[211]

The author of the book selected to illustrate open theism, Gregory A. Boyd, is the poster child for the link between process theism and open theism. His PhD dissertation was on the process theology of Charles Hartshorne. Boyd said:

> It is our conviction that the fundamental vision of the process worldview, especially as espoused by Charles Hartshorne, is correct.[212]

Boyd went on to say:

> My warmest appreciation must also be expressed to Charles Hartshorne. Though I disagree with him on a great many points, he has influenced my own thinking more than any other single philosopher, living and dead.[213]

---

[209] Hasker, William, *Christian Scholar's Review* 28:1 (Fall, 1998: pp. 111–139).

[210] Viney, Donald. *op. cit.*, point 7.

[211] One puzzling difference is in the temporal nature of God. Alfred North Whitehead believed that God is both temporal and atemporal; He is immanent; He is immortal. A good summary is found online at: Wikipedia, The Free Encyclopedia. *Process Philosophy*. Accessed 16 December 2012, from http://en.wikipedia.org/wiki/Process_philosophy. Also, Canale says much the same thing, maintaining that process theology developed a bipolar view of God, seeing Him as both timeless and temporal at the same time. See Canale, Fernando. "Evangelical Theology and Open Theism: Toward a Biblical Understanding of the Macro Hermeneutical Principles of Theology?" *Journal of the Adventist Theological Society*. 2/2 (Autumn, 2001): 16–34. p. 28. Open theists see God as temporal; trapped in time.

[212] Boyd, Gregory A. *Trinity and Process: A Critical Evaluation and Reconstruction of Hartshorne's Di-Polar Theism Towards a Trinitarian Metaphysics* (1992)(American University Studies Series VII, Theology and Religion). Vol. 119. Peter Lang: New York. 424 pp. See Preface. p. i.

[213] *Ibid.*, Preface. p. ii.

So there is good reason to believe that Boyd's theology, which resembles process theology in so many ways, was, in fact, derived from process theology.

B. SEARCH FOR SIGNIFICANCE

Another motive that could have impelled theologians like Gregory Boyd, William Hasker and Clark Pinnock toward open theism was their own personal search for significance. Could something in the writings of process theism have so caught their imagination, so opened their eyes to a new source of significance, that it motivated them to scour the Scriptures in an effort to find support for these exciting new viewpoints? If so, what could it have been?

Clearly, Satan has long understood that human pride is a powerful motive and an avenue into our souls. A subtle promise that stokes our ego, inflames our pride, and gives the vision that our names could be made great, is a powerful thing. Remember how Satan tempted Eve? He asked her about the tree and then denied that she would die, promising that she would be like God if she ate:

> "No. You will not die," the serpent said to the woman. "In fact, God knows that when you eat of it your eyes will be opened and you will be like God, knowing good and evil." Then the woman saw that the tree was good for food and delightful to look at, and that it was desirable for obtaining wisdom. So she took some of its fruit and ate it. She also gave some to her husband, who was with her, and he ate it.[214]

The oldest trick in Satan's book is to promise gullible humans they will be like gods. He appeals to their foolish pride. The idea is also found in 1 John 2:16, where the same progression is found. Eve saw the tree was "good for food" (the lust of the flesh), then that it was "delightful to look at" (the lust of the eyes), and then that it was "desirable for obtaining wisdom" (pride of life). 1 John 2:16 says in full:

> Everything that belongs to the world—the lust of the flesh, the lust of the eyes, and the pride in one's lifestyle—is not from the Father but is from the world.[215]

---

[214] Genesis 3: 4–6 (HCSB)
[215] (HCSB)

Pride is a universal human weakness, but the form it takes may vary from one culture to the next. Open theism is a movement coming out of Western culture and particularly from the United States. It is now clear to me, as an American, that one of our traits that is pronounced to an unusual degree is individualism. It was only by living in the Philippines for several years that I finally understood this. Filipino culture has a greater emphasis on community and is not as relentlessly Western as is the USA. Filipino culture allowed me to see American culture and its extreme individualism for what it is. So it seems to me that Americans exhibit pride in a way that emphasizes individualism—an inordinate desire for personal autonomy. This idea is not original with me. Francis Schaeffer said this about our society:

> As the more Christian-dominated consensus weakened, the majority of people adopted two impoverished values: *personal peace and affluence.*
>
> Personal peace means just to be let alone, not to be troubled ... to have my personal life pattern undisturbed in my lifetime ... Affluence means an overwhelming and ever-increasing prosperity ... an ever-higher level of material abundance.[216]

Schaeffer saw these impoverished values as having been greatly influenced by such Western philosophers as Jean-Jacques Rousseau (1712–1778). Rousseau promoted autonomous freedom, and that didn't just mean freedom from God. It meant freedom from all restraint. Schaeffer expressed it as: "freedom from culture, freedom from any authority, and absolute freedom of the individual—a freedom in which the individual is the center of the universe."[217] We Americans have definitely taken some of our basic values from Rousseau and thinkers like him. Our area of weakness—the focus of our pride—is to be tempted by the offer of greater autonomy: to reign at the center of the universe. This is where process theism comes in—it offers autonomy for human beings without completely breaking away from a belief in God.

---

[216] Schaeffer, Francis A. *How Should We Then Live? The Rise and Decline of Western Thought and Culture. op. cit.*, p. 205.

[217] *Ibid.*, p. 155.

Tom Ascol agrees with the view that open theism is a reflection of popular culture. He says:

> In many respects, Open Theism is a perfect theological fit for the contemporary American *zeitgeist*. In an age where empathy trumps truthfulness we are more comforted by someone who feels our pain than by someone who speaks honestly, unequivocally and consistently. Disappoint us if you will, fail to keep your promises if you must, but do not cease to reassure us that you really feel for us. The God of Open Theism perfectly fits this criterion.[218]

Obviously, open theists found something in the ideas of process theism that they liked since their theology agrees in significant ways. Boyd gushes out a promise about his book: "It will open your mind to an intriguing—and in my estimation wonderful—way of thinking about God and the future."[219]

Note that there is an "intriguing" idea of the *future* that is offered by process theism. Specifically, Boyd must be referring to the idea that we create the future though the operation of our libertarian free will.[220] At first glance, this idea does not sound too unusual. Evangelical Christians often talk in terms of working together with God to build his kingdom. We understand that our choices are real events which can cause other events to occur, but causation is not the same as creation. In the open theism view, the future does not exist. When we exercise our autonomous freedom, ultimately unconstrained even by God himself, we are not building the future, we are *creating* it from nothing. We have become like God. Oh, happy day! The promise of Satan to Eve has actually been fulfilled all this time, and it has taken open theism to reveal it to us. No wonder Boyd says it is "wonderful." There is one little problem: it is not true. We

---

[218] Ascol, Tomas K. "Pastoral Implications of Open Theism." *Founders Journal.* Fall 2001.pp. 9–22. This article is adapted from a chapter that appears in the book, *Bound Only Once*, edited by Douglas Wilson and recently published by Canon Press. Accessed 17 December 2012, from http://www.founders.org/journal/fj46/article2_fr.html.

[219] Boyd, Gregory A. *op. cit.*, p. 9.

[220] This will be defined below, but the idea is that our will is not determined by God in advance.

Christians are God's children, and joint-heirs[221] with Christ, yes, but we are not co-creators, autonomous from God.

It is understandable that a person who had such a wonderful insight might try to prove the truth of it in the Scriptures since scriptural proof was not a serious concern of process theologians. Writers like Boyd, however, consider themselves evangelical Christians, and the testimony of Scripture will be important to them. Boyd admits he combed the Scriptures for three years before finding evidence supporting process theism. He sums up his findings:

> About three years later, I became convinced that the customary view—
> that the future is exhaustively settled and that God knows it as such—
> was mistaken.[222]

Let us not go too far, though. I am not saying Boyd believes human-kind is completely autonomous. He and other open theists insist they believe God is still in ultimate control. However, this view of substantial autonomy, so in tune with Western values, seems to catch the spirit of the our age. It fits our view of how things ought to be. Clearly, open theists are excited—one might say intoxicated—with these new ideas, and once they have the vision, they are loath to give it up, no matter how much they have to diminish God in the process.

Brian G. Hedges gives a devastating critique of open theism that sums up much of what I have been saying:

> This concept of a God who can be surprised by our suffering, and yet remain empathetic, probably does appeal to some people—those who would rather have a grandfatherly-like God who feels sorry for them than an All-knowing and All-powerful Sovereign to whom they must submit. In reality, I have come to think that at least one of the reasons openness theology attracts people is because it shortens the distance between man and God and makes fewer demands of faith and submission. But this view of God leaves you bankrupt, because, in the final analysis, the god of open theism is nothing better than a crippled king who, though his heart is sympathetic, cannot or will not

---

[221] See Romans 8:14–17.

[222] Boyd, Gregory A. *op. cit.*, p. 8.

help us. Gratuitous suffering and evil have no purpose. They merely reflect upon the limitations of a god whose creation project went awry and is desperately trying to remedy the situation without violating the all-important freedom of his moral creatures. Open theism assigns God to a wheel chair.[223]

Perhaps this general critique is sufficient. Now let us consider certain key arguments of open theism and give them careful evaluation.

C. OPEN THEISM ARGUMENTS:

1. The future does not actually exist,[224] but because of God's control of present events, future events are partly settled and partly open.

2. God is omniscient, but he knows the future only to the extent that he has determined it. He has not determined everything and cannot know what he has not determined.

3. God rules in a sovereign way over creation, but he does not exercise meticulous control over every detail of history.

4. God has given human beings libertarian free will. That means God may not always get what he wants since humans might chose something else.

5. God experiences time in exactly the same way as we human beings do. He is not timeless, immutable or impassible.

6. God can achieve the future he wants, in broad terms, by continually adapting to the free choices of humans.

7. Some proponents add the belief that "simple foreknowledge"[225] (even if it existed, which they deny) would be useless to God.[226]

---

[223] Hedges, Brian G. "Book Review." *Founders Journal.* Fall 2001. pp. 23–24. Accessed 12 December 2012, from http://www.founders.org/journal/fj46/reviews.html.

[224] Saunders says that the future is not an "ontological entity." It does not exist. Sanders, John E., *The God Who Risks: A Theology of Divine Providence,* second edition. 2007. InterVarsity Press, Downers Grove, IL, pp. 203, 207.

[225] "Simple foreknowledge" is the concept that God knows the future, without determining it.

[226] These six points, and point G., which was given in the context of an argument, are from: Belt, Thomas, *Open Theism and the Assemblies of God: A*

4. WHAT IS WRONG WITH "OPEN THEISM"?

A. OPEN THEISM HAS A FATALLY FLAWED VIEW OF HOW GOD RELATES TO TIME.

It seems clear (as I discussed above) that the contention of the open theists that the future does not exist was drawn from process theism. Process theism had at its core several assumptions for which no proof was offered or even seriously attempted. One of these was the existence of God. Process theists (like the Bible itself) assumed God's existence and did not try to offer rigorous proofs of this assumption. A second assumption (no rigorous proof was offered) was that the universe was eternal. Time, space, matter, and energy have always existed, as has God himself. Process theists then attempted to develop, through philosophical speculation and logic, a view of what such a God would be like. Process theism was the result.

In the above discussion of "What is Time and Why Does It Matter?" I tried to give good reasons for holding to the traditional view of God and his relationship to time. This argument includes the idea that since God created time, he was and is not bound by it. Even though in his essential nature, since he existed before time began, he is timeless, he is also able to enter time and experience it. God is also shown in the Scriptures as being present in a place called "heaven," which is shown as not being of this earth. Jesus, for example, has ascended into heaven and is sitting at the right hand of God.[227] Process theists, on the other hand, have assumed that time always existed. So they logically conclude that God is not timeless but is limited to experiencing time as a succession of moments one after the other. We can understand how they reach that conclusion, but unless we agree with their assumptions, it would be illogical to agree with them.

Personal Account of My Views on Open Theism, presented to the Assemblies of God Commission on Doctrinal Purity, 2002. Accessed 12 December 2012, from http://www.opentheism.info/index.php/tom-belt/open-theism-and-the-assemblies-of-god-a-personal-account-of-my-views-on-open-theism/.
[227] 1 Peter 3:22

This illogical leap is exactly what advocates of open theism have done. Open theists do not reject the idea that God created the universe from nothing. They insist they part company with process theism on that point.[228] But it is exactly here that they went wrong. They reject one of the premises of a tightly-organized philosophical structure, striking at one of its primary, foundational supports and still say they agree with its conclusion. It seems they liked several ideas that were advocated by open theism, such as human co-creation, the "openness" of the future, and a God that is also "open"—a being that evolves, grows and interacts with his creatures. They also liked features of orthodox Christianity such as the Creation, the Trinity, and the Incarnation—God becoming flesh in the person of Jesus Christ. They then constructed a theology based on what they liked. One of the proponents of open theism, in an unguarded statement, said as much. John E. Sanders has admitted that open theists think God's timelessness is incompatible with a God who can interact with his creatures.[229] In other words, they are unable to imagine a timeless God who at the same time would be able to become a part of the normal human spacetime experience. In order to maintain the part of process theism that they liked (an open God), they felt forced to discard the idea of a timeless God.

The first foundational point on which open theism is based is nothing more than a bare assumption. Proponents say the future does not exist ,and God is not timeless. No scriptural proof is offered,[230] despite the fact

---

[228] At least one open theism proponent admits to rejecting the doctrine of creation from nothing: Thomas Jay Oord. See *For the Love of Wisdom and the Wisdom of Love.* A website by Thomas Jay Oord. September 26, 2011. Archived Blog Entry: *Is God Essentially Holy?* Accessed 22 August 2012, from http://thomasjayoord.com/index.php/blog/archives/is _god_essentially_ holy/#.UDWjp6O8rm4.

[229] Sanders, *op. cit.* See *God Who Risks*, rev. ed. pp. 199–209 and the chart on pp. 218–219. Also, Sanders, John E., "Divine Providence and the Openness of God," in Bruce Ware, ed., *Perspectives on the Doctrine of God: Four Views. 2008.* Broadman & Holman, Nashville, TN. pp. 225–228.

[230] Open theists do point to Scripture that shows God acting within time, such as Genesis 6:6. But this does not prove that God is not timeless in his *essential being.* Classic theism agrees that God is active in time, but denies

that these ideas oppose standard, orthodox Christian teaching which is based on the words of Scripture.[231] The best they can offer is a reference to some features of modern physics.[232] Other than that, they seem to be able to offer little but, "I believe this because I think it is true." This weak statement is not a good starting point for any argument, since if the premises are dubious, the conclusions will be equally so.

B. OPEN THEISM HAS A SIMPLISTIC VIEW OF DETERMINISM AND OMNISCIENCE

The second principle of open theism is concerned with what God knows and can know. *God is omniscient, but he knows the future only to the extent that he has determined it. He has not determined everything and cannot know what he has not determined.*

I have already shown above that open theism proponents have not proven that God is not timeless; nor have they established that the future does not exist. Without that proof, there is no basis to assert that "God cannot know the future unless he determines it." Some in the Calvinist tradition seem to have no objection to the idea that God knows the future only because he has ordained it.[233] Therefore, the question may seem moot to these Calvinists since they are certain the future has been ordained.

Be that as it may, Christians have advanced various models for expressing how God might foreknow the future and determine the future (which are slightly different concepts). Some, such as Saint Augustine of Hippo, mentioned above, saw the future as determined (foreordained)

---

that He is trapped in time.

[231] This despite the fact that Clark H. Pinnock admitted that the burden of proof falls upon open theists. See Pinnock, Clark H. *Most Moved Mover: A Theology of God's Openness (Didsbury Lectures).* 2001. Baker Book House. Grand Rapids, MI. p.18.

[232] This will be discussed in some depth below. But classical theism is quite resilient and not dependent on modern physics. Open theism, however, is quite vulnerable in this area and requires that a number of hotly contested scientific concepts be proven in their favor.

[233] *Tyndale Bible Dictionary,* eds. Walter A. Elwell, Philip Wesley Comfort, 2001, Tyndale, Wheaton, IL. "Foreknowledge." p. 494.

by God. This determination or foreordination was not so that God could know the future—Augustine would have had no doubts that God would have exhaustive foreknowledge of the future, in any event. He took his theology from many passages in the Bible that say God foreordained certain things, and he expanded it into a model that saw *all* things as foreordained. Some philosophers call this idea "hard" determinism and equate it with fatalism. Augustine greatly influenced the Protestant Reformers such as John Calvin.[234]

Other Christians have been troubled with this Augustinian concept because they simply could not see how such determination left room for humans to have any real ability to choose between good and evil. One of the great themes of Scripture is a look into the lives of people who meet or fail the test of choice. God's justice seems to consist of judging people's works and decreeing rewards for those who do good and punishment for those who do evil. Christ's atonement must also be considered, of course, since it provides for salvation by grace. There is a sense in which God's justice would be called into question if he ordained infallibly, with no possibility of free choice, that a person would commit a sin and then be punished for doing what he was forced to do.

These concerns gave rise to another school of thought, sometimes called *simple foreknowledge,* which said that God knows what will happen, in complete detail, but does not ordain the freewill of creatures. The common phrase in use is, "Foreknowledge does not imply foreordination." This idea is consistent with the Arminian-Wesleyan tradition.

There are combinations of these views. Within the Reformed tradition we see a strong concern to preserve God's sovereignty and a form of determination that leaves God's decrees as independent from his creatures' actions. Grudem (equating the Reformed tradition with Calvinism) says: "Calvinists would say that God's eternal decrees were not influenced by any of our actions and cannot be changed by us, since they were made *before creation.*"[235] Nevertheless, most in the Reformed tradition insist

---

[234] *Ibid.,* "Foreordination." p. 494.

[235] Grudem, Wayne. *op. cit.,* p. 345.

that our choices are real and voluntary. One statement of the Reformed view is the Westminster Confession of Faith (1643–46), Chapter 3: *Of God's Eternal Decree*. Paragraph 1 says:

> 1. God, from all eternity, did, by the most wise and holy counsel of his own will, freely, and unchangeably ordain whatsoever comes to pass: yet so, as thereby neither is God the author of sin, nor is violence offered to the will of the creatures; nor is the liberty or contingency of second causes taken away, but rather established.[236]

Open theism is a departure not only from the Reformed tradition but also from the Arminian-Wesleyan tradition. Arminians would certainly not agree that the future would be unknowable unless foreordained. Followers of Reformed views would strongly argue that nothing in the future is unknown by God. Open theists say that not everything has been ordained by God, and in this view they are not completely outside of mainstream thought. Some in the Arminian-Wesleyan tradition would have no problems with unordained events, but this does not really advance the open theism position. To put it another way: *Unordained does not mean unknown.* The open theism position does not advance unless it can be shown that *only* the foreordained future can be known. We could concede, for argument's sake, that not all the future is foreordained. But that, alone, does not prove the open theist's points.

The third principle of open theism is mostly a restatement of the previous discussion. *God rules in a sovereign way over creation, but he does not exercise meticulous control over every detail of history.* We can readily admit that this idea is partly within mainstream Christianity. Christians have various thoughts about whether or not God has ordained every detail about the future. So to say that God has not foreordained every detail is not heretical. However, this admission does not buttress the open theism position. If it is true: (a) that God is trapped in our time (our sequence of moment-by-moment events) and (b) that the future has no real existence, and (c) that God's omniscience is not complete, then perhaps this *lack of meticulous control* is a reasonable conclusion. However, point (a) is

---

[236] *Ibid.*, Appendix 1. p. 1181.

unsubstantiated, and point (b) is a naked assumption. Point (c) cannot be an assumption—for that is what open theists seem to be trying to prove. So the third principle is essentially a restatement of the idea that not everything is ordained by God. Again, the second and third principles are a clarification of what open theists believe rather than additional proofs of the correctness of their views.

C. OPEN THEISM IS BASED UPON THE MOST AUTONOMOUS VIEW OF FREE WILL.

The third principle of open theism is concerned with free will: what it is, what is needed to bring it about, and what limits it places on God: *God has given human beings libertarian free will. That means that God may not always get what he wants since humans might chose something else.* We might call this principle "hard" libertarianism.

I have mentioned above that one of the characteristics of the postmodern worldview is the tendency to "cherry pick" doctrines that one likes, without necessarily trying to derive them by a logical process. Hard libertarian free will denies limits on volition: "Human choices are free from the constraints of human nature or spiritual condition and free from any predetermination by God." This concept is a necessary part of process theism, but whether it was derived by open theists from that source or not, it is also obviously part and parcel of the openness of God paradigm. Open theists liked the openness paradigm of process theologians, and so they had little choice but to adopt the notion of libertarian free will and to reject all other forms of free will. Although open theists look to modern physics to support their views, they have some difficulty finding support for their view of free will in modern physics.[237]

---

[237] Physicist Stephen Hawking has called libertarian free will "just an illusion." He also said, "Quantum physics might seem to undermine the idea that nature is governed by laws, but that is not the case. Instead it leads us to accept a new form of determinism: Given the state of a system at some time, the laws of nature determine the probabilities of various futures and pasts rather than determining the future and past with certainty." See Hawking, Stephen and Leonard Mlodinow. *The Grand Design.* 2001. Bantam Books, New York. p.32.

The question of free will and what it is, exactly, is not a simple matter to be glibly tossed off. The various doctrines of free will all have advocates within the Christian tradition, and they are all difficult to harmonize with Scripture. Boethius, a sixth-century philosopher, even said there were degrees of freedom of the will:

> So it follows that those who have reason have freedom to will or not to will, although this freedom is not equal in all of them. [...] human souls are more free when they persevere in the contemplation of the mind of God, less free when they descend to the corporeal, and even less free when they are entirely imprisoned in earthly flesh and blood.[238]

It must be admitted Boethius had a point. Paul insists: "The person without the Spirit does not accept the things that come from the Spirit of God but considers them foolishness, and cannot understand them because they are discerned only through the Spirit."[239] This point would be a problem for libertarian free will as defined above, but perhaps some open theists would agree that spiritual deadness limits the ability to choose.

The libertarian concept of free will is not the only possibility. Some would say the only other choice is foreknowledge with *fatalism* (the complete absence of human freedom). Some open theists express the situation as follows: If God now knows what I shall do tomorrow, then it is logical to insist that either what I do tomorrow is already determined, or else tomorrow I have the power to defeat God's foreknowledge which would cause God to be in error. In other words, to have foreknowledge there must be fatalism, but this view is decidedly in the minority.

We must recognize there are other views of human freedom. One is called *compatibilism* or *soft determinism*. This view holds that divine foreknowledge is compatible (hence the name) with human freedom. This form of determination has arguments in its favor, but it may at first sound like a paradox. The paradox seems even worse when those who advo-

---

[238] Boethius, Anicius Manlius Severinus. *The Consolation of Philosophy.* 520–562 A.D.

[239] 1 Corinthians 2:14 (NIV)

cate this view admit that, although there is a difference between God's foreknowledge and God's foreordination, in both cases future events are never in doubt in the mind of God. If God foreknows something, it will happen. If God foreordains something, it will happen. Under the compatibilist view, if God foreknows (or foreordains) a future action that is freely chosen, that action will surely happen, but God's foreknowledge does nothing to make the choice less free. In this way, the two concepts are compatible. A more detailed discussion of this concept will be given below. Suffice it to say at this point, hard libertarian free will is not the only viewpoint having sound support, and, as I will try to demonstrate below, it is not even the best viewpoint.

Even if we agree that humans have libertarian free will in some sense of the word, it does not follow that "God may not always get what he wants." It is difficult to see this conclusion in any other way than a denial of the doctrine of God's omnipotence. Of course, there is a sense that when a person sins, God is getting something he does not want. Open theists think that when people choose wrongly, God's sovereign will has been thwarted. If so, that only calls his omnipotence into question. A better view, more harmonious with the Scriptures, would be to see human rebellion as something not wanted by God, but nevertheless, part of his sovereign will. Thus, God always gets what he wants, in an ultimate sense. But it appears that this "thwarted" sense is exactly what open theists prefer to believe. Once again, they prefer to cut God down to size.

D. OPEN THEISM PROPONENTS SEEM NOT TO HAVE CONSIDERED THE LOGICAL CONSEQUENCES OF THEIR "SMORGASBORD" THEOLOGY.

For those who might not understand what I mean by "smorgasbord" theology, a word of clarification is in order. A smorgasbord was originally a Scandinavian meal served buffet-style. In America some forty years ago, restaurants started serving meals with a wide selection, allowing patrons to take whatever dish they wanted for one flat price. So "smorgasbord theology" would mean a theological system where the doctrines were chosen eclectically depending on the taste of the theologian. Such a system is harmonious with a postmodern worldview. Whether or not open theism proponents agree they use this process is immaterial. The description refers to the result: what appears to be a mass of arbitrarily-chosen doctrines.

The fifth principle of open theism was: *God experiences time in the same way as we human beings do. He is not timeless, immutable or impassible.* I have already stated that open theists' concerns about God's immutable and impassible nature are exaggerated. The concept of time has already been discussed in detail. I have stated above that it makes no sense to agree that God created all things from nothing and then disagree that God is timeless.[240] In effect, open theists are saying God is in subjection to his creation. They also seem to ignore the concept of heaven, which, if it shows anything at all, shows that God is not trapped on this earth. There is no need to belabor that concept, but there is another line of argument that should be mentioned at this point.

Classic, orthodox Christianity has not only consistently maintained that God is timeless in his essential being; it has also insisted he is omnipresent in his creation. Omnipresence is a vital doctrine since it explains how God can be fully present with all of his followers simultaneously. Jesus could say, "For where two or three are gathered together in my name, there am I in the midst of them."[241] The same idea is found in a psalm of David:

> Where can I go from your Spirit?
> Where can I flee from your presence?
> If I go up to the heavens, you are there;
> if I make my bed in the depths, you are there.
> If I rise on the wings of the dawn,
> if I settle on the far side of the sea,
> even there your hand will guide me,
> your right hand will hold me fast.[242]

---

[240] It is not always clear what is meant when open theists say that God is not immutable or impassible. If they deny that God is immutable and impassible in his essential nature, then that is a serious error.

[241] Matthew 18:20 (KJV)

[242] Psalm 139: 7–10 (NIV)

There is no reason to suppose open theists have abandoned the doctrine of omnipresence, which is discussed by Wayne Grudem as follows: "God does not have size or spatial dimensions and is present at every point of space with his whole being, and yet God acts differently in different places."[243] Nor is there any assurance these theologians might not jettison the idea of omnipresence if it conflicted with their openness paradigm. In fact, the process of jettisoning omnipresence may already be underway. Clark Pinnock seemed to be open to the idea that God has a body (and he was not speaking of the Lord Jesus). Despite the fact that the Scriptures say that God is a Spirit (John 4:24) and that a spirit *by definition* is not embodied (Luke 24:39), Pinnock said this:

> I do not feel obligated to assume that God is a purely spiritual being when his self-revelation does not suggest it. … And how unreasonable is it anyway? The only persons we encounter are embodied persons and, if God is not embodied, it may prove difficult to understand how God is a person. What kind of actions could a disembodied God perform?[244]

This speculation is reckless. Pinnock seems to think a body is essential to perform any action.[245] Does he seriously think a body made of matter is essential to create the universe? This comment sounds like something a child might say, but coming from a mature theologian, it is difficult to understand. And if God has a body, how can he be omnipresent? I will try to show, based on their idea of a God trapped in time, how openness theologians may not be able to consistently fit the doctrine of omnipresence within their framework. As to what other attributes of God may fall out of openness theology in the future, only time will tell.

The idea that all created things are made of matter, energy, space and time is not particularly new.[246] Nor is the intuitive concept that matter and energy must be related in some fundamental way. This concept prob-

---

[243] Grudem, *op. cit.*, p. 173.

[244] Pinnock, Clark H. *Most Moved Mover, op. cit.,* p. 34. Also see pp. 80–81.

[245] This idea, that a spiritual being could not cause or influence anything material, is a common theme of process theism.

[246] This is not to deny the concept of "spirit" or spiritual creatures as taught in the Scriptures.

ably occurs to most people whenever a piece of wood is burned, since the burning releases heat and light. In a similar way, there is an intuitive sense that time and space are not completely dissimilar. They are both dimensions, one spatial and the other temporal, that are quite different from the matter–energy relationship. Modern physics has confirmed this view. One confirmation was the event which began the atomic age.

As I write this, I sit about seventy miles southwest of the site where the first atomic bomb was exploded on July 16, 1945. This device converted a bit less[247] than fourteen pounds of plutonium from matter to energy, releasing an explosive force equal to 18,000 tons of TNT. The famous equation that reveals a profound insight into the nature of matter and energy was proposed by Einstein: $E = MC^2$. Perhaps it is better to say that matter and energy are just different forms of the same thing.

In a similar way, modern physics confirms there is an intimate relationship between space and time. Einstein lumped the two together, calling the resulting concept "spacetime." Actually, though, it is better to credit another man with having this insight first: Hermann Minkowski (1864–1909). Minkowski spacetime is viewed as four-dimensional and often depicted as a light-cone diagram. Along the horizontal axis is space, and the vertical axis represents time. All real objects must move through time within the cones and must pass through the point at which the cones meet (the present). Shown in gray is what is called a "worldline" of a material object as it passes through time. If this concept is true, it shows that both the past and the future are real (ontologically real). In other words, the future does not happen but is already *there*.[248]

This whole concept casts doubt on the naked assumption of open theism that the future does not exist. Apparently space and time are intertwined in a complex way and are probably different forms of the same thing.

---

[247] Maybe as little as an ounce of matter was actually so converted before it all came apart.

[248] These concepts and the diagram are drawn from a website called "Einstein's Spacetime." From http://einstein.stanford.edu/SPACETIME/spacetime2.html.

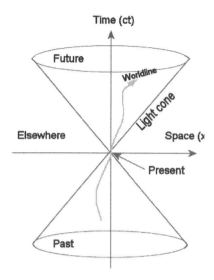

Figure 2: Lightcone Diagram[249]

Furthermore, the concept is not just a theory—it is confirmed by experimental science. For example, when an object moves through space, its speed through time slows down.[250] This being so, it would probably make no sense to say that God is bound to experience time moment by moment, as do all his creatures, and yet insist he is omnipresent. If God is omnipresent, then he would have to be also omnitemporal, if these relativistic concepts are true. Conversely, if he is not omnitemporal, then he is not omnipresent, either. That would mean the devotees of open theism would have to consign another attribute of God to the dustbin. In theology, as in life, we quickly find that everything is connected to everything else.

Nothing said above should be taken to mean that classic theology hangs or falls on the truth or falsity of Minkowski spacetime. Classic theology is not derived from any particular view of science. But if the above concept is true, then open theism is based on a false premise and its denial of God's omniscience lacks any shred of support.

---

[249] Image Credit: James Overduin. Used courtesy of the Gravity Probe B Image and media archive, Stanford University, Stanford California, U.S.A.

[250] Greene, *op. cit.*, p. 49.

E. Open Theists Assume God Controls the Future Loosely.

The sixth principle expounded by open theists is this: "God can achieve the future he wants, in broad terms, by continually adapting to the free choices of humans." Of course, if we react to what this principle literally says, we might find agreement. If we limit God's participation to that of a chess player, who must anticipate and then react to his opponents' moves, we will no doubt find, even with this arbitrary limitation, God still being very much in charge. He will be able, at the very least, to maintain close control over the destiny of humankind and the course of human history. The overt sense of this principle can be accepted with little problem so long as it is viewed as hypothetical and not an attempt to seriously describe reality.

I fear, though, that this is not seen as a hypothetical.[251] They are saying that God "doesn't sweat the small stuff." If open theists are suggesting that this idea is literally true, then at least three questions must be answered. Where do open theists get the idea that God would be satisfied with any such thing as achieving the future "in broad terms"? Where do they get the assurance that such a thing is even possible? Where in the Scriptures do they find this idea expressed? Let's consider these three questions separately.

1. Is there any support for the concept of a God with "loose control" over the universe?

For the origin of this idea, we need look no further than process theology. This idea of "loose control" permeates the entire corpus of process theologians' work. Hartshorne said God did not exert unilateral control over the universe.[252] He derived this idea from his view of God as bound

---

[251] Belt gives an explanation of this concept as follows: "God is not so insecure and unintelligent a Sovereign that the accomplishing of his ultimate purposes requires that he be limited to having to attend to only one certain route to the fulfillment of these purposes as opposed to several possible routes to their fulfillment." See Belt, Thomas, *op. cit.*, p. 9.

[252] Hartshorne, Charles. *Omnipotence and Other Theological Mistakes*. 1984.

in time and the future as necessarily open because time had no beginning. We are faced, again, with an idea that derives from a naked assumption of openness theology, that the future does not exist.

Process theism and openness theism are firmly rooted in scientific concepts of the nineteenth century. To try to prove otherwise, Tom Belt has made a valiant effort to try to show why the concept of an indefinite future[253] is compatible with modern physics. He said:

> ... for open theists the line of reasoning runs from the biblical to the scientific, not the other way around. That is, open theists are not "guided" by a commitment to a particular scientific view to interpret Scripture in openness fashion.[254]

This is, of course, highly laudable, and one would hope every Christian would view the proper place of science in this way. But the statement implies that open theists found their unique viewpoint in an unbiased study of God's Word, which is difficult to accept. An unbiased study of the Scriptures could never have led one to propose that the future did not exist. That idea must come from elsewhere, first, and only then be followed by intensive searches to find verses in the Bible to lend support to it. Incidentally, that effort must have been unrewarding. Open theists do find verses that support their view of an open God, but apparently none saying that the future does not exist.

Although Belt valiantly tries to show that there is a consensus among scientists supporting the notion of a nonexistent future, he is forced to admit that one must look at chaos theory and quantum mechanics to try to find this support. His argument, however, is lacking in specifics. He quotes Greg Boyd, a theologian who espouses openness theology, as saying that Einstein was totally mistaken in his view (that the difference between past, present and future is an illusion) because he was one of a number of physicists that based their view of reality on an "empirically

---

State University of New York, Albany, NY. pp. 20–26.

[253] Watch this closely, though. There is a difference between saying that the future is indefinite and the future does not exist.

[254] Belt, Thomas. *op. cit.*, see footnote 6.

groundless, metaphysically mechanistic assumption ..."[255] It is unclear, however, why we should take Greg Boyd's view on the implications of modern physics over Einstein's.[256]

Belt does not stop there. He also notes that William Lane Craig, who is not an open theist, defends the dynamic theory of time[257] in a recent book.[258] Whatever Craig might think about time being dynamic, however, he certainly did not deny in his book that the future could be known.[259] He said in response to the idea that God does not have an exact idea of the future: "Such a view seems so unbiblical that we might be surprised to hear that some persons think that it represents faithfully the doctrine of the Scriptures."[260] Craig finally concludes by saying that God knows all truth, including all future contingencies.[261] So it seems, Craig could only countenance a dynamic theory of time if he believed it was consistent with God's complete foreknowledge.

Finally, it must be said that Craig is not a scientist and so is not an authority who can usefully be cited in a discussion about the consensus of modern science. Though his ideas are interesting, he could not be said to be more competent than Einstein in the field of physics. For that, open theists should at least cite the views of a theoretical physicist.

Belt, apparently realizing this problem, found a qualified source in the person of John Polkinghorne, who is both a scientist and a theologian. It is true that Polkinghorne accepts the idea of a contingent future and therefore the idea that the future is somehow different from the past, as

---

[255] *Ibid.*

[256] The apparent source of the Boyd quotation is a blog: Boyd, Greg. *Scientific Support for the Open View,* 29 December 2007. Accessed 20 August 2012, from http://reknew.org/2007/12/scientific-support/.

[257] This is not the same as the view that the future does not exist.

[258] Craig, William Lane. *Time and Eternity: Exploring God's Relationship to Time.* 2001. Crossway Books, Wheaton, IL.

[259] It is not clear whether Craig is indebted to process theology for his views, but certainly, many theologians have adopted aspects of process theology, even though they reject the "openness of God."

[260] Craig, William Lane. *Time and Eternity. op. cit,* p. 247.

[261] *Ibid.,* p. 265.

opposed to Einstein or Sean Carroll. His argument is based in part on quantum indeterminacy. Belt maintains it is quantum theory that destroys classical theology in favor of openness theology. He quotes Boyd:

> At the very least, any who would want to continue to hold to the eternal definiteness of the future (in the mind of God) and thus to the non-ontological nature of quantum indeterminacy must now bear the scientific burden of proof.[262]

Polkinghorne is cited to establish this clear presumption against classic theology, but his views are hardly the "holy grail" that Belt and Boyd claim. Polkinghorne explains that there are two interpretations of quantum theory. One, called the conventional view, is that there are no causes for events within the quantum world. Note that this view is saying that causes do not exist, not that we do not know the causes. There are no causes to know. He goes on to say,

> To this conventional quantum interpretation, there is an alternative point of view, first worked out successfully by David Bohm. It asserts that all events are causally determined, but some of these causes (called in the trade "hidden variables") are inaccessible to us. That is the reason, in Bohm's view, why our actual knowledge has to be statistical. It is a matter, not of principle, but of ignorance. ... In the realm of non-relativistic quantum theory (that is, concerning the behavior of very small and slowly moving systems), the conventional theory and Bohm's theory give exactly the same experimental results. Yet the understand-ings they offer are radically different.[263]

Polkinghorne goes on to suggest (in the paragraph following the above quotation) that the reason for the strong preference of quantum physicists toward causelessness (or indeterminacy) is entirely a matter of taste.[264] It is not based on experimental results. Many physicists simply see

[262] Belt. *op. cit.*, Footnote 6. Also see Boyd, Greg. *Scientific Support for the Open View*, 29 December 2007. Accessed 20 August 2012, from http://re-knew.org/2007/12/scientific-support/.

[263] *The Polkinghorne Reader: Science, Faith and the Search For Meaning.* Thomas Jay Oord, ed. 2010. Templeton Press, West Conshohocken, PA. See Part 1, Section 1, "The Nature of Science."

[264] Stephen Hawking disagrees. In an online blog, "Does God Play Dice?" he

causelessness as more elegant, even though everyone seems to recognize that Bohm's ingenious ideas make "common sense."

This admission is a startlingly candid. The source put forward by Belt, in an attempt to put the burden of proof on classic theists (where the testimony of modern science is concerned), has admitted that experimental science has not proven the principle of indeterminacy. In fact, what we have here may actually only be an intractable measurement problem, arising from the fact that any attempt to reduce the standard deviation of measurements of a particle's momentum, will, by definition, widen the standard deviation of location measurements. Mathematically, it can be shown as follows:

$$\Delta x \Delta p \geq \frac{h}{4\pi}$$

Δ is the uncertainty (standard deviation), x is the particle's position, p is the particle's momentum, and h is Plank's constant. Clearly, as the uncertainty of the position goes down, the level of uncertainty of the momentum goes up and vice versa. It is not clear why a human measurement problem, though, should trouble the omniscience of the Creator (and inventor) of all these particles.

This belief that there are no causes to know (where quantum behavior is concerned) does remind one of open theist's beliefs that there is no future to know. It seems to have been seized upon as a matter of taste: to yield a doctrine that is more agreeable: more along the line of what one wants to believe. Of course, this mental leap implies a preexisting belief system that controls and regulates the doctrine. Clearly, quantum physics is still a work in progress, and it is difficult to say where it will be when it matures. John Hick had an insightful comment with respect to this issue:

> There is however a complication to this picture in the principle of indeterminacy or uncertainty in the behavior of the most fundamental particles. According to quantum mechanics, at the minutest subatomic

says that an experiment by John Bell yielded results that are inconsistent with hidden variables. Accessed 20 August 2012, from http://www.hawking.org.uk/does-god-play-dice.html.

level it is in principle impossible to measure precisely both position and velocity at the same time. There is thus an element of uncertainty or unpredictability at the heart of nature. It seems clear, however, that this micro indeterminacy so to speak cancels out at the macro level of objects consisting of trillions of sub-atomic particles. It does not create an indeterminacy in the world of humanly observable physical objects and processes.[265]

Interestingly, James Kakalios, a professor in the School of Physics and Astronomy, University of Minnesota, agrees with John Hick, the theologian–philosopher, on the wildly exaggerated claims concerning quantum mechanics and human existence. He explains:

We might have been spared countless inane pronouncements that "quantum mechanics has proved that everything is uncertain" if Heisenberg had simply named his principle something a little *less* catchy, such as, "the principle of complementary standard deviations."[266] ... While it is certainly true that all objects, from electrons, atoms, and molecules to baseballs and research scientists, have a quantum mechanical wave function, one can safely ignore the existence of a matter-wave for anything larger than an atom. ... Anything bigger than an atom or a small molecule has such a large mass that its corresponding de Broglie wavelength is too small to ever be detected.[267]

Therefore, we have no reason to suppose that indeterminacy at the particle level is relevant to the real world of human life. Let us assume it is real, though, and that indeterminacy is so persuasive as to prevent any prediction of the future: that the basic "stuff" of the universe is simply too chaotic for that. Under that assumption, how could human beings exercise our volition? The stuff of the universe would be so indeterminate that our volition would have nothing to act upon. Let us assume,

[265] Hick, John, John Hick Official Website. *"A talk given at King Edward VI Camp Hill School, Birmingham, March 2002."* Accessed 20 August 2012, from http://www.johnhick.org.uk/jsite/.

[266] Kakalios, James. *The Amazing Story of Quantum Mechanics: A Math-Free Exploration of the Science That Made Our World.* 2010. Gotham Books, New York. p. 82.

[267] *Ibid.*, p. 85.

however, that our body is different—made of determinate stuff—so that we can move our limbs, and the chemical reactions that carry impulses to our nerves are also determinate. That would still be no good. If the rest of our environment were indeterminate, we would have no ability to interact. How could we see unless light were determinate, at least at a large scale? How could any of our senses work? We could have the wish to exercise volition but not the means. So open theists cannot have it both ways. Either the universe is sufficiently determined that the future can be known at the level appropriate to human life and volition is also possible, or else the universe is so indeterminate that neither future knowledge nor volition is possible.[268]

Quantum physics is only one barrel of the double-barreled shotgun that Belt invokes to try to shoot down classical theology. The other barrel is chaos theory, but this theory will not deliver the killing shot, either. For one thing, chaos theory is different from quantum theory in that there is no claim that there is a fundamental property of the universe that makes some dynamic systems indeterminate. The quality that makes them so is a high sensitivity to initial conditions. This sensitivity is sometimes called the "butterfly effect," from the idea that a butterfly wing might be enough of an initial condition in such systems to cause a hurricane in Florida. "Chaos" is a shorthand version for the term "deterministic chaos," from the surprising concept that even if the system contained no random elements, the final result would not be predictable.[269]

Among the reasons that chaos theory is not particularly relevant are the boundary conditions. It may be true that extremely minute initial changes will lead to such different dynamic changes within the system that it is indeterminate from a practical as well as a mathematical viewpoint. It is difficult to show, however, why God would find the systems indeterminate. Superhuman precision of the initial state, not otherwise attainable except by God, would almost certainly make these systems

---

[268] This point could also be made with chaos theory, discussed below.

[269] Kellert, Stephen H. *In the Wake of Chaos: Unpredictable Order in Dynamical Systems*. 1993. University of Chicago Press, Chicago. p. 32.

deterministic, after all. At least it is a reasonable proposition, absent proof to the contrary—admittedly a difficult proposition to test. Furthermore, even open theists admit that God could intervene in his universe whenever it suited him to do so. No chaotic process could resist God's power. That being the case, there is good reason to believe that chaotic processes are no barrier to divine foreknowledge of the future. So chaos theory is not a prop that will sustain the idea that the future is unknowable.

A final point on quantum physics and chaos theory. We have seen that it is logical to insist that if these create an unknowable future, even by God, then they would also create a world where volition is impossible.[270] Despite this, let us assume that this conclusion is not true. Let us assume that quantum theory and chaos theory make the case that the future is dynamic and contingent. This assumption still does not prove that the future does not exist. Nor does it mean it is in principle unknowable. Two of Belt's own sources, John Polkinghorne and William Lane Craig, accept a dynamic view of the future, but nevertheless, still insist that God is omniscient and that he has exhaustive foreknowledge. Clearly, modern science has a variety of views concerning time, space and fundamental properties of particles, some of which[271] would be fatal for openness theism. Strangely, it does not seem to work the other way. God and his attributes, as taught in Scripture and as articulated by classic theology, do not seem to be threatened by the special or general theories of relativity, quantum theory or chaos theory. It is true that one or the other may favor the Reformed view as opposed to the Arminian-Wesleyan view. Orthodox, classic Christian theology can certainly be defended even if much of modern physics is provisionally accepted as truth. In other words,

---

[270] I recently learned that philosopher-theologian John Hick agrees with this point. He said: "For we are no more free if our thoughts and actions are randomly determined than if they are rigidly determined. Either way they are not freely determined by us. Given either strict determinism, or an indeterminacy due to subatomic unpredictability, human freewill would be excluded." Hick, John, John Hick Official Website. *"A talk given at King Edward VI Camp Hill School, Birmingham, March 2002." op. cit.*

[271] Such as Minkowski spacetime.

nothing here forces God to be reduced to exercising only loose control over the future, as open theists maintain.

2. What are the proofs that "loose control" over the universe by God is even possible?

This question, at first, appears to be strange indeed. It seems to challenge the omnipotence of God, but that is not the intent. The true God in any actual universe is clearly omnipotent and has limitless control over the universe. The question is getting at the model of the universe put forward by open theology. Does the open theism model, assuming its assumptions are correct, yield a plausible result?

Thomas does not think so. He doubts the idea of partial sovereignty is at all plausible. He compares the loss of authority suffered by Adam from the Fall to the loss of authority by the god of open theism:

> The open theist would have people believe that a similar thing has occurred with God. By choice God surrendered a degree of His sovereignty over His creation and will someday regain it at the second coming of Christ. The principal difference is that Adam surrendered his sovereignty in toto, but God surrendered only a part of His sovereignty. The obvious question is, however, Is there any such thing as partial sovereignty? If one surrenders even a fraction of his sovereignty, does sovereignty still exist? Webster defines "sovereign" as "supreme in power, rank, or authority." Someone who has surrendered even a fraction of that power, rank, or authority is no longer a sovereign. It is one thing for a sovereign to delegate responsibility, but it is another for him to surrender his authority as open theists say God has done. In that case God no longer exercises control over all that happens, with the result that creatures are operating independently of Him, without having to answer to Him for their actions. [272]

Let's take a critical look at the open theism model. First, the model assumes the future does not exist. Note that open theists say that it *does not exist*, not that it is indeterminate nor that it is dynamic. They say has no present reality at all. Secondly, they say God is trapped in time like a

---

[272] Thomas, Robert L. "The Hermeneutics of 'Open Theism.'" *The Master's Seminary Journal*. TMSJ. 12/2 (Fall 2001). p. 195.

fly trapped in amber. He cannot go forward in time, backward in time, or even leave our time. (I do not know how the open theism model explains heaven.) He is trapped in time for the duration of the universe. We had better hope he has no other universes to attend to! Thirdly, they say God can have some control over the future if he determines or forces it to be a certain way. But this option is necessarily limited since it is ultimately self-defeating: limiting or destroying individual libertarian free will. Fourthly, they say God is surprised in at least some cases. Things do not always turn out the way he expects.

At this point another objection might be raised: "I thought you had already conceded above, that even if God could only react like a chess player to the decisions of his creatures, he would still be able to maintain close control over human actions and the course of human history." I admit this point is a good one. I did say so, but open theists not only have to show, even with the limitations of their model, that God can to some extent control the destiny of seven billion people (which I accept), but he also has to react to the unpredictable decisions of uncountable numbers of malevolent fallen angels, with unknown but great powers. He has to deal with forces of nature, such as earthquakes, tidal waves, or volcanoes, any of which could happen with little warning. And, of course, the claim of open theism stretches beyond our little world to the whole of the universe. Clearly, God could deal with all of these things if he is truly the God of the Scriptures, but what about the god of open theism?

At this point we must stop. I no longer want to assume that the god of open theism is identical to the true God. For the rest of the discussion, when I am referring to the god of open theism I will use the term Open Theism God (OTG). When I use the word "God," I will mean the true God as revealed in the Scriptures. To continue, it does seems unlikely that OTG could possibly be omnipresent, under the assumptions of the open theism model, for the reasons discussed above. It gets worse. If OTG experiences time just as we do, then presumably the theory of relativity applies to him. Perhaps, if he is a spirit, he could achieve the speed of light but at the cost of being frozen in time.

If Pinnock's idea (that OTG has a physical body) is generally accepted by open theists and has to be incorporated into the model, then we are approaching some intractable problems. Pinnock asked, rhetorically, "What kind of actions can a disembodied God perform?" We could well ask: Can a physical body that is subject to the limits imposed by the theory of relativity permit OTG to exercise his omnipotence?

How could the OTG, who is not omnipresent, with a physical body subject to relativistic limitations, hope to achieve any sort of control over the universe? He would be stretched to the limit retaining some control over this world. The more we look at the issue, the OTG looks more like the Superman© of DC comics than the true God of Abraham, Isaac and Jacob. Whatever we might say of Superman, he is not up to the task of loose control over the universe and neither is the OTG. So the question remains. Is "loose control" over the universe by the OTG even possible? Open theism has not shown it to be so.

3. Where in the Scriptures do they find this idea expressed, that God is satisfied with "loose control"?

This appeal to the Scriptures is a problem for open theism. Isaiah 46:9–10 has this divine affirmation:

> Remember the former things of old: for I am God, and there is none else; I am God, and there is none like me, declaring the end from the beginning, and from ancient times the things that are not yet done, saying, "My counsel shall stand and I will do all my pleasure ..."[273]

This passage teaches that there are no limits on God's control. Clearly that control includes some very "small stuff." Jesus said in Matthew 10:29–30:

> Are not two sparrows sold for a farthing? And one of them shall not fall on the ground without your Father. But the very hairs of your head are all numbered.[274]

This kind of universal, detailed control by God is frequently mentioned. Here is another statement by God himself in Psalm 50: 10–12:

---

[273] (KJV)

[274] (KJV)

For every beast of the forest is mine, and the cattle upon a thousand hills. I know all the fowls of the mountains: and the wild beasts of the field are mine. If I were hungry, I would not tell thee: for the world is mine and the fullness thereof.[275]

One would wonder if loose control would be adequate to sustain the universe. God not only created all things, but he must also continually sustain all things. Note that this does not mean just the big things. *All* things. Paul says of Christ: "He is before all things, and by him all things hold together."[276] The same thought (speaking again of Christ) is found in Hebrews 1:3: "sustaining all things by his powerful word."[277] God's sustaining power must extend to the smallest particles.

With that understanding, there is little value in considering this matter further. The Scriptures consistently show God as having unlimited power, down to the tiniest details of his creation. This idea that he would be satisfied with any kind of loose control, or that such control would be sufficient to sustain the universe and keep it from becoming unmade, is not found in Scripture. It likely comes from process theism and was uncritically accepted by open theists along with so much else of that philosophical system.

Some open theists recognize that this argument cannot be won by resorting to Scripture. Tom Belt, by equivocating, seems to admit as much:

> We also agree that God is not limited to exercising such general sovereignty. He is perfectly free to intervene miraculously on occasion in highly specific ways, controlling whatever minutiae he wishes to control. We only disagree that this is the only, or even the characteristic, way God has chosen to relate to us.

Belt's attempt to evade the issue does not work. This concept still amounts to loose control. He still thinks "general sovereignty" is the normal situation. He assumes God will control "minutiae" only "on occasion" and not do so as a "characteristic way." Miraculous intervention or

---

[275] (KJV)

[276] (HCSB)

[277] (HCSB)

the control of minutiae comprise highly unusual and uncharacteristic acts on the part of God, or so he says. The problem for him, as we have seen above, is that the Scriptures see God as characteristically controlling even the fall of sparrows. The reason Jesus mentioned sparrows was not so much to reassure us about God's concern for birds but to comfort us with the insight that if he controls bird life so closely, he will take care of his followers even more closely. Clearly, he relates to us in highly specific ways, despite what Belt believes. And so the form of general sovereignty advocated by open theism is hard to defend.

F. "SIMPLE FOREKNOWLEDGE" WOULD BE USELESS TO GOD.

Open theists press their case by trying to show that a view of God's omniscience held by classic theism does not stand close scrutiny. Belt put the issue like this:

> For example, let us say God timelessly knows that Susan will be in a fatal car accident on her 21st birthday. Granted, this knowledge does not cause her death or determine her choice to go driving with her friends. We're only talking here about whether or not timelessly definite foreknowledge provides God a basis upon which he is able to act providentially. Can God use his knowledge of Susan's death to warn Susan not to go driving? Can God act in a miraculous way to prevent this accident? In fact, can God do anything on the basis of his knowledge that Susan will die to prevent her from dying? The answer to these questions is, of course, that God cannot intervene on the basis of simple foreknowledge in order to prevent this event from happening. Since God's foreknowledge is infallible, what he foreknows will happen will indeed happen. Not even God can act in order to change what he infallibly knows will come to pass. Simple foreknowledge, if it existed, would be useless to God in preventing foreknown evil and other undesired events.[278]

First, let us acknowledge that Belt is talking about simple foreknowledge. This sort of foreknowledge refers to events God has foreseen but not predestined to be as a part of his perfect will. Belt does not believe even

---

[278] Belt, Thomas, *Open Theism and the Assemblies of God. op. cit.,* p. 5.

an omniscient God has this kind of foreknowledge and is trying to show that if it exists, it is useless to him or to anyone else. Belt concludes with the thought that it is best to dispense with beliefs that explain nothing and contribute nothing.

There is a problem with the notion that there are events that are foreseen by God but not caused by him. Open theists overstate the case, to be sure, but all events foreseen by God must be allowed by him to happen in some sense. Clearly, if he foresaw an event that he did not wish to happen, he could stop it from happening. On the other hand, for God there are no unforeseen consequences arising from allowing an event or of preventing it from happening. If God allows an event because he foresees that it is the best way to achieve his plan for the future, it is hard to see how that would be different from a foreordained event.

Having said that, Belt does not make a coherent case, unless one accepts several implicit assumptions. Let us explore them. He clings to the view that God is trapped in time, so we should assume that, for the purpose of argument. And we must also, for the moment, accept that the future is definite but not necessarily desired by God. Finally, Belt assumes there is no overall plan developed by God in eternity past that encompasses fine detail, such as an individual person like Susan. We will accept the lack of a detailed plan, also, for the purpose of argument.

If we accept all these assumptions, then we must agree with Belt; indeed, we would insist simple foreknowledge is a horrifying idea. Belt understates the case, if anything. It is chilling to conceive of a God who is trapped in time, knowing full well that numberless cruel events are certain, but being unable to alter the future. It reminds one of the myth of Sisyphus, condemned to roll a rock up a mountain, only to see it roll back down again, for eternity. Simple foreknowledge is even worse because God is condemned to foresee tragic and inevitable events which he does not desire and cannot prevent, until the end of the world. Fortunately, we need accept none of Belt's assumptions. God, being omnitemporal, is not trapped in our time. There are no foreseen events that were not also chosen by God in eternity past. And God does have a perfect plan for the ages that means Susan's death has real meaning and value in the light of eternity.

One might almost hear open theists exclaim in response, like Darth Vader, "Aha! I have you now!" Then they might say, "You as good as admit Susan's death was chosen by God." Then they would fall back in horror at the very thought. Bob Enyart made the following comments in a debate with Larry Bray:

> Just as many Calvinists don't realize they are buying into a doctrine that says that God orchestrated the sodomy of every boy raped, they also don't realize that they are buying into God Himself being unable to have a single new thought for all of eternity future. Dr. Bray, can God write a new song? Calvinism says no. For then the future would be different, and that is not allowed because of utter immutability. But if God can no longer create, then there goes immutability, because before the foundation of the world He was able to create, and now He cannot. In reality though, God remains inexhaustibly creative. For He has a will, is free, and creative, so therefore the future is not settled but eternally open.[279]

Enyart thinks he has "Calvinists" caught in a trap. Either they must admit God orchestrated the "sodomy of every boy raped" or they must admit the future is open. They must admit God is locked into the strait-jacket of a deterministic future with no new thoughts or new songs forever or accept the open theist future. This argument, however, is a classic case of black and white thinking. Enyart is trying to limit the discussion to two alternatives and thinks if he can paint one black, through and through, then the only alternative is the model he likes. You could also call his "Calvinist" model a straw man which he can demolish in order to give the impression he has proven classic Christianity, as devoutly believed for nearly 2000 years, to be a pitiful and harmful illusion.

---

[279] Enyart, Bob. *Calvinism Debate between Bob Enyart and The North American Reformed Seminary(TNAR)'s Dr. Larry Bray - May 22nd, 2011.* post Wednesday at 8:44 p.m. Accessed 3 August 2012, from http://www.theologyonline.com/forums/showthread.php?t=74408.

Clearly, the matter is not really so simple. For one thing, open theism does not make the plight of the boy any better. The boy is still raped. Furthermore, the OTG[280] could see the rape unfolding, knew very well what was about to happen and did nothing to stop it. To make matters worse, since the OTG does not have a detailed plan for the future, there seems to be no overwhelming reason why the OTG could not save the boy. It would not mean changing his plan. True, he would be thwarting the libertarian free will of the rapist, but he would be honoring the free will of the boy. Open theists are buying into a doctrine that says the OTG could have prevented the evil, but because of either bad management or a lack of concern chose not to do so. If a man could have easily stopped a felony from occurring at no risk to himself and chose not to do so, he would be justly condemned as being cold hearted, if not an accessory to the crime. The open theism view is not the moral high road its proponents make it out to be.

The point about the lack of a detailed plan on the part of the OTG deserves more discussion. John Sanders, speaking for open theists, puts it like this: "Furthermore, God's plan is not a detailed script but a broad intention that allows for a variety of options regarding precisely how it may be reached."[281] In the classic view, God does allow suffering, but he also has a detailed plan of the ages.[282] The plan is perfect, as he is perfect, so we can have the assurance that no suffering is meaningless. We can have confidence in him if we realize he is not arbitrary—he is not just making things up as he goes along. If God's perfect plan could have been accomplished another way, without the suffering, then God would have chosen that way. However, the OTG has no such perfect plan. He can allow a variety of options and still achieve his goals. So there is no good reason that we can discern as to why he allows a particular act of wicked-

---

[280] Open Theism God.

[281] Sanders, John. "Is Open Theism Christian Theism?" p. 2. Accessed 23 August 2012, from http://www.opentheism.info/index.php/john-sanders/is-open-theism-christian-theism/2/.

[282] See Acts 2:23; Psalm 139:16; Job 14:5.

ness to occur. If the OTG seems arbitrary, it is probably because he is. It is not clear that in the open theist universe there is any meaning in suffering.

Open theists answer: "Hold on. We believe God gave his creatures free will. So it's no good if he simply steps in every time someone uses that free will to hurt someone else. That would defeat the whole point of creating humans as free moral agents." Perhaps we should let open theists speak for themselves. Thomas Jay Oord, theologian and author, put it this way:

> I am trying to propose a biblically supported view of God's nature that helps us make sense of why God doesn't prevent genuine evil. God can't prevent genuine evil, because God's nature of love always gives freedom and/or agency to others.[283]

We can agree there is a sense in which God does use evil to carry out his purposes. We must also agree that God is love,[284] but we do not have to agree that "love is God." God is love, yes, but on the other hand, he is more than that. We can also agree that love is always characterized by freely giving, and freedom is one gift. That does not mean true love always gives freedom in each and every possible case without any consideration for the greater good of all or the long-term good of the individual. We will look at some obvious examples of where a loving God nevertheless limits freedom. We will see that these limits pose problems for the open view. Open theists can only fall back on their stock answer. "God will not violate libertarian free will." Here we see a total fixation on the idea that God cannot restrain; love forces him to allow genuine evil. One wonders if Oord believes that because God's love is limitless, limitless evil must also be allowed.

To look at it another way: in classic theology this same concept exists. Because God has created man in his own image, he allows creatures the capacity to choose between good and evil. Naturally, such choices involve the possibility of suffering. In Belt's example of Susan who is to

---

[283] *For the Love of Wisdom and the Wisdom of Love.* A website by Thomas Jay Oord. February 24, 2010. Archived Blog Entry: *God Can't—and the Bible Says So.* Accessed 23 August 2012, from http://thomasjayoord.com/index.php/blog/archives/god_cant_—_and_the_bible_says_so/#.UDaG4qO06pQ.
[284] 1 John 4:8

die on her 21st birthday, there was/is presumably an element of volition and choice involved. In the case of the boy ravaged by the sodomite, we see a human will that chose to commit an abomination. C. S. Lewis has, rather famously, explained this idea in his classic book, *The Problem of Pain.* Lewis discusses the problem of the abuse of free will:

> We can, perhaps, conceive of a world in which God corrected the results of this abuse of free will by His creatures at every moment: So that a wooden beam became soft as grass when it was used as a weapon. … But such a world would be one in which wrong actions were impossible and in which, therefore, freedom of the will would be void. … So it is with the life of souls in a world: fixed laws, consequences unfolding by causal necessity, the whole natural order, are at once the limits within which their common life is confined and also the sole condition under which any such life is possible. Try to exclude the possibility of suffering which the order of nature and the existence of free wills involve, and you find that you have excluded life itself.[285]

Free will is not an end in itself, and classic theology never says God has to allow evil to exist to the maximum extent evil creatures might desire. The flood (recounted in Genesis, Chapter 6) was clearly decreed, in large part, to restrain evil upon the earth.[286] We see the beginnings of human government imposing capital punishment for murder, which is also clearly intended to restrain evil.[287] God confused the language of the whole earth, again to restrain evil and lessen its scope.[288] This theme of restraining evil continued through the destruction of Sodom and Gomorrah,[289] the giving of the law,[290] and God's judgment on the nations of the promised land.[291] It can also be seen in God's providential

---

[285] Lewis, C. S. *The Problem of Pain. op. cit.,* pp. 33–34.

[286] See Genesis 6:1; 5–7.

[287] See Genesis 9:5–6.

[288] See Genesis 11:1–9.

[289] See Genesis 18–19.

[290] See Exodus 33–34.

[291] See Acts 13:19; Deuteronomy 7:1. Note that God did not give the land to Abram in his day because the iniquity of the Amorites was not yet full. See

protection of his people. The Holy Spirit acts as a restraining force on the wickedness of humankind. Christ said the Counselor[292] would "convict the world about sin, righteousness, and judgment."[293] God does not give a blank check to the evil of this world, and the "ruler of this world," Satan, has no power over Christ.[294]

God sometimes allows evil and sometimes restrains it, but we have every reason to believe this activity is not simply an arbitrary exercise of power by God. One good reason is the confidence that God has a perfect, infinitely detailed plan, and evil is strictly limited to that permitted in his plan. Nothing is *ad hoc*. The OTG has no detailed plan and does not know the future. Open theists surely must not be saying that God has to allow all conceivable evil but they offer no coherent explanation as to limits that could be imposed that were not arbitrary reactions.

Open theists have accepted process theism's rejection of a detailed plan of God. They must reject it because it flies in the face of what open theism means. How could the future be "open" if God had a detailed plan? They attempt to justify this rejection by their contention that such a pre-ordained plan puts God in a trap. Bob Enyart was quoted above as saying that for all eternity future, God cannot create; cannot write a new song; nor can he even have a new thought, if what he calls "Calvinism" is true. Annoyingly, Enyart still clings to the same unspoken assumptions held by Belt (discussed above), except that he (for the purpose of argument) allows God a detailed, fixed plan. Enyart will only consider a providential, eternal plan of God in the context of an open theism universe, which is not fairly considering alternatives to his scheme. He allows God a definite, fixed plan, yes, but God remains trapped in time and experiences time in essentially the same way that his creatures do. Enyart concludes that God, therefore, could not have a new thought because that would change the plan, and the plan is fixed. What it would really mean is that you cannot

Genesis 15:12–17.

[292] The Holy Spirit.

[293] John 16:8 (HCSB) The Holy Spirit's restraining power is seen in Genesis 6:1, 2 Thessalonians 2:7. Also see John 14.

[294] See John 14:30.

have the one true God in an open theism universe.[295] The one true God is not trapped in time. He is free to envision and create other universes if he wishes. Truly, he can enter time and experience it authentically,[296] and interact honestly with his creatures exactly as described in the Scriptures. Since he is omnitemporal, he is not confined to any one time, any more than he is confined to any one space. Therefore, God can and does have new thoughts. He can sing new songs. He could even change his plan, but why would he want to? C. S. Lewis had a profound thought about this very idea:

> With every advance in our thought the unity of the creative act, and the impossibility of tinkering with the creation as though this or that element of it could have been removed, will become more apparent. Perhaps this is not the "best of all possible" universes, but the only possible one. Possible worlds can mean only "worlds that God could have made, but didn't." The idea of that which God "could have" done involves a too anthropomorphic conception of God's freedom. ... The freedom of God consists in the fact that no cause other than Himself produces His acts and no external obstacle impedes them—that His own goodness is the root from which they all grow and His own omnipotence the air in which they all flower.[297]

So open theists, like Enyart, resolutely refuse to confront the true, robust nature of classical Christian faith. They dare only spar with it after it has been crippled enough to safely approach. It seems they wish it so because otherwise the true nature of their attraction to the OTG will become apparent, even to themselves. It truly is "a fearful thing to fall into the hands of a living God."[298] The OTG seems more approachable and safer, somehow; certainly less demanding. In the classic book of C. S. Lewis, *The Lion, the Witch and the Wardrobe*, a conversation takes place

---

[295] One reason for this is, of course, because the open theism universe is a figment of the imagination.

[296] This idea was mentioned above, but to reiterate, it is sometimes expressed by saying that God is *immanent*.

[297] Lewis, C. S. *The Problem of Pain. op. cit.,* p. 35.

[298] See Hebrews 10:31.

between Lucy and Mr. Beaver concerning Aslan, the Lion, which is how Jesus Christ is portrayed in the land of Narnia:

"Aslan is a lion—the Lion, the great Lion."

"Ooh!" said Susan. "I'd thought he was a man. Is he—quite safe?"

… "Safe?" said Mr. Beaver … "Who said anything about safe? 'Course he isn't safe. But he's good. He's the King, I tell you."[299]

It is tempting to want a God who is more like us, but the true God is the only God that exists, and his voice can melt mountains. He is not safe. His foes fall before his breath like dry leaves before a tornado. He is like a blast from an atomic furnace. No one can look on his face and live, but he is good. He does love us, even more truly than we love ourselves. He is a God who is both present with us, *immanent*, and yet timeless in his own being. He has emotions, yet he is unchangeable in his own being. He is both infinite and personal. There is a "wildness" about God. He cannot be contained or made safe. It may stoke our ego to falsely think our free will can change the very being of God as we co-create the future. But, to the contrary, the Scriptures teach that God created us for his glory, and he considers us significant. Surely that is more than enough for us.

Where does this analysis leave us? For one thing, while we are inclined to admit simple foreknowledge would not be useful in an open theism universe, the analysis offered by such open theists as Belt and Enyart is not authentic since they refuse to turn loose of their implicit assumptions. They continue to criticize a crippled form of Christian orthodoxy instead of the real thing. They see God's decrees as limiting his sovereignty, while placidly accepting process theism's concepts of a God frozen in time. This final argument neither advances open theism nor even clarifies the issues. It is an attempt to "win" by scoring debating points. In the final analysis, it doesn't matter whether or not simple foreknowledge would be useful to God. The key issue is whether even God can know the future completely. It is one thing for Christians within the sphere of orthodox thought to disagree about the exhaustiveness of God's knowledge about the future.

---

[299] Lewis, C. S. *The Chronicles of Narnia: The Lion, the Witch and the Wardrobe*. 1994. Harper Collins, New York. p. 77.

But to say God *cannot* know the future in complete detail is little short of blasphemy. It is easy to see why some call the concept heretical.

FURTHER READING

Piper, John, Justin Taylor, and Paul Kjoss Helseth, eds. *Beyond the Bounds: Open Theism and the Undermining of Biblical Christianity.* Wheaton, Illinois: Crossway Books. 2003.

Frame, John M. *No Other God: A Response to Open Theism.* Phillipsburg, NJ: P & R Publishing. 2001.

DISCUSSION QUESTIONS

1. Why do some critics of open theism call it a "heresy"? Do you agree with using that term?

2. Why do open theists say not even God can completely know the future?

3. In what ways does modern science support or refute open theism?

4. What do open theists mean when they say God controls the future loosely? Do you agree?

5. Why do open theists say simple foreknowledge is useless to God? Do you agree?

CHAPTER 8
†

The Poverty of Open Theism

Book: *God's Lesser Glory: the Diminished God of Open Theism* by Bruce A. Ware.[300]

Issue: What is the danger of open theism?

Open theists continually accuse classic theologians of being taken captive by pagan philosophy: particularly by Greek philosophers, such as Plato. As true postmodern thinkers do, they attempt to deconstruct the classic concept of God by what amounts to name-calling. There is a clear attempt to smear classic theology by finger-pointing and shrill claims that it has been polluted and is not a scriptural theology at all. Of course, open theists are fine ones to talk. We have seen above how open theists have lifted most of their distinctive ideas from a modern philosophy called process theism. They illogically claim, "Our philosophers are better than your philosophers!" It is the classic case of the "pot calling the kettle black." This strategy often works to deceive the unwary; that is why it is so often used.

---

[300] Ware, Bruce A. *God's Lesser Glory: the Diminished God of Open Theism.* 2000. Crossway Books, Wheaton, IL.

1. HOW DOES "OPEN THEISM" INTERPRET THE BIBLE?

This idea that the early church somehow adopted pagan ideas, which caused them to misinterpret the Bible and misunderstand the nature of God, seems ridiculous at first glance. One has only to browse the writings of the early church fathers[301] to see how vigorously and persuasively they contended for the true faith against the ideas of pagan (mainly Greek) philosophers. Furthermore, all the distinctive ideas of open theists were also held by the Greeks, but open theists are not impressed. They see a telling correspondence of thought, particularly from Plato, in the early Christian concept of God. Boyd puts it like this:

> While some (including myself) argue that the development of the classical view of God was decisively influenced by pagan philosophy, classical theologians have always maintained that it is deeply rooted in Scripture.[302]

Enyart posted an online blog purporting to prove that God existed in time.[303] He said the idea that God was timeless was not found in the Bible; it was from Plato, that is, *pagan Greek philosophy.* He said the Greek and Hebrew terms in the Bible were different, and none of them meant "timelessness."[304] But the most authoritative lexicon available in English is the BADG which clearly lists one meaning of the Greek words *aion* and *aionios* as "timelessness" in regard to God. The same idea is found in the most authoritative theological dictionary—the TDNT.[305] The latter mentions "everlasting God" in Romans 16:26 as containing "not merely

---

[301] See *Ante-Nicene Fathers*. Ten Volumes. Available online at: Christian Classics Ethereal Library. From http://www.ccel.org/fathers.html/.

[302] Boyd, Gregory A., *God of the Possible. op. cit.*, p. 24.

[303] He seems to be unaware that classical theologians also believed that God exists in time. Classic Christian belief insists that God in his *essential nature* is timeless, which is quite a different thing.

[304] Enyart, Bob. On-Line blog. *Bob Enyart Live. Is God Outside of Time? The Bible Proves He is in Time.* Accessed 24 August 2012, from http://kgov.com/is-God-outside-of-time.

[305] See pages 43–47, above, for a thorough discussion of these terms.

the concept of unlimited time without beginning or end, but also of the eternity which transcends time."[306] So Enyart was profoundly wrong. The concept of "timelessness" is definitely found in the Bible.

It is ironic that we had to confront Rob Bell above,[307] when he tried to limit the Greek words *aion* and *aionios* to mean only two limited concepts, one of which was "timelessness." Now here, Enyart tried to say no Greek or Hebrew words *ever* meant "timelessness." Here were two church leaders trying to use a half-baked understanding of Bible languages to try to prove their point. It was almost like saying, "Don't argue with me. It says so in the Greek." Enyart, recognizing that English translations of the Bible did not agree with him, said these "translations do not flow from the grammar but from the translators' commitment to Greek philosophy."[308] Probably, he would say that the writers of the lexicons and Bible dictionaries were also infected with the curse of pagan Greek philosophy. Only he, Enyart, and those who agreed with him, could interpret the Hebrew and Greek properly. Unless Enyart were a Greek and Hebrew scholar who had given his life to the study of these languages, however, he would not be competent to venture an independent opinion that was not based on some pre-existing reference materials.

In order to test Enyart's and Boyd's claim that Christians have been infected with Greek philosophy, let us take another tack. Historians can make a strong case that the early Hebrew scholars were not influenced by Greek philosophy. That being the case, the rabbis' conception of God must be drawn from the Old Testament Scriptures exclusively. An exhaustive study by Fuller investigated this issue. Fuller confirmed that the rabbis were not influenced by Greek philosophy, and yet they arrived at a concept of God that was essentially identical to classic Christian theology on every point of dispute with the open theists. This finding clearly shows that classic Christian concepts of God derive from the Scriptures.

---

[306] Sasse, Hermann, Erlangen. "Aionios." In *Theological Dictionary of the New Testament, op. cit.*, p. 208.

[307] See pages 43–45, above.

[308] Enyart, Bob, *op. cit.*

Concepts that agree with Platonic thought are shown to be coincidental and not derivative.[309] Fuller concluded:

> Clearly, Christians must reject the claims of the openness view. Its historical claims are misinformed—the rabbis follow Moses and Isaiah, not Plato and Aristotle. Its theology is misguided—the rabbis maintain that God foresees and foreordains even future free actions. And its exegesis is mistaken—the rabbis interpret anthropomorphisms figuratively. In the end, the openness view requires too much. It requires us to believe that Christians and Jews have misunderstood history, theology, and exegesis for thousands of years.[310]

Clearly, the curse of Greek philosophy is simply a bogeyman, but what does Fuller mean about *exegesis*? Exegesis refers to the work of interpreting a text of the Bible. And *anthropomorphisms*, as the word is used here, are biblical passages that attribute human characteristics to God. With that understanding, we can discuss how open theism interprets the Bible to infer that God does not know the future completely. To an outside observer, it might seem open theists started with the concept of an open future and a God who was bound in time—both derived from process theism—and then searched the Bible for texts to justify their conclusions.

They deny this, of course. To the contrary, open theists claim classical theists are selective in how they interpret the Bible. Texts which show that the future is completely known and settled in the mind or will of God are interpreted literally. Texts that seem to show God changing his mind, or implying the future is not settled, are interpreted as being figurative or anthropomorphisms. Open theists claim to take both kinds of passages literally and see the future as "partly open and partly settled."[311] Boyd makes light of the

---

[309] Fuller, Russell. *The Rabbis and the Claims of Openness Advocates*. In: *Beyond the Bounds: Open Theism and the Undermining of Biblical Christianity*. 2003. John Piper, Justin Taylor, and Paul Kjoss Helseth, eds. Crossway Books. Wheaton, IL. pp. 23–41.

[310] *Ibid., p. 41.*

[311] Boyd, Gregory A. "God and the Future: A Brief Outline of the Open View". Accessed 25 August 2012, from http://www.pinpointevangelism.com/libraryoftheologycom/writings/opentheism/God_And_The_Future_Gregory_Boyd.pdf.

difference between literary forms. It does not matter to him, apparently, if the text is didactic (teaching something), prophetic, narrative, or poetry. He takes them all literally. Fair enough. We have been given warning.

Some open theists, such as Pinnock, apparently believe the Bible does not speak with one voice, not only concerning the degree to which the future is settled, but in many other cases as well. He said, "the Bible is not a flat text but a symphony of voices and emphases."[312] He also said Bible texts could not be trusted to be absolutely true, and what they meant when they were first written might not be what they meant today. He said:

> Biblical texts are not free of the issues of cultural relativism. Biblical revelation is progressive in character, requiring attention to where a text lies in the living organism of Scripture. What something meant originally and what it means authoritatively now may differ, at least at the levels of language and culture.[313]

However, the "gold standard" of biblical interpretation is called the "grammatico-historical" system. This approach considers the grammar of the language and the history of the setting in which the text was written. Milton S. Terry, who is as definitive on this subject as anyone, said:

> The grammatico-historical sense of a writer is such an interpretation of his language as is required by the laws of grammar and the facts of history.[314][...]

> A fundamental principle in grammatico-historical exposition is that the words and sentences can have but one significance in one and the same connection. The moment we neglect this principle we drift out upon a sea of uncertainty and conjecture.[315]

---

[312] Pinnock, Clark. "Catholic, Protestant, and Anabaptist: Principles of Biblical Interpretation in Selected Communities." *Brethren in Christ History and Life.* 9 (December 1986): 268, 275.

[313] Pinnock, Clark H. with Barry L. Callen. *The Scripture Principle: Reclaiming the Full Authority of the Bible.* Second Edition. 2006. Baker Academic, Grand Rapids, MI. Appendix. *The Inspiration and Authority of the Bible: Thoughts since 1984.* p. 267.

[314] Terry, Milton S. *Biblical Hermeneutics*, 2nd. Ed. n. d. Zondervan, Grand Rapids, MI. p. 203.

[315] *Ibid.*, p. 205.

So we need to consider carefully how open theists interpret the Bible. We should expect that they will treat the literary forms as equivalent. We can expect the text will be treated with suspicion. We can expect them to see the Bible contradicting itself. We cannot assume they will respect the original meaning of the text. We cannot even expect them to observe perhaps the most basic rule: "one meaning—many applications." With all these problems, we should not expect their interpretation of Bible texts to be reliable, but let us see whether or not our fears are unfounded.

EXAMPLES OF OPEN THEISTS' USE OF SCRIPTURE

First, look at the very verse that led Boyd down the path towards open theism: 2 Kings 20. This is a narrative passage[316] where King Hezekiah was sick, and the Lord sent him a message through the lips of Isaiah the prophet. Isaiah told the king he would die. Hezekiah wept and beseeched the Lord. Even before Isaiah had left the court, God told him to return with a new message. Among other things, Isaiah was told by the Lord to tell Hezekiah he would recover, and God would add fifteen years to the king's life.

Boyd puzzled over these verses, he says, and wondered if God had changed his mind. He asked: "Was God being sincere when he had Isaiah tell Hezekiah that he wouldn't recover from his illness?"[317] Boyd could not understand how Scripture could say God added fifteen years to Hezekiah's life if God had previously ordained the king's lifespan. Boyd claims that after three years of study he finally concluded the future was not exhaustively settled and that God did not know the future completely.[318]

To respond to Boyd, we must first emphasize that his reaction to this verse is idiosyncratic. There is actually little problem in harmonizing this verse with the view that the future is exhaustively settled and completely

---

[316] We need to be careful when considering narrative passages, since the purpose may not be didactic teaching. This will be discussed in more depth below.

[317] Boyd, Gregory A., *God of the Possible. op. cit.,* Preface. p. 7.

[318] *Ibid.,* p. 8.

foreseen by God. But there is difficulty in harmonizing Boyd's views with hundreds of prophecies and dozens of other verses that explicitly teach the classical view.[319] Let us look at this verse, specifically.

Boyd says God was deceptive in saying Hezekiah would die if the future were preordained so that he would repent and live. He also says that open theism saves us from thinking that God told a lie since God did not know if Hezekiah would repent or not when he told Isaiah to prophesy the king's death. When Hezekiah did repent, then *at that point* God decreed fifteen years would be added to the king's life. So the future of the king, previously unsettled, now became settled.[320] Boyd apparently believed that only this solution saved God from being seen as untruthful.

This verse became the linchpin of Boyd's theology. It is hard to see why, since using Boyd's own argument, open theism also fails the test. Piper explains:

> Boyd's own view also seems to make God disingenuous. Is God telling the truth when he says," You shall die, and not live," when he really means," You might die, but won't if you repent"? Boyd's criticism of historic Christian exegesis applies to himself at this point.[321]

So, however we look at the matter, there is an unspoken but clearly understood subtext to the prophecy. In other words, among the Israelites there was an understanding that God was both just and merciful and heard the penitent cry of the heart.[322] Piper goes on to explain this point:

> It is not true that one must always express explicitly the exceptions to the threats one gives or the predictions one makes in order to be honest. One reason for this is that there can be a general understanding in a

---

[319] See Psalm 33:11, 139:16; Proverbs 19:21; Isaiah 14:34, 31:2, 44:7, 46:9, 10; Malachi 3:6; Romans 1:2; Hebrews 6:17; James 1:18.

[320] Boyd, Gregory A., *God of the Possible. op. cit.*, p. 8.

[321] Piper, John. *Answering Greg Boyd's Openness of God Texts.* May 11, 1998. ©2012 Desiring God Foundation. Website: desiringGod.org. Accessed 27 August 2012, from http://www.desiringgod.org/resource-library/articles/answering-greg-boyds-openness-of-god-texts.

[322] Stallard, Mike. "The Open View of God: Does He Change?" *The Journal of Ministry & Theology.* Vol. 5. No. 2. Fall 2001. pp. 5–25.

family or group of people that certain kinds of threats or warnings always imply that genuine repentance will be met with mercy.[323]

Accordingly, despite Boyd, there is not the slightest evidence that God did not know full well what Hezekiah would do.[324] God foreknew that he would repent. There is nothing in the text that says God was caught by surprise. God has repeatedly said he would relent if a nation or kingdom (or individual) repented. The parable of the potter in Jeremiah 18 says as much:

> At one moment I might announce concerning a nation or a kingdom that I will uproot, tear down, and destroy it. However, if that nation I have made an announcement about turns from its evil, I will relent concerning the disaster I had planned to do to it.[325]

What is completely transparent to the classic view of Scripture is that God's decree to add fifteen years to Hezekiah's life was actually ordained in God's perfect plan before the creation of the universe. I will expand on this concept below, but suffice it to say, God is both timeless and yet present with us in time. Under the open view, how could God ensure Hezekiah would live fifteen more years? Nicole pointed out that under the open theism paradigm, God would have to override free will innumerable times to make sure that span of years came to pass, something open theists constantly assure us he is reluctant to do. He said:

> It is not clear how on "Open Theism's" premises God could make such an announcement fifteen years in advance, since the continuation of Hezekiah's life surely depended on many decisions of free agents, including himself.[326]

Bruce Ware had the same insight, which he expressed more fully:

> Is it not entirely conceivable that God's purpose behind these words was in fact to elicit from him such earnest, heartfelt dependence on God in

---

[323] Piper, John. *Answering Greg Boyd's Openness of God Texts. op. cit.*

[324] See Psalm 139:1–6, Job 42:2.

[325] Jeremiah 18:7–8 (HCSB) Also see Jeremiah 42:10. Jonah 3:10.

[326] Nicole, Roger. *"Open Theism" is Incompatible With Inerrancy.* Founders Journal. Spring 2003. pp. 14–21. Note 15.

prayer? … God granted to Hezekiah *fifteen years* of extended life—not two, not twenty, and certainly not, "we'll both see how long you live," but *fifteen years exactly*. Does it not seem a bit odd that this favorite text of open theists, which purportedly demonstrates that God does not know the future and so changes his mind when Hezekiah prays, also shows that God *knows precisely and exactly how much longer Hezekiah will live?* On openness grounds, how could God know this? Over a fifteen-year time span, the contingencies are staggering. The number of future freewill choices, made by Hezekiah and innumerable others, that relate directly to Hezekiah's life and wellbeing, none of which God knows (in the openness view) is *enormous.*[327]

We can conclude that 2 Kings 20 does not support the view of open theists, despite the pivotal role it played in the mind of Boyd. Of course, he also cites a number of other verses that he claims support his position. Since the failures of his analysis are consistent, it will suffice to consider only one of them. As a further example, Boyd cites Numbers 14:12–20 as a text that illustrates and supports the view of open theism. He says:

> In response to Israel's bickering, the Lord says, "I will strike them with pestilence and disinherit them, and I will make of you [Moses] a nation greater and mightier than they" (v. 12). Moses asks the Lord to forgive the people, and the Lord eventually responds, "I do forgive, just as you have asked" (v. 20).
>
> Unless the intention the Lord declared to Moses in verse 12 was insincere, we must conclude that he did not at that point intend to forgive the Israelites. It cannot have been certain at that time (let alone from all eternity) that God would forgive the Israelites. Hence, it seems that either the Lord is insincere, or the classical view of divine foreknowledge is mistaken.[328]

This is another case where Boyd is deriving a didactic teaching about God from a narrative passage. He believes God changed his mind, and God does not have foreknowledge as is usually believed. But this belief conflicts with other scriptures, such as Numbers 23:19–20: "God is not a man who lies,

---

[327] Ware, Bruce A. *God's Lesser Glory: the Diminished God of Open Theism. op. cit.*, pp. 95–96.
[328] Boyd, Gregory A., *God of the Possible.* p. 158.

or a son of man who changes his mind."[329] This passage is also from a narrative section, but it is a word from God himself. A prophetic word from God confirms this: "Furthermore, the eternal One of Israel does not lie or change his mind, for he is not man who changes his mind."[330] From the Psalms comes a powerful description: "He counts the number of the stars; he give names to all of them. Our Lord is great, vast in power; his understanding is infinite."[331] Finally, in Ephesians, in a didactic section, God has a comprehensive plan in which he causes *everything* to work out in accordance with his will.[332]

Clearly, the analysis by Boyd is inadequate on a number of levels. It will not do to say that he can harmonize the various teachings of Scripture by taking all of the above passages literally and asserting that the future is "partly open and partly settled," or that God sometimes changes his mind and sometimes he doesn't. We have a text implying that God changed his mind and a number of texts that say he will *never* change his mind. Boyd's solution is to literally accept the text he likes and to ignore all the others. He does not take all the verses literally and so does exactly what he accuses classic theologians of doing—arbitrarily affirming texts. Are we to be left with "dueling texts" and no way to resolve them? Happily, there is a simple solution. We will consider the form of the texts, of descriptive narratives as contrasted to normative teachings. Scholer explains:

> We must distinguish between normative teachings and descriptive narratives. The latter have relevance for determining authoritative principles in the New Testament but must be carefully related to normative teachings. They may clarify or qualify a didactic statement. ... Descriptive narratives which cannot be related to didactic statements may indicate material that is culturally relative. However, descriptive narratives may contain implicit teaching, and not all didactic statements are necessarily 'universal.'[333]

---

[329] (HCSB)

[330] 1 Samuel 15:29 (HCSB)

[331] Psalm 147:4–5 (HCSB)

[332] "We have also received an inheritance in him, predestined according to the purpose of the One who works out everything in agreement with the decision of his will." Ephesians 1:11 (HCSB)

[333] Scholer, David M. "Issues in Biblical Interpretation." *Evangelical Quarterly*

Boyd is going about the task backwards. Of course, it is proper to let the target text[334] speak for itself, without trying to force it into some preconceived mold. Once we have done that, and an apparent conflict seems to have arisen, it is proper to let the didactic texts interpret narrative passages. If we do this for Numbers 14:12–20, we will find that the narrative is discussing what happened *phenomenally* or "according to appearances."[335] It other words, it tells what happened from the standpoint of what an observer would have witnessed. It does not necessarily explain the mechanism "behind the scenes" that caused the events to be played out. Didactic texts describing the nature of God are the reverse. They explain, accurately but not necessarily completely, what we should understand about him. Now, the conflict can easily be explained. God did not actually change his mind, but he appeared to do so. Is this view the traditional one? Yes, it is, and it has been the settled view of Christians for many centuries. It is not clear why this view is so hard for open theists to accept since it nicely harmonizes all the above passages, which is something the open view does not do or even pretend to do.

There is one additional point that Boyd raises that should be met directly. He accuses the Lord of being "insincere" (a polite term for "lying") if he never really intended to smite them dead.[336] We could simply say God had his reasons and leave it at that.[337] Other possible explanations suggest themselves. Perhaps, long before God stated that this offense was worthy of death, he had already issued a decree in eternity past. He had in fact judged them and pronounced sentence upon them before the creation. In his infinite mercy (still in eternity past) he had chosen a future where Moses interceded and God had graciously decreed mercy.

(EQ) 88:1 (1988). pp. 19–20.

[334] Numbers 14:12–20

[335] For a discussion of the concept of phenomenal language see Ramm, Bernard. *The Christian View of Science and Scripture*. 1954. Eerdmans. Grand Rapids, MI. pp. 46–47.

[336] Remember though, that Hebrew has no tense, only stating whether the action was complete or not.

[337] We could also say he was being "insincere" if the open view was true since he did not say, "I will smite them dead unless they repent."

So in our universe, the one God has chosen, the people were spared, even though they were actually under the sentence of death for a time. To put it another way, from the divine (timeless) perspective, the people had been sentenced and then[338] spared (before the foundation of the world). So in that sense, God did not change his mind at Kadesh in the wilderness of Paran. In the flow of time which God was experiencing with Moses and the congregation, there was a time when the people were condemned to death and later a time when they were spared. So God neither lied (they actually were condemned) nor changed his mind (it was made up before the foundation of the world).[339]

The contrast between the timeless perspective of God and our human perspective is adequate to resolve the question that Boyd raises. There may be, however, an even simpler explanation.

Before anyone dares so much as to hint that God lied,[340] we must realize that the Hebrew text is a bit ambiguous. Certainly, Moses understood God to say that he was somehow in the process of smiting the congregation with a pestilence to destroy them. The tense is *imperfect*, however, and the words could mean "I will destroy them" or "I am destroying them" or "I am smiting them." God may have simply meant that the process of their destruction had already begun and was halted when God heard Moses' intercession. Again, this language is phenomenal and says nothing one way or another about God's decrees before the foundation of the universe. Clearly, though, we can reject Boyd's insinuation that God was insincere.

[338] This is a subsequent action in a logical sense, not a temporal sense, since it happened before time began.

[339] This point was summarized by Horton, taking seriously "... the dynamic outworking of God's redemptive plan in concrete history, taking very seriously the twists and turns in the road—including God's responses to human beings ... without denying the clear biblical witness to the fact that God transcends these historical relationships. Transcendence and immanence are not antithetical categories for us, compelling us to choose one over the other." See Horton, Michael S. *Hellenistic or Hebrew? Open Theism and Reformed Theological Method.* In: *Beyond the Bounds: Open Theism and the Undermining of Biblical Christianity.* 2003. John Piper, Justin Taylor, and Paul Kjoss Helseth, eds. Crossway Books. Wheaton, IL. pp. 23– 41.

[340] Contradicting verses like Numbers 23:19–20.

George L. Klein, Professor of Old Testament, at Southwestern Baptist Theological Seminary, responded to an e-mail question concerning an exegesis of 2 Kings 20 and Numbers 14:12. I asked him:

> But I am wondering if there might also be an issue with Hebrew grammar. The Hebrew in 2 Kings 20:1 is not actually in future tense, but imperfect. Could it not actually be saying "You are dying"? Or in Numbers 14:12 could it be saying "I am [in the process of] destroying them"?[341]

He kindly answered:

> I agree with your observations about the imperfect verb in 2 Kings 20:1. Various modal understandings, in addition to your own, are possible. Although I am far from an expert on open theism, its approach to verses like this trouble me greatly for their overly simple, narrow understandings and interpretations which the text doesn't require. Likewise, in Numbers 14:12 the verb translated "I will strike" could be rendered modally, such as "I want to strike," "I ought to strike," or "I should strike." It pains me to see anyone treating imperfect verbs so woodenly as if they all equated to future tense verbs in English. For that matter, the Hebrew verbal system is not tense (time) based anyway. So to make an argument assuming that these verbs are essentially temporal is quite mistaken.[342]

Klein's reaction to my question certainly should make anyone pause before uncritically accepting the exegesis offered by Boyd. Boyd's analysis of these texts does not adequately consider the grammar, the literary form (genre), or the historical setting. He seems to use a "cafeteria-style" exegesis, wherein he finds texts that can be made to support his preconceived theology and ignores the ones that do not. This approach is not a respectful treatment of the sacred Scripture.

Enough of this look at Boyd and his views. Suffice it to say that the open theists' analysis of Scripture consists of page after page of more of

---

[341] E-mail from Jim Fox to George Klein. Monday, August 27, 2012, 1:05 PM. Subject: Exegesis of 2 Kings 20 and Numbers 14:12.

[342] E-mail from George Klein to Jim Fox. Wednesday, August 29, 2012 11:35:33–0500. Subject: Exegesis of 2 Kings 20 and Numbers 14:12.

the above. It simply amounts to forcing texts into a pattern already in the mind. There is an old saying: "A text of Scripture is like a condemned criminal. If you torture it enough, you can make it say anything you want it to." Selective use of texts, with no attempt to seriously deal with numerous passages that teach the opposite of their views, make their conclusions humanly pre-ordained and of little value in recovering the original meaning of the text. Clearly, open theists were convinced in the arena of philosophical speculation, long before they approached the Scriptures. They need not expect that many evangelical Christians will follow that path.

2. DOES "OPEN THEISM" LEAD TO A DENIAL OF AN INERRANT BIBLE?

Open theism proponents seem to be abandoning belief in the inerrancy of the Scriptures—yet another example of the deterioration of evangelical Christianity and an attempt to reach an accommodation with the culture. This betrayal was foreseen by Frances Schaeffer[343] who predicted that a loss of belief in the inerrancy of Scripture would set evangelical Christians on the path toward apostasy. If we lose here, we will not be able to stand against the pressures of our culture.

As evidence of this accommodation, we need look no further than the case of Boyd, who has been cited above. His website says he was "professor of theology for sixteen years at Bethel University, founder and pastor of Woodland Hills Church, St. Paul, Minn."[344] Boyd spares no effort in promoting the concept of open theism. He also candidly admits he has abandoned the idea of an inerrant Bible: "I'd like to suggest that the truly dangerous view is the one that believes the Bible must be 100 percent accurate to be God's inspired Word." He then lists a catalogue of biblical difficulties that would be the credit of any atheist website. Clearly, Boyd is proceeding down the path predicted by Frances Schaeffer.

[343] Schaeffer. *The Great Evangelical Disaster. op. cit.,* pp. 46–47.

[344] *Reknew.* A website by Greg Boyd. May 24, 2012. *Answering an Objection to a Cross-Centered Approach to Scripture [Q&A].* Accessed 22 August 2012, from http://gregboydreknew.blogspot.com/2012_05_01_archive.html.

We need not think that Boyd is an isolated exception. Another open theism proponent, Thomas J. Oord, said this:

> Some modern Christians attempt to establish absolute truth by claiming the Bible is absolute truth. This typically means claiming the Bible has absolutely no errors whatsoever. The Bible is inerrant, they say.
>
> The modern project of establishing the absolute truth of the Bible by affirming its inerrancy, however, collapses upon itself. The Bible itself cannot support the project, because it has multiple errors of various types. Fortunately, the vast majority of errors are of minimal consequence.
>
> As a response, some modernists [sic] claim the original biblical manuscripts were error-free. But his [sic] response offers no help for establishing that the Bibles we actually have now are absolutely true.[345]

Finally, we should mention Clark Pinnock's defection. He was once a strong proponent of the inerrancy of Scripture. He was even an associate for a time with Frances Schaeffer. It was not long after he began to accept open theism that he also began to question and finally abandon inerrancy.[346] By the end of his life, he had become what Francis Schaeffer warned us of—the academic who gave in to the spirit of the age.[347]

There seems to be little reason for optimism about the future for open theism. If a belief in the inerrancy of the Scriptures is lost, if past experience is any guide, there will be little ability to resist further compromise with the culture.

---

[345] *For the Love of Wisdom and the Wisdom of Love.* A website by Thomas Jay Oord. May 12, 2012. Archived Blog Entry: *Postmodern and Wesleyan 2.* Accessed 22 August 2012, from http://thomasjayoord.com/index.php/blog/archives/postmodern_and_wesleyan_2/#.UDWe-qO8rm4.

[346] Koop, Doug. *Clark Pinnock Dies at 73.* Obituary. Christianity Today. Posted 8/17/2010,12:14 PM, p. 2. From http://www.christianitytoday.com/ct/2010/augustweb-only/43-22.0.html?start=2.

[347] Schaeffer, *The Great Evangelical Disaster. op. cit.*, p. 119.

3. WHAT CONCLUSIONS CAN WE REACH ABOUT "OPEN THEISM"?

Open theism is a profoundly flawed and unsatisfactory system of theology. Scripture has the concept of the "fruits of the poison tree." If the tree is poisonous, the fruits will be poisonous too. Not all Christian teachers are bringing fruits that nourish the sheep. Matthew 7: 15–17 says:

> Watch out for false prophets. They come to you in sheep's clothing, but inwardly they are ferocious wolves. By their fruit you will recognise them. Do people pick grapes from thornbushes, or figs from thistles? Likewise, every good tree bears good fruit, but a bad tree bears bad fruit.[348]

In the last two chapters we considered seven points that are typically used to justify the basic beliefs of open theism:

1. Open theism says the future does not exist. I maintain that no one could possibly derive this idea from an unbiased reading of Scripture. It had to come from a philosophical system outside the realm of orthodox Christian theology. It seems clear that this concept was lifted from process theism, where, apart from the premises that engendered it, it simply languishes, without visible means of support.

2. Open theism says God knows the future only in part; he has decreed only a limited number of events that must occur and undetermined actions of creatures with free will are unknowable. This conclusion stands or falls on the idea that the future does not exist. But this idea has not been established, so this limitation on God has not been established, either. To the contrary, it flies in the face of Scripture, which often speaks of a real future.

3. Open theism says God does not exercise meticulous control over the future. I conclude this idea is not greatly different from the previous one. Christians might argue about whether the future is completely foreordained or whether parts are simply foreknown. Notwithstanding these arguments, Christians agree that, either way, God knows

---

[348] Matthew 7: 15–17 (NIV)

all. As Peter said, "Lord, you know all things …"[349] Without laying the groundwork with sufficient proof, this idea does not advance the open theism case. It merely restates an Arminian doctrine.

4. Open theism says humans have *hard* libertarian free will. Their entire system depends on this being true in a strong sense. Unfortunately for open theism, this idea is far from being established. Classic theism is not of one mind on the issue but does not hang or fall on which version of free will is correct. Open theism is fragile and depends on human freedom being absolute and autonomous (see below).

5. Open theism says that God is trapped in time. Proponents show from Scripture that God is active in time, but cannot explain the Scriptures showing God to be timeless. They try to argue that the consensus of modern science affirms the future does not exist, and therefore, God must experience time in the same way that human beings do. To the contrary, however, there is no consensus on this issue from science. Theories of special and general relativity deny the open theist view. Chaos theory and quantum indeterminacy, rightly understood, are not proofs in favor of the open theism position either. Some sources suggested by open theists do support the idea of a dynamic or contingent future, but that is not the same as saying the future does not exist.

6. Open theism says God can achieve the future he wants, in broad terms, by adapting to the free choices of his creatures. However, it is not sufficient to say that God might be able to do so. The question is: Why would he want to? Would "broad" control be sufficient to sustain the universe? I must conclude that this idea is problematic and not supported by the Scriptures. Open theism can find Scriptures that show God interacting with humans, but there has been no convincing case that God would ever be satisfied with "broad" control.

7. Finally, open theism maintains that simple foreknowledge would be useless to God. Their analysis does not really interact with orthodox Christian thinking, since open theists refuse to relinquish the idea that God is trapped in time (even for the sake of argument). This being the case, the arguments of open theists take on a hectoring tone, using "black-and-white thinking" and "straw-man" arguments. Open theists simply have not made the case that God is unable to have full knowl-

---

[349] John 21: 17 (NIV)

edge of all determined and foreseen events in the future. Certainly this view is contrary to the testimony of Scripture.

4. WHAT IS THE LIKELY FUTURE OF "OPEN THEISM"?

Open theism is not a theology unique to a particular denomination. Propounded by evangelical theologians, it has arisen for the most part within the academy rather than local churches. On the other hand, advocates for open theism have not confined themselves to arguing their viewpoint in scholarly articles or seminary textbooks. This idea has compelled them, from the early days of the movement, to write and publish books designed for a popular audience. Today the viewpoints of open theism are zealously promoted on the internet and especially by social media.

All this advocacy has not gone without notice. Christian leaders have been appalled by the views of open theists and have remonstrated with them. Finally, efforts have been made to remove open theists from positions of influence. For example, Clark H. Pinnock, a theologian who had espoused open theism, was challenged by members of the Evangelical Theological Society and was nearly expelled in 2002.[350] Johan D. Tangelder, in another summation of Pinnock's life, said:

> Pinnock's intention is to remain true to the historic gospel, but his views have left him wide open to serious criticism. R. C. Sproul has said publicly that Pinnock is a heretic for teaching limited omniscience. Norman Geisler said that Pinnock's work is a part of a "dangerous trend within evangelical circles of creating God in man's image."[351]

Tangelder also noted that even before Pinnock embraced open theism, he had abandoned his belief in the inerrancy of Scripture. His view has

---

[350] Koop, Doug. *"Clark Pinnock Dies at 73."* Obituary. *Christianity Today.* Posted 8/17/2010 12:14 PM. p. 2. From http://www.christianitytoday.com/ct/2010/augustweb-only/43-22.0.html?start=2.

[351] Tangelder, Johan D. *The Teaching of Clark Pinnock.* Banner of Truth website. Reprinted with permission from "Christian Renewal" Vol. 20, No's 3,4, & 5), P.O. Box 777, Jordan Station, Ontario, LOR ISO, Canada. From http://www.banneroftruth.org/pages/articles/article_detail.php?42.

been described as an overemphasis on the role of the human authors and an inadequate view of the divine role.[352]

There have been further instances of pushback against open theism. Another theologian, John Sanders, was terminated from his position at Huntington University because of his "notoriety" in promoting open theism.[353] The Southern Baptist Convention[354] adopted the *Baptist Faith and Message* (2000) partly to deal with open theism. In the section on God, are these words:

> God is all-powerful and all-knowing; and his perfect knowledge extends to all things, past, present, and future, including the future decisions of his free creatures.[355]

The committee that authored the updated version of the *Baptist Faith and Message* explained why this wording was chosen:

> In the context of modern denials of the omniscience, exhaustive fore-knowledge, and omnipotence of God, we have reaffirmed the teachings of the Bible and the consistent teaching of our Baptist tradition, as reflected in Article II: "God."[356]

Unfortunately, this kind of forthright stand against open theism seems to be more the exception than the rule. We can only hope that as the deviation from evangelical Christianity becomes more and more obvious, other denominations will speak out to warn Christians about the danger of this false doctrine.

As mentioned above, open theists are already abandoning a belief in the inerrancy of the Scriptures. One open theist, Thomas Jay Oord,

---

[352] *Ibid.*

[353] Guthrie, Stan. "Open or Closed Case? Controversial Theologian John Sanders on Way out at Huntington," *Christianity Today*, December 22, 2004). Accessed 6 February 2013, from http://www.christianitytoday.com/ct/2004/decemberweb-only/12-20-32.0.html.

[354] Southern Baptist Convention.

[355] *2000 Baptist Faith and Message.* Article II, "God." Southern Baptist Convention. From: http://www.sbc.net/bfm/bfm2000.asp.

[356] *Ibid.*

admits to rejecting the doctrine of creation from nothing, which is a logical next step in the path away from orthodoxy. We also saw that Clark Pinnock was open to the view that the triune God was embodied, which reminds one of Mormonism. There is evidence that open theists are moving towards universalism,[357] as discussed above in the case of Rob Bell, or annihilationism.[358] Either way, open theists are moving to reject orthodox views of salvation and hell. Feminism? Do not expect open theists to stand strong against pressures from radical feminists.[359] Darwinism? Do not expect a strong stand against evolution. Open theists have built their house upon the sand—there is no reason to believe this is a house that can stand strong.

The sad thing about open theism is that with its emergence we evangelical Christians have lost our innocence. There was a time, not so long ago, when C. S. Lewis could say:

> Everyone who believes in God at all believes that he knows what you and I are going to do tomorrow.[360]

That was true within my lifetime; it is true no longer. Open theists have changed how they think about God and want us to change also. They want us to see God as very much like us in many ways: fallible, vulnerable, open to change. They think this new way of seeing God makes him more attractive to the present generation.

[357] John Sanders advocates a view called *inclusivism* which says that some will be saved, even without trusting Jesus. See Wikipedia, The Free Encyclopedia. *John E. Sanders. Sanders on Inclusivism.* Accessed 23 August 2012, from http://en.wikipedia.org/wiki/John_E._Sanders.

[358] *Annihilationism* is the view that the damned in hell will eventually be destroyed. Greg Boyd admits to believing this in his blog. See Boyd, Greg. *Are you an annihilationist, and if so, why?* 19 January 2008. Reknew Blog. Accessed 23 August 2010, from http://reknew.org/2008/01/are-you-an-annihilationist-and-if-so-why/.

[359] Some open theists say that the Bible allows us to name God in feminine ways and consider "patriarchalism" in the Bible as "oppression." See Clark H. Pinnock and Robert C. Brow, *Unbounded Love: A Good News Theology for the Twenty-first Century.* 1994. InterVarsity Press, Downers Grove, IL. pp. 52; 116.

[360] Lewis, C. S. *Mere Christianity. op. cit.*, p. 148.

Perhaps, in the past, we believers may have given the impression that we thought God was not much involved in his creation at all. If so, we were misunderstood and that could have had unfortunate consequences, but the Bible does not show God that way. Truly, the God of Scripture has a plan for the ages. He has complete foreknowledge of every sparrow that falls. The future exists, and it is known in complete detail by our heavenly Father. He loves us more truly than we love ourselves. Jesus, the Son of God, came and died for us. God is involved in each of our lives every minute of the day. And we must not forget that he has also known each of us by name from before the creation of the world.

The OTG[361] knew each of us about the time that our parents did, and he did not know our name until they named us. We can pray to this god, but he may not be able to help us. If the spirit of the OTG leads us to make a decision, it still could turn out wrong because he can make mistakes. He has a plan for the future, but it is a general one, and he does not know whose names will be in the book of life.

I fail to see how this OTG can be attractive to the current generation or how this concept can improve our prayer life. The one true God, the God of the Bible, is alone worthy of worship. May all those who try to create a god in their own image come to see the error of their ways. May the false concepts of open theism be revealed for what they are. And may all Christians give praise, honor and glory to the one true God and Father of our Lord Jesus Christ.

FURTHER READING

Ware, Bruce A. *God's Greater Glory: The Exalted God of Scripture and the Christian Faith.* Wheaton, Illinois: Crossway Books. 2004.

---

[361] We had defined "OTG" as "open theism god."

DISCUSSION QUESTIONS

1. Open theists say that Christians have been heavily influenced by pagans in our conception of God. Do you find this argument persuasive?

2. Rob Bell tried to insist that words usually interpreted as meaning "eternal" actually meant "timeless." Now Enyart is trying to say that no Hebrew or Greek words ever meant "timeless." Since standard reference sources disagree with both these views, what conclusions can we draw?

3. Open theists deviate from the basic rule: "one meaning—many applications." They insist that a text can have more than one meaning. What problems are this deviation likely to cause?

4. Open theists seem to be insensitive to basic Hebrew Grammar. What are the implications of this?

5. Why are the concepts of open theism finding such wide acceptance among young people?

CHAPTER 9
†

A Possible Bridge
Molinism to the Rescue

Book: *Salvation and Sovereignty: A Molinist Approach* by Kenneth Keathley.[362]

Issue: Can the divide be closed?

Considering the seemingly irresolvable nature of the conflict between competing models of salvation and sovereignty, is there any hope for a resolution? Open theism is a dead end. Classic solutions of Arminius and Calvin do not lack defenders but seem to be gathered into armed camps. A Baptist approach as proposed by Hankins is not without merit but, ultimately, is not compelling. Is there anything else out there? Kenneth Keathley believes that there is a better solution.

1. WHAT IS "MOLINISM"?

The term *Molinism* derives from a Jesuit theologian named Luis de Molina (1535–1600). The major thesis of Keathley's book (above) is that Molina's ideas close the gap between Calvinism and Arminianism. In order to understand how this closure might be possible, we need to look at the

---

[362] Keathley, Kenneth. *Salvation and Sovereignty: A Molinist Approach*. 2010. B&H Publishing Group, Nashville, TN.

major tenets of Molinism. In a review of *Salvation and Sovereignty,* Steve W. Lemke gives a good summary of the Molinism model:

> Like Bohr's model of the atom, Molinism is a heuristic device, a plausible theological construct to help us conceptualize what appears from a human perspective to be inconceivable—how God can be absolutely sovereign and humans can have genuine libertarian freedom at the same time. Molinism is not demanded or required by Scripture, but as Keathley points out, it is consistent with Scripture at many points.[363]

Molina visualized God's creation of the universe to have occurred in three logical steps, which some call *moments.* It is crucial to realize that this conception is a *model* of what might have happened and still is happening. The idea is to fit what has been revealed in Scripture into a coherent system. This model is useful to demonstrate that the teachings of Scripture, particularly on the weighty issue of salvation, are coherent, reasonable, and not contradictory. It is not appropriate to claim that this model, or any model, is certainly true or that it is the only possible way to understand how God created the universe.

The first concept to understand is the *moment.* Keathley points out that early theologians such as Duns Scotus and Thomas Aquinas had used this term, as do Reformed theologians.[364] A moment is a stage or a step in a sequence. In this context, a moment is also a category of God's knowledge. We have to understand that these moments form a logical sequence but do not deal with chronology. They existed before the beginning of time.

Two moments are not particularly controversial. The first logical moment is God's *natural knowledge.* This term simply means that God knows all possibilities. He knows everything that could happen. He knows everything that must be true. He knows everything that is intrinsically impossible. Some define this knowledge as things that derive truth independent of God's will and therefore cannot be false. Keathley calls this concept the *could* moment or everything that could happen.[365]

---

[363] Lemke, Steve W. "Salvation and Sovereignty: A Review Essay." *The Journal For Baptist Theology & Ministry.* Vol. 7, No. 1. (Spring 2010) p. 73.
[364] *Ibid.,* p. 16.
[365] *Ibid.,* p. 17.

A subsequent logical moment is God's *free knowledge*. This term means God's knowledge of the universe he created. The term *free* means that God was free to create or not. He could have created this world or another. He was not under compulsion. However, since he did create this world, his knowledge about it is complete. Keathley calls this concept the *will* moment or everything that *will* actually happen.[366]

Molinism proposes that there is actually a third moment, which is sometimes called *middle knowledge,*[367] that logically comes between God's natural knowledge and his free knowledge. This is the knowledge of what volitional creatures (such as angels or human beings) would freely choose to do in any given set of circumstances. It also includes the concept of feasibility. God knows that only some possible worlds are feasible. Keathley calls this concept the *would* moment or everything that would happen. Armed with his knowledge of the set of feasible worlds, God chooses one world to actualize. God's choice of one world is logically subsequent to his knowledge of feasibility. So middle knowledge comes between what worlds are possible and the one world that God actually created. Keathley summarizes:

> From the infinite set of possible worlds that *could* happen (God's natural knowledge), there is an infinite subset of feasible worlds which *would* accomplish his will (God's middle knowledge). God freely chooses one of the feasible worlds, and he perfectly knows what *will* happen in this actual world (God's free knowledge). In the Molinist model, God sovereignly controls all things, yet humans possess real freedom for which they must give an account.[368]

God's middle knowledge (or *scientia media*) was the most original concept of Molina. To reiterate, he visualized this to be the complete knowledge of events which occur as the result of God-given volition. God has perfect foreknowledge of these volitional actions since he knows what his free creatures would do under any set of circumstances. For example,

---

[366] *Ibid.*

[367] This is sometimes given in Latin as *scientia media*.

[368] *Ibid.,* p. 18.

consider a contingency: "When Tim gets up tomorrow morning, the first thing he will do is scratch his head." Let us imagine this truth is infallibly known by God, but it did not have to be true, and in a sense, God is not the primary author of the head scratching. Tim is the causal agent. God knows it will happen, however, by means of middle knowledge.

A scriptural example would be Matthew 11:21–24, where Jesus tells Chorazin and Bethsaida: "If the mighty works which were done in you had been done in Tyre and Sidon, they would have repented long ago in sackcloth and ashes."[369] Here Jesus knows what would have happened in a counterfactual contingency.

Keathley goes into this model in more detail, but he includes the following statement in his introductory material:

> Within [God's] natural knowledge of all possibilities—everything that *could* happen—God possesses a perfect knowledge of all feasible worlds—all possibilities which *would* accomplish what he wanted to have happen. This knowledge of all viable possibilities is "located" (so to speak) between God's natural and free knowledge—hence the term middle knowledge. God's middle knowledge contains all of the choices and decisions that free creatures would do if they were created in a particular world. When God chooses to actualize one of these feasible worlds, He knows certainly what *will* happen. Notice: *could, would,* and *will.*[370]

In other words, God uses the choices and free decisions of his creatures to give shape to the world that he created. In this way their decisions are truly free, but these decisions are also chosen by God. The result is that God has complete, sovereign control over his creation, yet his creatures make free choices for which they can be held accountable. Craig summed it up as follows:

> Molina's doctrine has profound implications for divine providence. For it enables God to exercise providential control of free creatures without abridging the free exercise of their wills. In virtue of his knowledge of

[369] (KJV) Also see Exodus 13:17; 1 Samuel 23:8–14; Jeremiah 23:21–22; Matthew 11:21–24; 1 Corinthians 2:8.

[370] Keathley, Kenneth. *op. cit.,* p. 18.

counterfactuals of creaturely freedom and his freedom to decree that certain circumstances exist and certain free creatures be placed in those circumstances, God is able to bring about indirectly that events occur which he knew would happen as a direct result of the particular decisions which those creatures would freely make in those circumstances. … Thus, God knew, for example, that were he to create the Apostle Paul in just the circumstances he was in around AD 55, he would freely write to the Corinthian church, saying just what he did in fact say. It needs to be emphasized that those circumstances included not only Paul's background, personality, environment, and so forth, but also any promptings or gifts of the Holy Spirit to which God knew Paul would freely respond.[371]

Craig certainly covers the main, and most attractive, aspects of Molina's doctrine. He shows how it is possible to maintain a strong view of God's sovereignty and yet also allow for free volitional choices on the part of his creatures. Craig mentions a concept that should be explained further: *counterfactuals of creaturely freedom*. The term is a misnomer, since, in the context of middle knowledge, the universe had not yet been created, so none of the contingencies were as yet really counterfactual or contrary to fact. Nevertheless, the term refers to contingencies such as: "If it were sunny, Jim would go for a walk." All counterfactuals relating to the volition of creatures can be expressed in the form: "If it were the case that A, then it would be the case that B."

Following creation, such statements are literally counterfactual. Such as statement is found in Matthew 11:23:

And you, Capernaum, will you be exalted to heaven? You will go down to Hades. For if the miracles that were done in you had been done in Sodom, it would have remained until today.[372]

God clearly knows the truth value of counterfactuals. He knows what would have happened in a circumstance that did not actually occur.

---

[371] "'Men Moved By The Holy Spirit Spoke From God' (2 Peter 1.21): A Middle Knowledge Perspective on Biblical Inspiration." *Philosophia Christi* NS 1 (1999): pp. 45–82.

[372] (HCSB)

So Molinism allows us to see how these two statements can both be true:

1. God is meticulously sovereign over his creation.
2. Human beings have genuine freedom which allows them to make free choices for which they can be held accountable.[373]

In other words, by choosing to create a world which includes circumstances where creatures will freely choose certain actions, God is able to bring about those actions without encroaching on their free will. This view reconciles divine sovereignty with human freedom which is why Keathley and others find the doctrine so attractive. Furthermore, this reconciliation is not the only one found in Molinism. In fact, Keathley finds six other cases where reconciliation is possible:

2. THE POWER OF RECONCILIATION.

There are many cases where truths are taught in tandem in Scripture, and they are often seen to be in tension. I mentioned some of these truths above in the discussion of Calvinism and the five points summarized by the acronym TULIP. Keathley holds that only three of the five can be supported scripturally and prefers the ROSES acronym devised by Timothy George: (Radical depravity, Overcoming grace, Sovereign election, Eternal life, and Singular redemption).[374] Keathley discusses tandem truths and ROSES as follows:

A. GOD IS BOTH GOOD AND GREAT.

We know God is good. He has revealed himself to be kind and loving, both in Scripture and through the revelation of his Son.[375] We also know God is all-powerful, so he is clearly great. Despite this power, some people are not saved, even though God has said he desires the salvation of all. How this can be true? Did God really not want them saved? Or was he

---

[373] Keathley, Kenneth. *op. cit.*, p. 9.

[374] George, Timothy. *Amazing Grace: God's Initiative—Our Response.* 2000. Lifeway, Nashville, TN.

[375] See 1 John 4:8–12.

not powerful enough to save them all? Keathley sees Molinism as giving sufficient underpinning to answer these questions.

In what Keathley calls the "Antecedent/Consequent Wills Paradigm" humans do have real decision-making capacity. He puts it like this:

> The antecedent/consequent wills position seems to be the clear teaching of Scripture. God antecedently "loved the world in this way: He gave His one and only Son," that consequently "so everyone who believes in Him will not perish but have eternal life." Christ antecedently orders the gospel preached "to every creature," but he consequently decrees that "he that believeth not shall be damned." The antecedent/consequent wills paradigm fits nicely with the Great Commission.[376]

So we can see that God does love the world. He made provision for the salvation of all, but for those who do not believe, God justly decrees that they will not be saved. Thus, God's love, his justice and his power are all displayed. Molinism's contribution is that it reveals how the decision to believe in Christ can be free from compulsion, and God is shown to be in complete control.

B. Human Freedom is Both Derived and Genuinely Ours.

The "R" of ROSES concerns *radical depravity.* This term simply means that the Fall of Adam and Eve radically removed our freedom to choose to follow God. Yet God has chosen to restore to fallen human beings a measure of freedom.

An important concept of Scripture is that God created us in his image. In Latin, the term is *imago dei* or "image of God." Keathley points out that one important part of this image is the "real ability to choose."[377] In order to exercise freedom, we need two prerequisites: first, we must have liberty or permission from God to choose, and secondly, we must be given the

---

[376] Keathley, Kenneth. *op. cit.*, p. 58.
[377] *Ibid.*, p. 10.

ability or power to make choices. These were assumed in the discussion about the goodness and greatness of God, but here they are made explicit.

Keathley argues against *causal determinism,* the idea that the choices made by a person are determined by his nature and his circumstances. If these were determined by God, then God's will would be the cause of all things.[378] To the contrary, Keathley urges the concept of *soft libertarianism* or *concurrence* which insists human freedom means the freedom to do something or not to do it. Man is seen as a causal agent, so far as these decisions are concerned. This argument is a practical application of the general principle, mentioned above, that God is meticulously sovereign, but human beings are genuinely free.[379]

Keathley does put some boundaries on his soft version of libertarianism. He suggests God's enablement of free choices is limited to *will-setting moments.*[380] The freedom to choose has clear boundaries and limits on options. Keathley explains:

> Humans are ultimately responsible for their moral decisions in a way the other creatures of the earth are not. This is because as causal agents, they are—in a limited, derived way—the originators of their respective choices. This ability is a gift bestowed by God and is a way in which humans reflect the divine image. At certain significant will-setting moments, persons possess the real ability to choose or refrain from choosing. However, even though we retain the freedom of responsibility as causal agents, our choices affect our freedom of integrity.[381]

Even though our character and our environment may not absolutely determine our choices, our choices do form our character. In extreme cases, our character may become so warped toward sin that we lose the ability to do anything else. We remain responsible, however, because this inability that has become part of our character was our own fault. In all

---

378 *Ibid.,* p. 9.
379 *Ibid.*
380 *Ibid.,* p. 70.
381 *Ibid.,* p. 99.

cases, our moral character sets limits on our choices, both in a positive and in negative sense.[382]

C. God's Grace is Both Monergistic and Resistible.

The "O" of ROSES concerns *overcoming grace*. This term refers to the grace that God gives to accomplish the salvation that he has determined.

We first need to define the term *monergism* to clarify what Keathley means. Monergism means that our redemption is completely due to God. He is the sole worker and the only one to accomplish our salvation. The grace of God is sufficient and not based on human effort or merit. However, Keathley also says that God's grace can be resisted. In fact, many reject the gospel, even though salvation is freely offered by God. We can see that God is the sole author of salvation, but human beings are totally responsible for sin.[383]

Keathley rejects the idea of irresistible grace and sees it as being in conflict with Scripture, pointing out that God invites sinners to repent (see Isaiah 1:18). This rejection, of course, is in conflict with one of the basic tenets of Calvinism. Keathley considers and rejects three Calvinist views on irresistible grace (the non-conversionist position, the conversionist regeneration-precedes-conversion position, and the conversionist effectual-call position). Most Calvinists believe that regeneration comes *before* conversion, which is a startling idea. Others, such as Millard Erickson, realize that many passages clearly teach conversion comes first.[384] But even Erickson insists God's grace is irresistible and given only to the elect. Keathley concludes the idea of irresistible grace conflicts with clear invitations given in God's Word:

The Bible ends with a universal invitation: "Both the Spirit and the bride say, 'Come.' Anyone who hears should say, 'Come.' And the one who is thirsty should come. Whoever desires should take the living water as a

---

[382] *Ibid.*

[383] *Ibid.,* p. 11.

[384] *Ibid.,* p. 115. Keathley references Erickson, M. *Christian Theology,* 2nd ed. (Grand Rapids: Baker, 2004), pp. 944–945.

gift" (Rev. 22:17). The bride here takes part in issuing the appeal, so the invitation of this verse cannot be narrowed to only the elect.[385]

One of the most helpful parts of Keathley's discussion of God's grace is a clear demonstration that faith is not a work nor is it a virtue to be rewarded. Therefore, even though faith is necessary, God is still the sole author of salvation. Keathley calls his view *Overcoming Grace*.[386]

D. GOD'S ELECTION IS BOTH UNCONDITIONAL AND ACCORDING TO FOREKNOWLEDGE.

The first "S" of ROSES concerns *sovereign election*. This term simply means that God "elected" or chose some people for salvation.

Most Calvinists, according to Keathley, believe God decrees the salvation of the elect but merely permits unbelievers to be lost. This asymmetrical view is actually inconsistent for the Calvinist but logically follows from Molinism. The Molinist position is that God makes his sovereign choice based on his foreknowledge, but that foreknowledge involves many possible worlds. Foreknowledge does not determine salvation, and Molinism agrees with Calvinism that choosing the elect is not due to any foreseen merit or faith. When God actualizes a foreseen world with certain people freely accepting Christ by faith, those people were thereby chosen unconditionally.[387]

Keathley summarizes the Molinist position:

> Molinism provides a much better answer. Why does the reprobate exist? Because of God's sovereign will. Why is he reprobate? Because of his own unbelief. When God made the sovereign choice to bring this particular world into existence, He rendered certain—but did not cause—the destruction of certain ones who would reject God's overtures of grace. According to Molinism, our free choice determines how we will respond in any given setting, but God decides the setting in which we actually find ourselves.[388]

---

[385] *Ibid.*, p. 117.

[386] *Ibid.*, Chapter 4.

[387] *Ibid.*, p. 11.

[388] *Ibid.*, p. 154.

E. The Saved Are Both Preserved and Will Persevere.

The "E" of ROSES concerns *eternal life*. This term is essentially the same as the "P" in TULIP for *perseverance of the saints*. Although it is true that not all who claim to be Christians will go to heaven, those who are truly saved have the assurance God will preserve them until the end. In other words, eternal life begins with salvation.

Keathley first presented the material explaining this point to the John 3:16 Conference at First Baptist Church of Woodstock, Georgia, in 2009, and it is also included in a chapter of *Whosoever Will: A Biblical-Theological Critique of Five-Point Calvinism*. Keathley addresses two key issues: how we can know we are genuinely saved and the security of our salvation.[389] Keathley shows how Molinism provides a model which "affirms that everyone who trusts Christ for salvation is securely preserved and every saved person possesses a faith that is guaranteed to remain."[390]

F. Christ's Atonement is Both Unlimited in its Provision and Limited in its Application.

The second "S" of ROSES concerns *singular redemption*. It refers to the often-debated issue of the atonement: whether it is general or particular.

General atonement is generally thought of as an Arminian position, while particular atonement is Calvinist. There are fine shades of this argument, but the general point of contention is whether or not Christ's sacrifice was for all people or whether he paid only for the sins of the elect. Not all Calvinists hold to particular atonement but most agree with this view. Keathley argues for the view that the atonement is unlimited and specifically, "that it is sufficient for all but efficient only for those that believe."[391]

---

[389] *Ibid.*, Chapter 6.
[390] *Ibid.*, p. 12.
[391] *Ibid.*

The problem with the limited view is that it negates the "well-meant offer of the gospel" to the lost. Those holding this view can hardly say to an unbeliever, "Christ died for you" because if the person is not one of the elect, then Christ did *not* die for them. However, this idea hardly accords with the entire thrust of the gospel. It is to Keathley's credit that he has taken the opposite tack.

Keathley concludes with the following:

> The Molinist model of salvation and the sovereignty of God endeavors to maintain the biblical balance of certainty and contingency, confidence and urgency. Our sovereign God saves. Despite that God granted genuine freedom to us; despite that we promptly abused that freedom to descend into darkness and death; despite that, as fallen creatures, we loved our sin and were without love for Him—despite all these things, God is perfectly accomplishing His plan of salvation. And He is doing so in a way that maintains His perfect integrity from evil and does not turn humans, whom He created in His image, into robots. Salvation is of the Lord, all of grace and for His glory.[392]

3. THE POWER OF MOLINISM

Molinism is seen by Keathley as the bridge to close the gap between Arminians and Calvinists. It melds a Calvinist view of God's sovereignty and an Arminian view of human freedom.[393] It recognizes that God's foreknowledge is comprehensive and certain, yet it explains how God is not the direct cause of human decisions. It avoids the error of *fatalism* which holds that all choices are necessary, without the option of choosing otherwise. It also refutes the notion of *causal determinism* or the idea that all human choices are determined by one's nature or character or environment, so we cannot possibly choose otherwise. Finally, it reveals that God is not the author of sin.[394]

The reason for rejecting fatalism and causal determinism is simply because these theological notions are not taught in Scripture. In fact, they

---

[392] *Ibid.*, p. 210.

[393] Ibid., p. 5.

[394] *Ibid.*, p. 8.

are difficult to reconcile with the Bible in any meaningful way. They are extrapolations or deductions, proposed as a mechanism to understand God's sovereignty. We might admit that the simplest way to understand omnipotence is to insist God alone is a causal agent. However, if human agency can be shown to be compatible with divine sovereignty and omnipotence, there is no reason to deny humans also make real choices as causal agents.

Does Molinism accomplish this reconciliation? I think it does. Of course, Molinism is not to be seen as the answer to all thorny theological issues. I shall cover some of these shortcomings below. Molinism may not even be the best answer to questions about salvation. But it does deliver on its key promise. It gives a reasonable explanation as to how God can be sovereign in his decrees and yet allow human beings to have freedom and responsibility for their actions. It is a coherent view of providence.

Molinism can be distinguished from Arminianism. Arminian doctrine holds that God looks into the future and elects for salvation those whom he foresees will freely accept him. Calvinists, in an almost visceral reaction, reject this passive role for God. It is not hard to see why. This view makes God foresee a future he did not ordain. But if God did not ordain it, where did it come from? If the future did not come from a personal cause, is it impersonal? Is the future somehow outside of God's control? Is human volition simply a given?

Molinism seems, on the whole, better able to harmonize the Scriptures than either the causal determinism of Calvinism or the simple foresight of Arminianism. It answers the above questions. We see that the future is determined by a personal God. It is not outside of God's control. Man has volition as a causal agent simply because God has ordained it would be so.

Let us sum up the crucial issue of salvation from a Molinist standpoint: God precisely knows in what circumstances humans will make free decisions to respond to his grace. Therefore, he actualizes a world in which each one receives enough grace for salvation if only he or she will make use of it. Of course, God knows exactly who will and who will not respond, but in every case the grace is sufficient. The credit for salvation lies completely with God, and the blame for damnation lies completely with those who reject him. So the fault does not lie with God even though some persons freely resist his grace.

4. THE LIMITS OF MOLINISM

Keathley candidly admits Molinism does not remove all mystery from God and his relationship with humankind. He goes even further and admits it does not even clear up all questions regarding our salvation. But he insists we must never use our theological models to negate the clear teachings of Scripture.[395]

He lists three areas where Molinism does not provide a complete answer:

1. The mystery of evil remains. Molinism does not show why angels or human beings fell and continue to fall into sin or why most people reject the offer of salvation.
2. It is not clear why God chose to actualize this particular world out of the myriads he could have chosen.
3. Exactly how God knows what free creatures will choose and decide remains unknown. This puzzle is sometimes called the "grounding objection." Nevertheless, given God's omniscience, it seems presumptuous to entertain the idea that our future choices would not be known by him.[396]

Another difficulty with the concept of Molinism is technical. It concerns the idea that if I were to be placed in circumstances C, God knows how I would freely choose to behave (chosen behavior = b). This relationship can be diagrammed as C→b. Let this symbol mean that if I were placed in circumstances C I would choose to take a walk. So God certainly knows that C→b is true, and he knew that before the creation of the world. On the other hand, there is no way for God to create me and put me in circumstances C and have me do anything else but go for

[395] *Ibid.,* pp. 12–13.
[396] *Ibid.,* p. 13.

a walk. He could create someone else or put me in circumstances other than C if he does not want me to take a walk, of course, but C→b does put some limits on the worlds God can actualize. Molinism shows how God can have advance notice of the free choices of every creature prior to creation. It also implies there are some worlds God cannot create, even though they would be logically possible.

So God knows what volitional choices we will make in circumstances C, but Molinism visualizes the range of these choices to be limited. God seems to be unwilling or unable to expand that range. People will respond as they will respond, and that is the end of it. C→b is a fixed response, but this concept leaves a curiously passive role for God.

Another puzzle relates to C. How could we make a choice in C freely, if our choice is determined by C, and yet we do not get to choose C? Do circumstances completely foreordain our choice, even though God does not?[397] If so, then we have environmental determinism which would smother human liberty as effectively as fatalism. Perhaps circumstances influence our choice but do not determine it. If so, then what do circumstances have to do with the matter? Perhaps C could be taken to comprise both circumstances and our character. There is something about us, our DNA, our heredity, our instincts, our predispositions that determines our choice which means it is nature that determines our choice. Then, of course, we have natural determinism, and again it is hard to see where freedom comes in.[398]

There is a particular kind of determinism that Molinists do not deny, and that is the pervasive impact of the Fall, and sin generally, on the ability of lost sinners to choose to follow Christ. Their fate is predetermined, and all would be lost without the prevenient grace of God. Molinists (as briefly mentioned above) believe our choices in will-setting moments can affect our moral character to the point that future choices are affected. The

---

[397] A Molinist would deny this, saying that circumstances are non-determining.

[398] Again, Molinists would deny nature to be an absolute determining factor, given the grace of God and the power of the Holy Spirit.

downward spiral into depravity (illustrated in Romans 1:16–32) shows the perverse effect of continued sin.

In desperation, we might say that C includes circumstances, our environment, our nature, our moral character and all the rest, but that none of it is absolutely determinative. Our will is influenced by all these things, but our will still retains the power of choice. Well and good. If that choice does not come from our own character, however, how can we receive any credit or blame for it? Molinism rejects determinism but does not seem to fully come to grips with these questions.

Molinism does not explain why God appears to be so passive, but this limitation is, in a way, convenient for Molinism. To be sure, if God actively changes our hearts so that we respond differently in circumstances C, then he could easily micro-manage our every choice—which brings us back to causal determinism. In other words, if God simply changed me so that instead of C→b (in circumstances C I freely choose to take a walk), it is now C→~b (in circumstances C I freely choose to refrain from walking), he could have an alternate decision without changing C. So these convenient limits on God prevent Molinism from falling into the arms of Calvinism. Molinism does not explain why the limits on voli- tion should exist. Furthermore, the limits on volition and the idea that they are fixed seem also to be a limit on God himself. This limitation is a puzzle. Certainly, it is unreasonable to impose limits on omnipotence unless we are dealing with a paradox. True, God cannot square a circle or take any other paradoxical action, but limits on volitional choices seem to be an entirely different matter. No paradox is obvious, so these limits comprise an unexplained feature of the model.

Even worse, if God could easily change C→b to C→~b in the case of the walking decision, then He could do the same in the case of a decision for salvation. And if he could adjust me so that I choose to be saved in circumstances C and did not do the same for someone else, would that mean I was one of the elect and another was not? It is easy to see why Molinism prefers to see C→b as a given that God passively accepts because any other view leads back to Calvinism and the Reformed view of predestination, and then Molinism fails to be an alternative, reconciling model.

Objections to Molinism come most vocally from those who lean towards Calvinism. They describe Molinists as "philosophically sophisticated Arminians."[399] The substance of their objections is that the Molinist view of God's sovereignty seems to be "less robust" than that presented in Scripture. It is said that Molinists usually deny the doctrines of total depravity and limited atonement. Finally, Molinists are said to typically deny that God is atemporal and immutable.[400]

Limited atonement and total depravity were perhaps points of disagreement with Molina, himself, but the concept of middle knowledge would lend itself to any understanding of the atonement or the depravity of man. Furthermore, there seems to be nothing in the middle knowledge concepts of Molinism that would require one to deny that God is atemporal or immutable. Certainly, Keathley disagrees with the doctrine of limited atonement, holding a nuanced view called *singular redemption* (see above).[401] But Keathley's understanding of the depravity of humankind (he prefers the term *radical depravity*) closely corresponds with the Calvinist view, and he doesn't object to the concept of God as immutable and atemporal in his essential being. This latter criticism seems to be one of guilt by association.

Perhaps, however, it still seems to Calvinists that God's decisions are held hostage by human decisions in the Molinist concept of God's use of middle knowledge. That is a matter that should be carefully assessed. It may be that any concept of humans as causal agents is simply unacceptable to many Calvinists. If so, then Molinism may not be able to

---

[399] See web page: Gotquestions.org. *What is Molinism and is it biblical?* Accessed 2 September 2012, from *http://www.gotquestions.org/molinism. html* .

[400] *Ibid.*, This web page also insists that Molinists believe that: *God has middle knowledge of all feasible worlds, and He chooses to create the world in which the most people would be saved.* It is not clear that all Molinists would claim to know that.

[401] Keathley, Kenneth. *Salvation. op. cit.*, p. 12.

completely reconcile Calvinists and Arminians. But it is a step toward resolving the conflicting viewpoints.

Another problem with Molinism is that it is not clearly taught in the Scriptures. Of course, one could correctly respond that neither is Arminianism nor Calvinism spelled out in God's Word. All are models which may be derived from Scripture but go beyond it in at least some points. Nevertheless, since scriptural silence is a common criticism of Molinism, we need to address it.

The essence of Molinism is the concept of middle knowledge, which concerns knowledge possessed by God not only logically prior to creation but even logically prior to the selection of a world to create. So it concerns the things of God that were logically prior to Genesis 1:1. Therefore, it is no wonder it is not clearly spelled out in the pages of Scripture. The Bible does include texts showing that God knows what would have happened in circumstances other than what actually took place (cf. 1 Samuel 23:10–13; Matthew 11:20–21), but firm proof is not found in its pages. Craig admits this:

> Since Scripture does not reflect upon this question, no amount of proof-texting can prove that God's counterfactual knowledge is possessed logically prior to his creative decree. This is a matter for theological-philosophical reflection, not biblical exegesis. Thus, while it is clearly unbiblical to deny that God has simple foreknowledge and even counterfactual knowledge, those who deny middle knowledge cannot be accused of being unbiblical.[402]

Keathley defends his conviction, however, that Molinism is more than just a philosophical system. He insists that if it were only some sort of overlay imposed on Scripture, it would be a bad idea. To the contrary, he maintains:

> How strong a scriptural case for Molinism can be made? ... (1) The ingredients that seem to necessitate Molinism are provided by the Bible;

---

[402] Craig, William Lane. "The Middle-Knowledge View," in *Divine Foreknowledge: Four Views,* ed. James K. Beilby and Paul R. Eddy. 2001. InterVarsity Press, Downers Grove, IL. p. 125.

and (2) rather than being exotic examples of metaphysics, "possible world" concepts are notions we use and understand in everyday life. The ideas central to Molinism—such as possible scenarios and counterfactuals—are not strange at all. Rather, we find they are contained within the very grammar of the Bible.[403]

Perhaps we may safely conclude that even if Molinism is not explicitly taught in Scripture, it is at least harmonious with its teachings. With that, we can agree with Keathley that Molinism is a helpful model of God's sovereignty and human freedom. Therefore, Molinists seem to be bridging the chasm between Calvinists and Arminians. Unfortunately, to the Calvinists, Molinists look a lot like Arminians. On the other hand, to Arminians, Molinists seem to be much like Calvinists. So the bridge is more like a shooting gallery than a place of reconciliation. Calvinists still see any hint of man as a causal agent to be an unacceptable diminution of God's sovereignty. And Arminians see what looks suspiciously like determinism in the whole matter of counterfactual knowledge, particularly since Keathley says God exercises meticulous control over all events.[404] Logically, though, Molinism is tailor-made for a reconciling role. It is insightful and has great explanatory power. Unfortunately, the reconciliation offered by Molinism has been more potential than actual.

FURTHER READING

Perszyk, Ken, ed. *Molinism: The Contemporary Debate.* Oxford: Oxford University Press. 2011.

---

[403] Keathley, Kenneth. *op. cit.*, p. 19.
[404] *Ibid.*, p. 22–25.

DISCUSSION QUESTIONS

1. Does Molinism seem to be a reasonable bridge between the competing camps?

2. Does "middle knowledge" seem to be a reasonable concept?

3. What are the strong points of Molinism?

4. How does Molinism explain the way that God can be sovereign in his decrees and yet allow human beings to have freedom and responsibility for their actions?

5. How does Molinism seem to leave a curiously passive role for God?

CHAPTER 10
†

Chosen Contingency
Another Possible Bridge

Issue: Is there another way to bridge the divide between Christians?

Over the past forty years or so, my wife and I have had to confront the basic questions that give meaning to life. During that time, I gradually developed a mental image that seemed to give reasonable answers to the issues of God's sovereignty and man's salvation. I did not base my system on Molinism nor was it based on the Calvinist or Arminian views. Like Hankins, I wanted a Baptist position that was true to the Scriptures. The framework that I give below I call the *chosen contingency model*, for the lack of a better term. I have found it to be helpful, and I present it here in the hope that others will also find it so.

1. WHAT IS THE CHOSEN CONTINGENCY MODEL?

The Chosen Contingency Model (CCM) explains the creation of the universe as God's selection of one contingency out of a host of possible options. The model realizes that God, in his essential character, is outside of time or timeless. It recognizes that God's omniscience does not require him to weigh possible options and decide which is best, as human beings must do. He simply knows all things, in a sweeping act of awareness. He is fully sovereign, and his decision to create any universe at all, or any specific universe, was due precisely to his own good pleasure. Nevertheless, it is useful for us to model the logical steps God could have used in creating the universe—the world in which we find ourselves. Critics of Christianity have called Christian beliefs logically incoherent and contradictory. If we can reasonably demonstrate how to harmonize key beliefs, the arguments of these critics lose force.

Luther, Calvin, Arminius and others labored to present consistent systems to explain the things of God. I intend the CCM to refine and build on their work and the labor of many others. None of these ideas should be viewed as anything more than suggestions, offered in an attempt to be helpful, and subject to further refinement.

2. WHAT LOGICAL STEPS WOULD EXPLAIN CREATION?

Let us review briefly some information I covered in Chapter Nine. Theologians distinguish two kinds of knowledge possessed by God. The first is *natural knowledge*[405] which was all that God knew prior to the decree to create the universe. This knowledge included an understanding of all possible universes he might create. It also included all logical constraints. An example of a logical constraint is that God cannot create an object that is too heavy for him to lift. This limitation (despite God being all-powerful) is because such an object would be a paradox. God has full knowledge of paradoxes.

The second kind of knowledge is called *free knowledge*. His decree to create was "free" in the sense that no one or nothing outside of God was able to force his decree in any way. Therefore, free knowledge means all

---

[405] See Frame, John M. "Scientia Media" from *Evangelical Dictionary of Theology*, ed. W. Elwell, 1984. Baker Book House, Grand Rapids. pp. 987–988. Natural knowledge or necessary knowledge is described as follows: "Many theologians have said that God knows the world by knowing himself. He knows what is possible or impossible in the world by knowing what he can or cannot do: this knowledge is called the knowledge of simple intelligence or necessary knowledge (since it follows from the very nature of God's being)."

knowledge about the universe he did create. When he created the universe, all times were future, and he knew all future events. This foreknowledge means all future events were in some sense predetermined, but as we shall see, that does not mean God has removed free will.

Now let us look at the model which I call the CCM. We can define five logical steps of creation as follows:

A. DECREE TO CREATE A UNIVERSE. This step means God decided he would utilize his creative abilities to create something outside of himself. Nothing is implied at this point as to what that might be. We must remember that these are logical steps, not steps in time, since time did not exist prior to the creation.

B. ESTABLISHMENT OF DESIGN CRITERIA. He established criteria, although we have only a dim understanding as to what they might be. Yet we can make inferences based on what we can observe from his creation and his revelation in the Scriptures.[406] These criteria defined what God would create.[407] Let us imagine that God first dealt with the most basic structural elements of creation. He decided he would use subatomic particles as building blocks which would form atoms, molecules and elements. He would create energy to power the system. He would create space to have somewhere to put it. He would create time so objects could have duration and interact. He decided fundamental values relating to these building blocks, such as a decision to make protons just 1,836 times larger than electrons.[408] He established the other natural laws, such as Newton's laws of motion and the speed of light. Having decided this much, he would have already markedly decreased the set of possible universes. This step would establish the stage for the great drama of the

---

[406] See Romans 1:20. "For the invisible things of him since the creation of the world are clearly seen, being perceived through the things that are made, even his everlasting power and divinity; that they may be without excuse." (HCSB)

[407] Ephesians 1:11. This is also implied in John 1:1.

[408] This ratio of protons to electrons is fortunate for us since if they were only a bit bigger or smaller, they could not form the molecules we require for life.

ages. Next would come the actors for the stage. Living creatures would require additional definition.

So design criteria would have defined more than basic structure. We can also picture God using higher-level criteria such as:

1. The creation must bring glory to his name.[409]

2. The creation must reveal God's attributes—for example, love, grace, mercy, justice, wisdom, power, holiness and goodness.[410]

3. The creation must give a level of autonomy to the inanimate universe, as well as to plants, animals, human beings and angels.[411] In other words, it must be elegant.[412]

4. The creation must maximize the freedom and spiritual growth and development of his intelligent creatures.[413]

5. The creation must include a specific number of unique, individual humans and angels.

6. The creation must include a material universe comprised of matter, energy, space and time.

7. The creation must include a spiritual universe.[414]

8. The creation must be conducive to the formation of creatures worthy to receive God's love and to have fellowship with him.

C. EVALUATION OF ALL POSSIBLE UNIVERSES. As the next logical step, God evaluated an inconceivably large number of universes.[415] Knowledge

---

[409] Philippians 3:3; Psalm 86:9

[410] Compare Psalm 8:1, 19:1f, 50:6, 89:5.

[411] The Bible mentions cherubim and seraphim, but these are probably types of angels.

[412] I shall discuss below what I mean by "elegance."

[413] Leibniz suggested this. See below.

[414] This may or may not be part of the material universe. It is not clear, for example, if heaven is part of this universe, a separate dimension in this universe, or an entirely separate universe. Of course, it is quite clear that spiritual beings such as angels or fallen angels (demons) have access to this universe. And fallen angels may be *confined* to this universe.

[415] This would be a finite number, even though incomprehensibly large from a human perspective.

of these universes is part of God's natural knowledge. He only needed to consider possibilities that were coherent (that did not involve logical contradictions) and which met the design criteria. There is no sense that God simply picked one available universe as the best of a bad lot. He limited his choice only by his own pleasure (which included his own criteria) and logical constraints. Those clearly failing to meet the criteria, or which were logically incoherent, could be summarily rejected. The other contingencies could be then evaluated and one chosen contingency selected. This step (Step C) is the key to the CCM. There will be a separate section that gives more detail about this evaluation process.

D. DECREE TO CREATE THIS UNIVERSE. This decree involves two closely related steps, but it is best to consider them as one. Having evaluated all possible universes, God chose the best (substep one) and decreed that it be brought into existence (substep two). God perfectly tailored the chosen universe to accomplish his good pleasure. This decree brought about everything that would happen in the future and is, naturally, a decision made before the universe was created. Knowledge of this universe is, by definition, God's free knowledge. I affirm that God's foreknowledge of this universe came logically before his decree to create, when he chose the best possible world. God's foreknowledge does not depend alone on his foreordination since foreordination is expressed by his decree to create. Foreordination alone, however, would be enough to foreknow all things exhaustively. In other words, God buttressed his foreknowledge by two truths (his decree to create and his foreordination of his creation), either of which would allow God to foreknow the future completely.

E. GOD CREATED THE UNIVERSE. The Scriptures reveal that the creation was a process, beginning with God's decree.[416] Genesis reveals that the creation took six days, followed by a seventh in which God rested from creating. We are still in this seventh day of creation. Apparently God is resting from his creative activities, but he still sustains his creation so it continues to exist. He also involves himself in every detail of the outworking of his eternal plan, in a continuous action called *concurrence*.

---

[416] See Genesis 1:1.

God's providence, then, is still active, even though the time of his creative actions has passed.[417]

3. HOW DID GOD EVALUATE ALL POSSIBLE UNIVERSES?

As mentioned above, God's knowledge about all possible universes is part of his natural knowledge. The CCM does not require *middle knowledge*. Middle knowledge, as I discussed above, was proposed by a Jesuit priest named Luis de Molina. This knowledge is said to consist of contingencies that come about by volitional decisions of intelligent creatures (men and angels). Molina saw God as knowing what creatures would decide, given a set of circumstances. He did not see middle knowledge as properly being part of God's natural knowledge since natural knowledge involves possibilities that exist independently from God's will. Molina's argument is an appealing one[418] and should not be lightly set aside.[419]

In the CCM, the set of all possible universes does exist independently from God's will, so it is part of his natural knowledge. These possibilities define the potential limits of what might be created and are not comprehensible by human beings. Human knowledge of the boundaries of the set of possible universes is not the overriding concept—the overriding concept is to understand that there were alternatives available to and known by God. Since God naturally knows all possibilities, there seems to be no logical reason why a third category of knowledge, as per Molina, is necessary. For this reason, the CCM will not make use of this concept. This is not to say Molina was wrong. In fact, Molina's focus on contingen-

---

[417] There is the possibility that God has not *completely* ceased creative action. One could argue that God still creates the immortal soul of every child at the time of conception. There may also be other exceptions, even now, and God will surely use his creative power to form the new heavens and the new earth at the end of this age. But as a general rule, it seems safe to say creation has ceased for the time being.

[418] Probably if I had been aware of Molinism, I would not have bothered to work out my ideas of "chosen contingency." But as it turns out, the chosen contingency model is not the same thing as Molinism.

[419] Molina's concepts will be briefly reviewed below.

cies brought about by the volition of intelligent creatures is a useful place to concentrate the analysis.

A. The Case of *Groundhog Day*

Groundhog Day is a 1993 film starring Bill Murray who plays TV meteorologist Phil Connors and Andie MacDowell who plays a TV news producer named Rita. The film is a postmodern look at a time loop in which Murray finds himself. It is postmodern because it never tries to explain what caused the situation or what caused its resolution. The viewer is responsible to create his own narrative to explain what happened. However, the situation begins on February 2 with Connors covering (for his TV station) the annual appearance of Phil the groundhog in Punxsutawney, Pennsylvania. Connors ends up spending the night there, awakening in his hotel room to find that February 2, 1992, repeats itself. He has the memory of the previous February 2, (and all subsequent repeats of February 2), but no one else remembers. Everyone but Connors always acts in the same way, unless Connors does something different. Then they will respond to him which can cause a cascade of changes for that day. Nevertheless, the next morning brings a complete reset back exactly as it was on the first February 2. Connors repeats the time loop over and over again—for years. He learns French; he becomes an accomplished pianist, and he learns to ice sculpt. Finally, Rita falls for him, and only then does he break out of the time loop and enter February 3.

This film gives a helpful analogy of the way that God could intuitively understand contingencies throughout the history of the universe. God could comprehend a universe of alternatives with Phil Connors responding to the same situation with differing variables. God would not have to guess what Phil Connors might do—he would see him react in a kind of virtual reality. So this film is a picture of the logic that undergirds the CCM, but of course, God's understanding of these contingencies takes place *before* creation.

B. THE CASE OF ADAM AND EVE

God made man[420] in his image and gave man dominion over the earth.[421] I affirm "being made in the image of God" included autonomy which is empowerment from God to make free choices between alternatives. As an exercise of that autonomy, God gave Adam the responsibility for naming the animals. God brought them to Adam, and whatever Adam called them became their names. This concept leads us to view Adam as a causal agent, having been delegated that authority from God. That does not mean Adam was a first cause. It does mean God foreordained the future, which was a future where Adam would give names to the animals. It does mean God was sustaining creation during this naming process. It does mean God was acting concurrently with Adam at every moment. It also means that Adam, because of God's good pleasure, had dominion over the earth, that naming was part of the exercise of that dominion and that Adam exercised freedom in choosing the names. His will was still as free as can be conceived. Note that this all happened before the Fall. Adam and Eve were innocent of sin and in a perfect environment. They had not yet fallen, but that was to come.

The story of the Fall hardly needs retelling. Suffice it to say that the serpent (Satan) deceived Eve and appealed to her pride. She disobeyed God's command not to eat the fruit of the tree of the knowledge of good and evil. She gave Adam the fruit, and even though Adam was not deceived, he also ate. This decision to sin, deliberately to disobey the express command of God, had catastrophic consequences. Adam and Eve became fallen creatures and were expelled from their perfect environment, the Garden of Eden. God cursed the serpent; he cursed the ground with thorns and thistles; he cursed Adam's labor; in fact, he cursed the whole earth. Man's will was no longer free.

Since I believe God ordained the future that included Adam's and Eve's sin, does that mean God is the author of sin? To "author" sin is usually taken to mean bringing it into being and incurring guilt in the

---

[420] This term applied to both Adam and Eve.
[421] See Genesis 1:26–31.

process. James 1:13 says God never tempts anyone with evil, and God is not tempted with evil.[422] Furthermore, 1 John 1:5 says: "God is light, and there is absolutely no darkness in him."[423] So God is not the author of sin.

There is a problem here. Arminians say that Calvinists, by insisting that God ordained all things, make God the author of sin. However, the Arminians' case is little better since they admit God foreknows sin and does nothing to stop it, which at the very least, makes him an accomplice to it. Can we say, somehow, that when God created the world, knowing full well that Adam and Eve would sin, he is nevertheless not guilty of it? I say "yes." I maintain it *is* possible to account for the presence of sin, even the cataclysmic sin of Adam and Eve and still see that God is guiltless even though he foreordained it.

First, we need not say that when God created the best of all possible worlds, he had to create a world with no sin. All we must say is that *if* the present world (universe) is the best of all possible worlds, any change, even if it were seemingly an excellent change, would cause things to be worse, due to humanly unforeseen adverse consequences. People often assume that in God's design criteria for the universe, there must have been a specification that no sin would be allowed. In that case, the presence of sin would be a failure of execution; but God never says he decreed (before the world began) there would be no sin in this world.[424] He apparently does decree this in the new earth,[425] but not in the present universe. Why does he (for now) allow sin? Apparently it is the inevitable result of giving creatures sufficient autonomy to make choices. Sometimes, creatures who are causal agents will choose poorly and break God's law. That is sin.

Let's talk through the case of Adam's sin. When God evaluated all possible universes, he clearly considered those that would have been the same in every respect up to the point that the serpent tempted Eve. At

---

[422] James 1:13 "No one undergoing a trial should say, 'I am being tempted by God.' For God is not tempted by evil, and he himself doesn't tempt anyone." (HCSB)

[423] (HCSB)

[424] To reiterate, I insist that God is not the *author* of sin.

[425] See Revelation 21 and 22.

that point, they diverged to form different contingencies. In some possible worlds, Adam did not eat the fruit; in others, Adam did eat and thereby sinned. God had to decide which choice would better fulfill his design. One criterion that I suggested was, "The creation must reveal God's character—e.g. love, grace, mercy, justice, wisdom, power, holiness and goodness." God could have been coercive and compelled Adam to choose not to sin, but would that have revealed God's justice in the proper light?

We can visualize God concluding that he had gifted Adam with his presence. He had given Adam a perfect environment. He had warned Adam by speaking to him face to face. Adam clearly understood that the fruit would bring death. There is no evidence that Satan had been given authority over Adam; Satan could not force the first pair to do anything. Adam's will was not corrupted by sin—he was still an innocent, unfallen creature. God had been carefully forming Adam's character, and Adam was now at the point that he should have been able to resist the temptation to eat the fruit. So God decided that to do more would be unjust. God knew exactly where the fine line is between giving Adam the grace to resist Satan and *coercing* him to resist. As the contingency played itself out, Adam chose to sin, and God (honoring his perfect justice) determined to select the sin alternative to be his chosen contingency. God allowed Adam to sin because it was just to do so. In other words, God's justice is perfect.

God did not tempt Adam. The serpent—or perhaps more correctly Eve—did that. We need not analyze why God permitted the serpent to have access to the garden. That analysis would be similar to the analysis of Adam's sin. Sin is utterly against the character of God, but sin on the part of the creature may not be the worst possible outcome in the mind of God. Remember, there is always a sense in which it can be truly said that God allowed Adam to sin because the alternative would be worse.

Some might say the CCM is the same as Molinism and the concept of middle knowledge. Molinism, however, has difficulty explaining how God knows what a volitional agent would do in a given set of circumstances. This problem is sometimes called the "grounding objection." The often-made point is that if the choice is truly free, not even God could know what the person would do in advance. On the other hand, if God arranged circumstances so the person would always make a predictable choice, the decision would be determined and so would not be free.

In the CCM, the answer to these questions is trivial. God knows what a creature would do in any given alternative because (if we may speak of it this way) God can "run" a simulation and watch the creature and *see* what he does.[426] The movie *Groundhog Day* shows what this simulation might look like. Another analogy might be a computer virtual reality simulation. These simulations can include a virtual world with virtual people with artificial intelligence and can be extraordinarily detailed. God is essentially timeless. He could run such a virtual simulation a million times, adjusting variables each time, if that is what it took to know the precise parameters of Adam's volition. He is all-powerful, so the simulation could be equally powerful. This assessment might be called the "brute-force" approach. There is no doubt that if God had to use something like a brute-force approach to comprehend fully what Adam would do, he could do it.[427] So human (or angelic) volition creates no difficulty for God's exhaustive foreknowledge.

So let us consider volition, God's grace, and the line between assistance and coercion. God's sovereign choice of a contingent future is based on his character. His character determines his choice, and his choice must demonstrate his character. We must assume that since God intends Adam to exercise a free choice, he knows how much grace he can supply, without assistance becoming coercion. So the contingencies foreseen by God finally came down to these two:

1) God provides a level of grace to Adam which would amount to coercion. This provision would affirm God's mercy but would not perfectly demonstrate his justice.[428] Adam does not sin.

---

[426] We don't have to think of God actually doing this in any crudely literal way. This is an illustration to show how God's prescience is equal to the task.

[427] This is an analogy to show what is possible for God.

[428] God is merciful and will not punish the innocent. But his justice also means that the guilty must be punished. See Nahum 1:3: "The Lord is slow to anger but great in power; the Lord will never leave the guilty unpunished

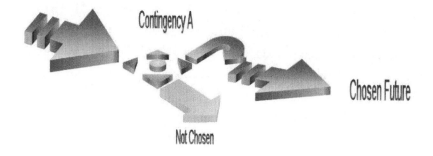

Figure 3: The Chosen Contingency

2) God provides a sufficient level of grace. Adam's volition is empowered to the point that he is able, if he chooses, not to sin. He has volitional freedom. No coercion is involved. This sufficiency affirms both God's mercy and God's justice. Adam chooses to sin.

Therefore, God affirms choice 2. It is the chosen contingency. God has now foreordained that Adam will commit sin, as God also foreknew. God incorporates this contingency in his eternal plan and in his unfolding decree which will result in the creation. We see that even though there would have been possible alternatives where Adam did not sin, none were acceptable to God, for one reason or another. The above discussion considers only one possible limiting factor—that when God wants to display creaturely volition, he will not provide more grace than needed for that display.[429] There are other factors that would play a part, of course.

Figure 2 shows the situation in a diagram. The arrow on the left is the timeline of the chosen timeline of history that God has constructed up

---

..." (HCSB) If Adam's volition was inclined to sin, absent coercion, then to prevent the sin would arguably be unjust.

[429] See Ephesians 4:7. "Now grace was given to each one of us according to the measure of the Messiah's gift." (HCSB)

to the point of Adam's sin. This arrow comprises all of God's choices up to that point. The junction "Contingency A" represents Adam's decision to sin. The arrow that fades out is the option not to sin and is not part of the chosen timeline. The "Chosen Future" is the contingency chosen by God. It is pertinent to note that the total of these sequential choices by God comprised the entire history of the world.

Does this viewpoint answer the grounding objection? Yes, it does. If in no other way, God knows what Adam will do in the same way that the designer of an engine knows the engine will work. He builds a simulation or perhaps an actual prototype and runs it to see if it works. Of course, in God's case, he certainly does not have to build a test universe; he knows intuitively. God knows how much grace and influence can be brought to bear to prevent coercion yet lift the person to the point that the decision is free. In 2 Peter 2:9 we read: "The Lord knows how to rescue the godly from trials and to hold the unrighteous for the day of judgment, while continuing their punishment." This model assumes that an omnipotent God can always ensure the decision is never indeterminate. Still (to put it in the crudest anthropomorphic terms), even if God examined one million simulations, providing grace enough to enable a free decision but not so much as to compel, and the results were indeterminate, God would still have a happy solution. If Adam continued to choose one way as often as another, God could choose either decision, whichever was best, knowing it was a free choice of his creature either way. All else being equal, we would expect God to choose the contingency with no sin.

Some might ask: "Isn't it true that everyone will always do that which they most want to do—at any moment, in any given situation?" Some conceive of God causing a person to choose either option "A" or option "B" by simply changing the circumstances prior to the decision. If God wants Adam to choose option "A," he merely alters the factors that influence Adam's choice until he most desires option "A" and will unfailingly choose it. In this way, Adam can freely choose what God desires. Ware puts it like this:

God, through his middle knowledge, can know whether he should permit an agent to choose according to his greatest desire or whether to alter the circumstances.

In response to this idea, I must say that no doubt God does exactly this, at times. He can, in effect, force the decision he wants. We need to realize that if he does so, God will not only be the ultimate cause of the action, as he is in all cases, but also the proximate cause. If God simply "piles on" circumstances until a person unfailingly chooses one option, then the outcome is not in doubt. True, the choice was only free in the sense that the person involved did what he most desired. Nevertheless, he thought his decision was free, and we must admit this belief is significant. It is an immense advantage when the human agent does not have the sense of being forced to do something against his will. It is easy to imagine many occasions when God may well want to force us to do certain things, and by using this method, we are quite unaware of his direct involvement. This idea is consistent with what we experience. We are not conscious of God forcing us one way or the other, even if he sometimes does so.

Under the CCM, there is no assumption that a person will always make the choice that he most desires. We have all had the experience of desiring to do something but by force of will resisting the impulse. This event might be an illusion, but it is a convincing illusion. Under the CCM, there is no need to try to decide if a person will always do what he most desires, or whether he will choose to do his duty, regardless of desire. God has the power to integrate all such considerations. Since he knows and can visualize all possible alternatives and circumstances by virtue of his natural knowledge, he can simply select the best option *that the person freely chooses.* Of course, if no freely chosen option is acceptable, God can then change the circumstances so that the person has no option. To put it in theological terms, God may allow a person full, free will in his choice of some options, God may restrict the choices so as to limit free will, or God may determine that an option is fixed (hard determinism).

Clearly, though, God loves to encourage volition among his creatures. He delights in giving freedom. One assumed design criterion was that he would "maximize" freedom. Furthermore, when we confront issues affecting our salvation or works of righteousness, God is zealous to give us grace. Grace is given to broaden our choices, to increase our freedom, to enable us to choose righteousness even when our heart would otherwise most ardently desire evil. Still, Jesus confirms there are limits to grace, beyond which he cannot justly go. He said:

> Woe to you, Chorazin! Woe to you, Bethsaida! For if the miracles that were done in you had been done in Tyre and Sidon, they would have repented long ago, sitting in sackcloth and ashes.[430]

So Jesus knows the boundary between sufficient grace, which allows for volition, and an excessive amount. The works he did in Chorazin and Bethsaida were sufficient, and he did no more even though they did not repent. These cities justly deserved their coming woe.

This idea that Adam's volition had an effect on the foreordained future would not satisfy many Calvinists. It means God adjusts his decree to create, based in part on Adam's will. It means Adam is, in some derived sense, a causal agent. This human agency, they would say, limits God's sovereignty. God is limited in what he will create and that limit is based on something outside himself. The essence of God's free knowledge is that it is free—not dependent on anything except God's good pleasure. If Adam makes a free choice, then God is not free. God's sovereignty is compromised, and so the CCM is not an acceptable model, or so goes the argument.

Certainly, the desire to preserve the absolute sovereignty of God is laudable. It must be affirmed in the strongest possible terms that God is fully sovereign. He was not in any way compelled to create anything, much less the world that he did create. There is no way any creature could cause God to do or fail to do anything he did not wish. We can agree that God created the world solely to satisfy his good pleasure. If we say no more than that, we can leave the matter knowing that we have described it accurately, if not comprehensively.

---

[430] Luke 10:13 (HCSB)

To Calvinists, I must point out a couple of truths. We all have to be reminded that even though God is sovereign and all-powerful, he cannot do everything. For example, if he chooses to create Billy Graham, he cannot at the same time have a universe where there is no Billy Graham.[431] By creating Billy Graham, he has limited his sovereignty. This limitation is due to a logical principle called the law of non-contradiction. A statement about the universe cannot be both true and false at the same time. It involves a logical law which means it applies to God as much as it does to any of us. Few would say that creating Billy Graham denies the sovereignty of God, even though we must all admit it does *limit* God's sovereignty.

So we must recognize that not everything that narrows God's options is a limit to his sovereignty. If God limits himself, his sovereignty is unimpaired. Now let us return to the idea that God created a universe where Adam sinned because God respected Adam's free choice to sin. Is this situation a limitation on the sovereignty of God imposed by a creature? The answer has to be "No." It is true that Adam's choice to sin was a basis on which God chose to create, but Adam's choice was not the ultimate cause. The ultimate cause was God's decision to consider Adam's choice. Like the choice to create Billy Graham, the decision to consider Adam's choice limited the scope of God, but it was a self-imposed limit, along the line of "You can't have your cake and eat it, too."

The response by many Calvinists might take this form: "Yes, the decision to honor Adam's choice is one thing. Yet how can God develop a plan for the ages, if he has to select from a range of options that are limited to those chosen by his creatures? This restriction limits the plan of God to one of reaction rather than action." One can see this complaint has plausibility. To answer, we must be reminded that God considers all possible universes—not just the ones in which persons make free choices. Secondly, there is no reason why God couldn't simply ordain the choices of his creatures whenever it pleased him to do so. Volition may not be the most salient consideration in all cases.

God can impel a person to choose a contingency, and the Scriptures indicate that he does so, on occasion. Exodus 2:21 and 7:3 say that God

---

[431] Unless, of course, He creates more than one universe. But any given universe cannot both have Billy Graham and not have Billy Graham at the same time.

hardened Pharaoh's heart so he would not let God's people go. This thought is reconfirmed in Romans 9:16–18.[432] God is shown to be in charge. He caused Pharaoh to make the choice he made. We are not obliged to believe, however, that God would hold Pharaoh judicially responsible for his sinful choices if God compelled those choices. We can be confident that God's judgments will be fair and impartial.[433]

With this confidence, we see that God has the prerogative of overriding the free will of his creatures whenever it pleases him. His justice compels him, however, to take freedom into account when he judges individuals for their works. His righteous judgments are perfect. There is a particular case, however, when such action on the part of God is problematic and that is the case of individual salvation of fallen human beings. Let us take a look at one famous example.

C. The Case of Billy Graham

Billy Graham was saved in 1934 during a revival preached in Charlotte, North Carolina, by evangelist Mordecai Ham.[434] Graham said he felt he had to "do" something when he went forward and stood at the front of the revival tent. He had heard the message and felt the compulsion to go forward. Then he realized it was "the moment to commit myself to Christ." First, he mentally assented. He accepted that what he knew about Christ was true. Emotionally, he wanted to give the Lord love in return for Christ's matchless love. Then, with intention, he turned himself over to Christ's rule in his life. Graham believed that when he checked his decision on a card, with a real sense of purpose, it was at that moment that he made his real commitment to Christ and became a child of God.

1. *God must draw fallen men and women to himself.* Since sin affects every part of us all, we have lost the freedom to accept Christ. We are

---

[432] Romans 9:18 says: "So then, He shows mercy to those he wants to and He hardens those He wants to harden." (HCSB)

[433] See 1 Peter 1:17; Genesis 18:25; Job 37:23; Psalm 19:9; 119:62.

[434] Graham, Billy. *Just as I am.* 1997. Harper Collins. New York, NY. See Chapter 2 and particularly p. 30.

slaves to sin.[435] God must give us the grace to believe in him. In John 6:44 Jesus explains: "No-one can come to me unless the Father who sent me draws them."[436] Paul makes the same point: "For it is God who is working in you, enabling you both to desire and to work out His his good purpose." (Philippians 2:13).[437] We must recognize that God loves the *world* as in John 3:16. This word "world" cannot be limited to the elect but must include everyone.[438] Yet God does love his church in a special way.[439]

This drawing of the creatures that God loves must be thought of as a process. Jesus revealed a bit about this process in the Parable of the Sower in Luke 8. He first explained there were four types of soil (hearers of God's Word), but only one of those who heard the word produced any fruit. In Luke 8:9–18 we see a basic principle:

a. God gives light. God works to reveal some of his truth to us in the same way that the sower sows seed.

b. We respond to the light either by moving towards it or by moving away from it. The light reveals our character (what kind of soil we are), whether we desire the light. Our response determines the third step.

c. God grants more or less light. If we make a positive response, God gives more light, and the process begins anew. If our response is negative, we move away from the light and have less opportunity to be enlightened. Jesus said:

> For there is nothing hidden that will not be disclosed, and nothing concealed that will not be known or brought out into the open. Therefore consider carefully how you listen. Whoever has will be given more; whoever does not have, even what they think they have will be taken from them.[440]

---

[435] John 8:34

[436] (NIV)

[437] (HCSB)

[438] John 3:16. "For God so loved the world, that he gave His only begotten Son, that whosoever believeth in him shall not perish, but have everlasting life." (KJV) John, in fact, consistently contrasts the "world" with those who are followers of God. See Carson, D. A. *The Difficult Doctrine of the Love of God*. 2000. Crossway Books. Wheaton, IL. p. 17.

[439] See Ephesians 5:25.

[440] Luke 8:17–18 (NIV)

God clearly uses this process of light giving to form our character.[441] Of course, God can use many circumstances to do the same. In Romans we see that God's love, the power of the Holy Spirit, and even afflictions come together to form our character and give us hope:

> Therefore, since we have been justified through faith, we have peace with God through our Lord Jesus Christ, through whom we have gained access by faith into this grace in which we now stand. And we boast in the hope of the glory of God. Not only so, but we also glory in our sufferings, because we know that suffering produces perseverance; perseverance, character; and character, hope. And hope does not put us to shame, because God's love has been poured out into our hearts through the Holy Spirit, who has been given to us.[442]

2. *No two fallen people are the same.* Every person is unique. The potter analogy in Romans 9 reveals this truth, where God is making one pottery vessel for honor and one for dishonor. God has power over the clay, and the formation of human beings is in his hands. Obviously, God has chosen to create large numbers of unique, individual persons, each with different gifts, talents and inclinations. Jesus made the same point when he compared people to four kinds of soil. Some are resistant to God's efforts to draw them, others are less so.[443] Of course, all need God to draw them. None of us, with our fallen mind, will, and emotions, would ever submit to God. We need him to draw us, but not everyone responds in the same way.

The question might be asked: "Why would a loving God create a person who is resistant to his word?" It does seem cruel to create someone who may be said to be created for God's wrath. Yet we know that God, being a God of love,[444] is not cruel. Perhaps God wants to create a

---

[441] This concerns the spiritual growth of the Christian, but God can do much the same to bring an unsaved person to the point of a decision to accept (or reject) Christ.

[442] Romans 5:1–5 (NIV) See James 1:2–4; Philippians 4:11–12; Hebrews 5:8. Also: Ware, Bruce. *God's Greater Glory.* 2004. Crossway, Wheaton, IL. p. 168.

[443] See James 4:6.

[444] 1 John 4:8b

complete set of persons. Perhaps "hardness" is part of the definition of a specific person. If the hardness found in the "hard soil" person is an integral part of who he is, then if God changed that hardness, he would not be creating him but someone else. As the Scripture says:

> Or has the potter no right over the clay, to make from the same lump one piece of pottery for honor and another for dishonor? And what if God, desiring to display His wrath and to make His power known, endured with much patience objects of wrath ready for destruction? And what if He did this to make known the riches of His glory on objects of mercy that He prepared beforehand for glory—on us, the ones He also called, not only from the Jews but also from the Gentiles.[445]

Perhaps, then, to obtain the full spectrum of humanity, God decided to create people who ran the gamut from the hardest of the hard soil to those with an "honest and good heart."[446] Some will never cease their rebellion against God without spiritual coercion. These might be called "objects of wrath." They would not repent in any possible contingency where they made a free choice. Possibly God's justice impelled him to give them life and to give them a chance to repent, even though he foreknew they would only serve to allow him to display his wrath and power. Others would be objects of mercy, with hearts so tender that they immediately repented in all contingencies. Probably most of us would fall somewhere in the middle. We can be sure God's justice will take into account the burden some individuals bear due to their precise nature. Ultimately, however, God is sovereign and has the right to create whomever he will.

We must not forget that the gate to Christ's kingdom is narrow, and Jesus himself said relatively few would find it. He also said: "For the gate is wide and the road is broad that leads to destruction, and there are many that go through it."[447] Many can be thankful that Billy Graham was one of those who found the narrow gate since he in turn touched the lives of so many.

---

[445] Romans 9:21–24 (HCSB)

[446] Luke 8:15b (HCSB)

[447] Matthew 7:13b (HCSB)

3. *Salvation comes to Billy Graham.* So we can see that before the foundation of the world God decided to create Billy Graham with a nature that influenced his ability to respond. Apparently his heart was not created hard, like a path. As a fallen creature, he still had to depend on God to give him the grace he needed to be able to follow Christ. As a sinner, he was guilty of rebellion before God.[448] To be justified, he had to obtain God's righteousness which is given by faith to all who believe.[449] His salvation was not based on his works, and even the faith he needed was a gift from God.[450]

To sum up, God considered a contingent world in 1934, Charlotte, North Carolina, Mordecai Ham's revival tent. We have to realize that God, even before the foundation of the world, knew Billy Graham by name. God gave him the grace he needed to overcome his slavery to sin. God also gave him the faith he would need to be saved. God had often shown Billy a glimpse of his light. Billy's response, whether he moved towards or away from the light, helped form his character. He had made thousands of small choices. Then his time came. The Holy Spirit touched him, and he realized he should go forward in that revival tent. He was able to remember what he had been taught, and he believed in Christ. He was emotionally involved and responded to Christ's love. His will was involved when he intentionally turned himself over to Christ and accepted him as Savior and Lord. The lasting commitment came, as Billy Graham has testified, when he filled out a small decision card. So we can see that his mind, will, and emotions were all involved in his decision to follow Christ.

God saw all of this event in a preview, considering a contingent world. He saw that the decision to follow Christ was genuine. God had helped him along the way, and Billy Graham believed. It was a free, genuine decision that gave glory to God and allowed him to display both his justice and his mercy. God was pleased, so he accepted this contingency

---

[448] Romans 3: 9–18, 23

[449] Romans 3:22, 27–28

[450] Ephesians 2:8. "For by grace are ye saved through faith; and that not of yourselves: it is the gift of God: Not of works, lest any man should boast." (KJV)

and made it part of his plan. We realize, of course, that Billy Graham's salvation decision in 1934 was part of God's plan from before the foundation of the world. We can see that the salvation was not based on Billy Graham's works. We can see that Billy Graham freely believed, but it was God who worked with him every step of the way. It was God's chosen contingency. Remember, however, that this explanation is neither Calvinist nor Arminian; it is based on the CCM.

4. BILLY GRAHAM—A DISCUSSION OF HIS SALVATION

Let us look at four questions relating to this example:

A. How Does the CCM Differ From the Arminian View?

The Arminian view, as it is usually expressed, is that God looks into the future and foreknows those who will choose to follow Christ, and so he elects those people to salvation. In the CCM, God does not simply foresee "the future." He foresees all possible futures and, in the end, chooses the future that pleases him. So God foresaw that Billy Graham would choose Christ, but God also chose the future in which Billy Graham chose Christ. God chose the best possible future and that included Billy Graham. Under the Arminian view it does seem that God's choice is limited. His election of a person comes logically after the person's decision is foreseen. In the CCM, although God does respect Billy Graham's volition, it is God's choice that determines who is saved. In other words, if Billy Graham chose to follow Christ only under such conditions that would not reveal God's justice,[451] then God would not choose a contingency where Billy Graham was saved, and God would not determine him to be one of the elect.

---

[451] Justice is only one example of an attribute that God intends to demonstrate.

B. How Does the CCM Differ From the Calvinist View?

As the Calvinists do, the CCM takes seriously the verses that speak of God's sovereign election in eternity past. Calvinists resist any attempt to define what process God may have used in choosing his elect. Clearly, they would insist, election is not based on works since election takes place before a person is born. Romans 9 explains:

> Yet, before the twins were born or had done anything good or bad—in order that God's purpose in election might stand: not by works but by him who calls—she [Rebekah] was told, "The older will serve the younger." Just as it is written: "Jacob I loved, but Esau I hated."[452]

Calvinists would also argue that those foreknown by God were predestined, those predestined were called, those called were justified, and those justified were also glorified. How many who are called by God are saved? Calvinists would say all who are called by God are saved.[453] Calvinists commonly maintain that people are elected before they believe. To followers of Calvin, God's choice of whom to save is totally inscrutable. The CCM, however, does not look at it in exactly the same way.

The context of Romans 8:28–30 seems to give assurance to those Christians who love God, telling them they have always been secure and will always be secure. If persons are Christians, they can be assured they have never been in danger of being lost. Jesus said: "Everyone the Father gives me will come to me, and the one who comes to me I will never cast out."[454] What is being presented is one side of the coin—the eternal perspective of God. Of course, from that perspective our salvation has never been in doubt, ever since God's decree to create and even before

---

[452] Romans 9:11–13 (NIV) (name added) This is not to say that this election is concerned with the eternal salvation of Jacob or Esau. But it does show that election precedes birth. Indeed, Revelation 13:8 says that the book of life was written from before the foundation of the world.

[453] Romans 8:28–30

[454] (HCSB)

that. From our perspective, however, we are still required to believe, to exercise volition, to use the faith God has given us.

Under the CCM, when God chooses a contingent future that includes our believing in faith, we have been elected. God did not have to choose that future. The circumstances of our coming to faith have to bring glory to God; otherwise he would not select it. Much more is in play than God simply looking into the future and foreseeing whether or not we come to faith. God does not consider just one possible future but myriads of them. Truly, it can be said that God calls us. For those who respond in the chosen contingent future, the call is always effective and effectual. Our names are written in the Lamb's book of life.[455] For those who resist, God knows two truths: 1) The call was sufficient in a judicial way; those who resist cannot blame God. 2) The failure to accept was due to their hardness of heart and a persistent unwillingness to follow Christ. It was not an effectual call, both in the sense that the person failed to respond and also in the sense that God knew it would not be effectual. It was sufficient for them to have been able to respond, should they have wished.

In the final analysis, the CCM does explain how God can be said, sovereignly, to elect those who believe, and at the same time it affirms the truth that "whoever believes in him shall not perish." Calvinism does not provide an explanation how both can be true, even though many followers of Calvin believe both are. As an example, let us consider a statement from Francis Turretin, a well-known Reformed theologian of seventeenth century Geneva, after the time of Calvin:

> ... that God on the one hand by his providence not only decreed, but most certainly secures, the event of all things, whether free or contingent; on the other hand, however, man is always free in acting and many effects are contingent. Although I cannot understand how these can be mutually connected together, yet (on account of ignorance of the mode) the thing itself is (which is certain from another source, i.e., from the Word) not either to be called in question or wholly denied.[456]

---

[455] See Exodus 32:32–33; Psalm 9:5; Revelation 3:5, 13:8, 17:8, 20:12, 15.

[456] Turretin, Francis. *Institutes of Elenctic Theology Volume One: First Through Tenth Topics*. 1992. Presbyterian and Reformed Publishing Company,

So even though he was not able to reconcile the two, Turretin agreed that human beings had freedom or volition and that freedom involved contingencies. He apparently did not see God as choosing contingencies prior to creation, however.

I have touched on the idea of *irresistible grace* and do not find it useful as it is normally expressed. As to other controversies, such as the issue of limited atonement, which (under Calvinism) holds that Christ died only for the elect, the CCM illustrates why Christ's sacrifice can truly be for the sins of the whole world,[457] or unlimited in terms of potential, yet limited in terms of its effect. The atonement is sufficient to justify all, in a judicial sense.[458] In other words, no one at the throne of judgment could use the excuse that Christ's sacrifice would not have been effectual in their case. It is Christ's atoning work that enabled God to take Billy Graham through the process described above when he accepted the Lord. Reformed theology is a tightly-reasoned and unified scheme of thought, and the doctrine of limited atonement fits nicely within that model. But the CCM comes from an entirely different viewpoint: limited atonement does not figure in it, just as irresistible grace doesn't. The other points of TULIP,[459] the acronym used to identify some key Reformed beliefs, seem to be in harmony with the CCM. *Total depravity* can be affirmed. *Unconditional election* can also be accepted, insofar as it holds that election is not based on works. Finally, *perseverance of the saints* is harmonious with the CCM, though the CCM probably contributes little to establish this concept. So there are points in which the CCM is clearly compatible with Reformed theology, and it has some potential to visualize how other concepts could be harmonized.

Phillipsburg, NJ. p. 1: 512.

[457] 1 John 2:2

[458] It is the judicial effect of the atonement that is absolutely certain and which applies to every sinful human heart.

[459] To reiterate, TULIP stands for: Total depravity; Unconditional election; Limited atonement; Irresistible grace; and Perseverance of the saints. These are the "Five Points" of Calvinism.

C. BILLY GRAHAM HAD TO BELIEVE TO BE SAVED. ISN'T THIS REQUIREMENT A WORK?

The Scriptures distinguish between faith and works. Belief proceeds from faith and is, therefore, not a work as the term is used in Romans 2:27. In Romans 4:5 Paul said, "To the one who does not work but trusts God who justifies the ungodly, their faith is credited as righteousness." This verse clearly shows that faith (or belief) is the only thing one can employ in the context of salvation that is not considered to be work. It must be said, however, that some Calvinists insist God elects without preconditions of any kind, and they also resist any attempts to explain God's choice. Under the CCM, God elects those who freely choose him, *but that choice must occur in the contingency that best honors the criteria he has established.*

D. BILLY GRAHAM MAY NOT HAVE BEEN COERCED, BUT IN THE CASE OF PAUL, IT APPEARS GOD GAVE HIM NO CHOICE.

One might conclude, quite understandably, that God coerced Paul to become a Christian. Paul saw a bright light from heaven. Then he heard the voice of the risen Lord Jesus and was struck blind. He was told to go into the city and was unable to see for three days. Then a believer called Ananias placed his hands on Paul who regained his sight and was filled with the Holy Spirit. He was then baptized. It is hard to see how anyone would not have believed under those circumstances! This is an account of perhaps the most extreme and powerful conversion in the New Testament.[460]

Yet the Scriptures do not say Paul was coerced. It appears God knew what it would take to convert Paul. He was a man of strong will, and his face was set like flint against Christianity. We can well believe it took extreme measures to get Paul's attention. Would it have been impossible for Paul to have refused to believe? "Impossible" is a strong word. I

---

[460] Acts 9; 22; 26

cannot say it would have been impossible, in the absence of a clear word in Scripture. It is also possible God might compel salvation in unusual circumstances. If God had chosen Paul to fulfill his perfect plan, then he may well have supplied circumstances to such an extent that Paul had no choice.

Having admitted that either compulsion or volition may have been possible, where are we now? We should not assume God denied human volition. Perhaps a lesser man would have had his volition compromised, but we need not assume this was true in Paul's case. Either way, however, this account is harmonious with the CCM.

5. WHAT TENDS TO SUPPORT THE CHOSEN CONTINGENCY MODEL?

When I was first trying to understand the issues involved, I came to wonder if an avenue toward harmonizing Scripture might lie with God's decrees before the foundation of the world. The Arminian idea (that God foresaw the future as it unfolded and then elected to salvation those whom he foresaw accepting Christ) seemed simplistic. Why couldn't God have had a more active role in choosing the exact future he wanted? Surely God must be more than a passive observer of the future unfolding. The Calvinist idea that God decided the future by hard determinism seemed to be more reasonable than seeing him as a mere observer. But unfortunately, hard determinism seemed to leave no place for human freedom. It reminded me of my grandson moving his plastic toy soldiers over the living room floor.

What if, before creation, God considered all possible future states of the universe, made full use of contingencies involving the free choices of his creatures, incorporated his direct intervention when needed and then chose the best of all possible futures? I considered this hypothesis to be a possible resolution of the conflict, and it formed the heart of the CCM. Although these considerations would logically be prior to the creation of the universe, they were not prior in time since God, in his essential nature, is timeless.

With this basic concept in mind, I began to look at ideas that had been proposed by others. I wanted to see if the CCM was original. I found these questions had been discussed by Christians ever since the days of the apostles. I also learned that my solution had, for the most part, already been proposed. In a way, that was comforting. I see the wisdom in the adage, "If it's new; it's not for you." Let us look at three proposals that offered helpful insights:

A. GOTTFRIED LEIBNIZ — BEST OF ALL POSSIBLE WORLDS

Gottfried Leibniz (1646–1716), a German mathematician and philosopher, presented a theodicy (and coined the term) in 1710, in an essay called *Théodicée*. Leibniz also popularized the expression that the current world is the best of all possible worlds. He explained that God could have created other possible universes or "worlds," but chose this one instead. In other words, the fact that this world exists represents a decree or choice by God. Since God is infinitely powerful, wise and loving, he would have decreed the best possible world. Leibniz suggested that God intended to maximize the freedom, spiritual growth and development of his creatures, demonstrate his goodness, and display a variety of features circumscribed by fixed laws. Leibniz recognized that logical constraints do exist (such as the law of non-contradiction) which limit the worlds that God could make. Leibniz concluded that the best possible world would be logically possible and maximize the criteria he proposed.[461] Leibniz is probably the main source of the model I am proposing.

B. LAPLACE'S DEMON

It would seem that a description of scientific determinism would have little bearing on an investigation of God's ultimate relationship

---

[461] See *Wikipedia, The Free Encyclopedia.* "Irenaean theodicy." Accessed 30 Aug. 2012, from http://en.wikipedia.org/wiki/Irenaean_theodicy.

to his creation. Surprisingly, Pierre-Simon Laplace (1749–1827),[462] a French mathematician and astronomer, presented ideas which help to clarify our thinking on this topic. One of his concerns was to disprove the idea that God must periodically intervene in a supernatural way to fine-tune the "natural laws" that govern the universe. He believed God had designed those laws better than that. He also began to speculate as to whether a lesser being than God could predict the future with absolute precision. Laplace had the idea that if we precisely knew everything about the present, then we could predict the future.[463] His ideas centered on a hypothetical intellect which came to be known as *Laplace's Demon*.[464] He famously stated:

> We may regard the present state of the universe as the effect of its past and the cause of its future. An intellect which at a certain moment would know all forces that set nature in motion, and all positions of all items of which nature is composed, if this intellect were also vast enough to submit these data to analysis, it would embrace in a single formula the movements of the greatest bodies of the universe and those of the tiniest atom; for such an intellect nothing would be uncertain and the future, just like the past, would be present before its eyes.[465]

The value of Laplace's Demon to our argument is that it expands our vision, not that it could be done. Under this theory, if we assumed that the position and momentum of all the atoms in the universe (the number of atoms is estimated to total 10^{80}—which would be ten followed by eighty zeros) could be defined, then their future state could also be defined. Laplace's Demon would then be like the mystic's crystal ball. Of course, this idea was never more than a theoretical model. Quantum physics and Heisenberg's uncertainty principle suggest such precision

---

[462] Pierre-Simon, Marquis de Laplace (1749 – 1827).

[463] Carroll, Sean. *From Eternity to Here*. 2010. Dutton, New York, NY. p. 120.

[464] I believe that the term "demon" as used here refers to a slang term for a calculating engine.

[465] Laplace, Pierre Simon, *A Philosophical Essay on Probabilities*, translated from the 6th French edition by Frederick Wilson Truscott and Frederick Lincoln Emory. 1902. John Wiley & Sons, New York, p. 19.

of measurement with respect to subatomic particles is impossible. One can measure the momentum of a particle or the location of a particle, but one cannot know both with exactitude.[466] If this uncertainty is valid, it almost suggests God built something into the fabric of the universe to prevent us from building Laplace's Demon: a fortune-telling machine. Even so, would it be possible for God to do more than consider all possible worlds (as Leibniz theorized) and to go even further? Could he consider all possible combinations and contingencies for every one of the 10^{80} atoms and their subatomic particles, from the beginning to the end of time?[467] Since we know God is infinitely powerful, there seems to be no fundamental problem with this idea. The number of possibilities would be unimaginably large but would still be finite. It would be far easier for an infinite God to intuitively know all the possibilities than it would be for us to deal with the future positions of two balls on a pool table. It would also have been far easier for God to understand all the options than it would have been for him to create all of these particles from nothing in the first place. We need not consider that the measurement problems of quantum physics would defeat God. Simply considering all possibilities, of course, would be a brute-force approach. Even with no optimization, however, it would not be outside the range of God's power.

Another concern of Laplace, as mentioned above, was his conviction that God's natural laws were well enough designed as to avoid the need for God to intervene constantly and supernaturally to fine-tune them. Newton was concerned that the calculated motion of the planets gave no assurance the solar system was stable and concluded God had to intervene every so often to prevent disaster. Laplace was sure this continual intervention was not needed and was able to refine the calcula-

---

[466] Carroll, Sean. *op. cit.*, pp. 119–120.

[467] I mention the "end of time," meaning the end of time foretold in Revelation 21:1 and the creation of a new heaven and a new earth. This avoids the problem of God considering an infinite number of possible futures. It could be argued that an evaluation of an infinite number might be a paradox, and the concept of an end of time avoids that problem, at least for the purpose of discussion.

tions to support his view.[468] One can see why Laplace was concerned. We don't need to disbelieve in miracles to see a problem with Newton's view. Perhaps one way of looking at the problem is that of elegance. A solar system that operated quite well, autonomously, without the need for God to fine-tune it, would be more elegant than the alternative.[469] An elegant universe clearly shows God's glory, which is a point in Laplace's favor. This analysis does not suggest everything in the universe is determined by remorseless, impersonal laws of cause and effect – such a viewpoint would be unscriptural.

C. Luis de Molina—A Middle Way

Let us briefly review Molina's contribution. Molina (1535–1600) was a Spanish Jesuit priest who tried to reconcile the precise problem we are discussing: the seeming conflict between predestination and human free will.[470] The tenets of Molinism have been discussed in detail in Chapter Nine, above.

Under Molinism there is a great emphasis on counterfactuals[471] of freedom or middle knowledge. This thought is similar to the "possible worlds" of Leibniz who said our world was the "best of all possible worlds." So is Leibniz's idea actually a form of Molinism? Perhaps, although Molina's vision seems to be more detailed.

As mentioned above, Molinism is not the same as the CCM, but there are similarities. The CCM does not depend on middle knowledge nor does it require strong libertarian free will.[472] The CCM does not see God

---

[468] Whitrow, G. J. (2001) "Laplace, Pierre-Simon, Marquis de", *Encyclopaedia Britannica,* Deluxe CDROM edition.

[469] We shall see below that God is involved, though his providential sustaining or conserving of the universe and his *concurrence* in all that happens. But that does not take away from the concept of natural law and of autonomy.

[470] Keathley, Kenneth. *op. cit.,* p. 5.

[471] To reiterate, the term "counterfactuals" is a misnomer, since the contingencies in view are in advance of any "facts." The universe was not yet created, so the counterfactuals were alternatives but not counter to any facts.

[472] The weak form of libertarian free will advocated by Keathley seems quite harmonious with CCM. See Keathley, Kenneth. Salvation and Sovereignty. *op.*

simply choosing from a set of alternatives; rather, it sees him creating alternatives in an interactive way.

6. WHAT MIGHT BE USED TO REFUTE THE CHOSEN CONTINGENCY MODEL?

The CCM is based on assumptions regarding time that are reasonable and based on the Scriptures. Yet because time is so mysterious, it must be said they are debatable. For one thing, the model assumes time is part of creation, which means it is relative. Some would disagree and insist time is absolute. In other words, an "absolutist" would say that even if the universe had never been created, time would still exist. Another question about time is whether it flows like a river. This debate is sometimes seen as the difference between A and B theories of time. I thoroughly discussed the concept of time in Chapter Six and further explored the matter in Chapter Seven, as it involved the claims of open theism. Nevertheless, I will briefly explore a few additional implications of time and how they affect our model.

A. WHAT IS TIME AND WHY DOES IT MATTER TO CCM?

We need not be advocates for either A or B theories of time. The truth may be that A-series time is an adequate description of time as we experience it, while B-series time is the underlying reality as God created it. A recent thesis by Hanne Kristin Berg proposed a resolution in which both theories could be considered compatible and even necessary to gain a complete understanding of time.[473] CCM is compatible with both theories. While, technically, the CCM does not depend upon the B-series conception of time being true, it is much easier to explain and understand if all time is seen as equally real from God's viewpoint.

---

cit., p. 9.

[473] Berg, Hanne Kristin. *Philosophy of Time: Combining the A-Series and the B-Series.* MSc Thesis. Universiteit van Amsterdam, 2010. Institute for Logic, Language and Computation. Accessed 13 September 2012, from http://www. illc.uva.nl/Research/Reports/MoL-2010-13.text.pdf.

Steve Bishop raises several objections to the B-series idea that we should consider:

- It regards our experience of time as an illusion—a "psychological quirk."[474]
- It is difficult to reconcile with the doctrine of the incarnation and conflicts with the Nicene creed. It would imply that there was a time before when the Son was not begotten.[475]
- It conflicts with the idea that God created the universe from nothing or *ex nihilo.*
- It does not explain how one event can cause another.

Of all these, only the last objection has validity if we consider that God is free to experience the universe from his eternal, timeless perspective but equally free to experience time with his creatures.[476] The B-series view seems to say that our perception of time does not reflect the underlying reality. We saw that Einstein called it a "stubbornly persistent illusion." Others have used various terms to present this view which is seen as psychological rather than real. We might ask how such a persistent, universal perception can be regarded as false. On balance, "false" is too strong a word. Probably the A-series is true in some sense of the word. We should not, however, insist that our subjective experience is the decisive factor to consider. It is well to remember that our perception of space always puts ourselves at the center of the universe. It is a remarkably persistent illusion, but we will be making a colossal mistake if we think the world

---

[474] Bishop, Steve. "God, Time and Eternity." *Quodlibet Journal*: Volume 6 Number 1, January – March 2004. Accessed 13 September 2012, from http://www.quodlibet.net/articles/bishop-eternity.shtml#_ednref15. Note that all of these points were raised by Bishop.

[475] Bishop cites: Paul Helm "Eternal creation." *Tyndale Bulletin* 45(2) (1994).

[476] See Lemke, Steve W. *The Transdimensional God: A Proposal Regarding God, Time and Providence.* New Orleans Baptist Theological Seminary for the 2003 Southwest Regional Meeting of the Evangelical Theological Society. Accessed 22 September 2012, from http://www.nobts.edu/faculty/itor/lemkesw/personal/Transdimensional%20God%20and%20Time.pdf. Lemke proposes a model called *transdimensionality* which agrees very well with the concept that God is essentially timeless, yet can enter into time as he pleases.

revolves around us. Bishop's first point is valid, but it does nothing to prove that the B-series concept is false.

The second point, which Bishop derived from Paul Helm, seems to have been based on a misunderstanding. Helm did not say B-series time caused a conflict with the Nicene creed. He said, rather, that if we considered God to be subject to time *of any sort* in his essential nature, then we would have problems with the doctrine that the Son was eternally begotten from the Father. This argument has nothing to do with A-series time as opposed to B-series time. There is nothing in the concept of B-series time to suggest God is not timeless in his essential being. Since that is the case, the B-theory is not a difficulty for the Nicene creed. Bishop never explains why the incarnation would pose a problem for God if B-series time were correct, and it is hard to imagine why it would, unless Bishop imagined B-series time would somehow lock God out of the universe. Whatever Bishop may think, we see nothing about B-series time that (even theoretically) limits God in any way.

Similarly, the idea that God created the universe *ex nihilo* seems to mesh well with the idea of B-series time. It is only necessary to propose that God created the universe as a four-dimensional spacetime block to account entirely for B-series time. Some B-series advocates see the concept of "becoming" as incompatible with B-series time, but it would be incoherent to say the universal block of spacetime could not itself have had a beginning. Within the block, once time has begun it might be correct to say "becoming" is *no longer* a feature since all things and all times would then exist in some sense of the word.

The final point, that B-series time does not explain how one event causes another (causation), is well taken. B-series time, standing alone, is incoherent. It seems necessary to hold that when God created time, he (as the ultimate cause) had to infuse it with the necessary principle that changes and events are caused by previous events.[477] In other words,

[477] See Craig, William Lane and James D. Sinclair. "The *Kalam* Cosmological Argument." *Library of Philosophy and Religion Series*, edited by John Hick. New York: Barnes and Noble, 1979. p. 124. Accessed 14 September 2012, from http://commonsenseatheism.com/wp-content/uploads/2009/05/

even if B-series time is the deep level of reality, it still must be infused with A-series time to explain how there is any logical sequence of events. This need for a logical sequence also comprises an argument which holds that B-series time must have had an intelligent creator.

To conclude: the CCM assumes God created time, that he is not subject to time (but can enter it), and the future is real. The CCM does not require that either A-series time or B-series time be taken as a complete description of reality. Both theories have elements which harmonize well with scriptural revelation and our own experience.

B. Problems With the Idea of God's Timelessness

The idea that God is timeless, in an eternal present in his essential being, is found in Scripture. The concept was also found in early Greek philosophers such as Plato. Christian philosophers such as Boethius[478] explicitly taught it, and this idea is sometimes referred to as the "Boethian position."[479] McCann considers the Boethian view to have a glaring deficiency. God does not have foreknowledge of what his creatures will do until after the creation. This is how McCann phrases it:

> The difficulty is that in order for God to exercise full providence over the world, he needs to know *as creator* how the decisions and actions of creatures with libertarian freedom will go. It is hard to see how that is possible on the Boethian view, for even if God is outside of time, his activity as creator is still *ontologically prior* to the activities of free creatures on this account, whereas his knowledge of those activities is *posterior* to them. Thus it seems impossible that God's creative will could be guided by his knowledge of our actions, even if, from his time-

craig-and-sinclair-the-kalam-cosmological-argument.pdf. The point about the need for A-Theory time is put like this: "The past did not spring into being whole and entire but was formed sequentially, one event occurring after another."

[478] Boethius, *The Consolation of Philosophy*, Bk. V, pr. 6.

[479] McCann, Hugh J., "Divine Providence", *The Stanford Encyclopedia of Philosophy (Spring 2009 Edition)*, Edward N. Zalta (ed.). Accessed 14 September 2012, from http://plato.stanford.edu/archives/spr2009/entries/providence-divine/.

less perspective, such knowledge is finally available to him. If this is correct, then even the Boethian God runs an immense risk in creating the world. He can only hope that we will use our freedom justly and wisely, perhaps making some allowance for the possibility that we will not, but otherwise simply trusting in the outcome. So although God's omniscience may be restored by placing him outside of time, he is in no way empowered by it.[480]

We would have to agree there is a serious problem if it was only after the creation that God gained his comprehensive, timeless view of all future history, but where did McCann get this idea? Boethius never said any such thing. Furthermore, it seems more logical for God to decree future history and then create it. This concept is proposed in the CCM. In other words, God's knowledge of creation, to include the actions of his creatures, is *ontologically prior* to the creation in the CCM. Therefore, the concern of McCann with the Boethian position does not apply to the CCM.

C. PROBLEMS WITH THE IDEA OF MIDDLE KNOWLEDGE

McCann then considers the solution proposed by Molina (discussed above). He raises some practical difficulties with Molinism in the context of a decision about whether or not to attend a concert. He then supposes that God knows, using middle knowledge, that McCann, when placed in circumstances C, will attend the concert tonight. He diagrams this contingency as: $C \square \!\!\!\rightarrow p$. Then he says:

> In principle, then, nothing need occur in the actual world that does not have God's prior recognition and consent, at least. There may, of course, be much that does not go as God would prefer. It is important to realize that middle knowledge does not restore complete sovereignty to God. If $C \square \!\!\!\rightarrow p$ is true, then there is no way for God to create me in circumstances C and have me do anything but decide to go to the concert. The best he can do is alter my circumstances to fit some true subjunctive of freedom that has another outcome. And the same goes for the subjunctives of freedom that hold of all other creatures God

---

[480] *Ibid.*

might create. This means there is quite a range of worlds which, though logically possible, are not *feasible* for God, in that they are beyond his reach as creator. From God's point of view, free creatures will behave as they will behave, and that is that. Still, God can know in advance of creation what worlds are feasible, and can plan accordingly, which is a vast improvement over the Boethian view.[481]

This criticism assumes that God will never overrule his creatures' free will. It is not clear that Molina insisted on this assumption as an integral part of his theory, but whether or not it is a key feature of Molinism, it is not a key feature of the CCM. For one thing, the CCM does not even assume full libertarian free will is possible in a fallen world. For another, the CCM would consider a decision that is impelled by a person's own character, desires, lusts, is nevertheless free. If the decision is derived from who we are, then we must be said to be responsible for the decision, whether or not it meets the definition of libertarian free will. Clearly, a fallen world limits human choice.

So the CCM assumes God's full sovereignty. He can select worlds that are logically possible and can overrule free will whenever he pleases. On the other hand, the CCM assumes God has selected design criteria that will eliminate some worlds because they do not meet his objectives, *even though they are logically possible.* Furthermore, under the CCM, as in Molinism, there will be circumstances when God will accept the free choice of a creature, such as $C \diamond\!\!\to p$ because that best meets his perfect will. Even if $C \diamond\!\!\to p$ were a sinful action, God might still choose it if all the alternatives where the creature refrained from sinning were unacceptable. Under the CCM, God is free to plan the future he wants. He does not have to simply, passively[482] choose from among actions selected by his creatures.

McCann does not believe God could know, whether using middle knowledge or any other way, what a truly free creature might do in

---

[481] *Ibid.*

[482] McCann admits that Molinism reduces the passivity of God but does not eliminate it.

circumstances C. Specifically, he raises the grounding objection. He describes the objection in this way:

> It is not a necessary truth that if placed in circumstances C, I will decide to attend the concert tonight. Nor can we allow that God might learn the truth of $C \, \square\!\!\rightarrow p$ from my actual behavior—that is, by observing that I actually do, in circumstances C, decide to attend the concert. For God could not make observations like this without also finding out what creative decisions he is actually going to make, which would destroy the whole purpose of middle knowledge. Instead of being guided in his creative choices by knowing what decisions creatures would make *if* they were created, God would be presented from the beginning with a *fait accompli*—with the reality that he was *going* to create certain creatures, and they were going to behave in certain ways.[483]

I do not intend to challenge McCann in his criticism of Molinism. On the one hand, it is true Molinism does not give a clear explanation as to how God knows what free creatures will do when placed in a set of circumstances. It is not enough to say he can make a reasonable guess in most cases. It is also true that there is no observing the creature—Molinism assumes observations must come only after creation. So McCann concludes middle knowledge does not help in predicting the actions of creatures.

Does this objection apply to the CCM? I must admit that part of the argument has merit. These decisions on the part of free creatures are not *necessary*. In plain English, they are not a truth like 2+2=4. It is a necessary truth, that on a given evening (if there is a concert), McCann will either choose to go to the concert, or he will not choose to go to the concert. He cannot do both, and he cannot do neither. The way he decides is not a necessary truth. Also, McCann is correct that it is too late for God if he creates and only then observes from his timeless vantage point what a person might do. Furthermore, God could do that without needing middle knowledge. All this analysis applies just as much to the CCM as to Molinism.

[483] McCann, Hugh J., *op. cit.*

The CCM gets around the grounding objection in the following way:

1. God knows all possible futures.

2. God can accurately visualize a person (in a possible future) in a situation $C \mathrel{\square\!\rightarrow} p$ in a manner analogous to virtual reality. The simulation of reality is so exact that it predicts the actual situation with 100 percent accuracy.

3. So God knows what a person will do in $C \mathrel{\square\!\rightarrow} p$ by direct observation.

4. If the situation proves to be indeterminate, then God can quite properly[484] choose either option for his chosen alternative since either one would represent a free choice.

So the problems with middle knowledge as raised by McCann and others do not apply to the CCM. For one thing, the CCM does not use middle knowledge. For another, the CCM explains God's knowledge of what free creatures might do as simply being part of his complete understanding of all possible alternatives.

D. Problem of Degrees of Human Freedom

This issue is similar to the grounding objection in that it is a problem of middle knowledge. Let us examine it to see if it is also a problem for the CCM. We have seen that middle knowledge consists of God knowing what a person would do in $C \mathrel{\square\!\rightarrow} p$, with C being a set of circumstances and p being the volitional action. As seen above, McCann calls these circumstances that govern volition "subjunctives of freedom." Zimmerman calls them "conditionals of freedom" or "CFs." Strangely, according to Zimmerman, Molinists believe God does not actually cause these conditionals of freedom or CFs—rather, he discovers them:

> As a good libertarian, the Molinist must say the CFs are contingent. Were they not, then what I do in any given circumstances would be settled, ahead of time, as a matter of iron-clad necessity. Furthermore, as a good libertarian, the Molinist agrees God cannot just make free

---

[484] By "properly" I mean a choice that maximizes a creature's free will.

creatures freely do whatever he wants. But if God could choose which CFs were true, he could do exactly that; so, creaturely CFs must be contingent truths over which God has no control. According to Molinism, then, it is as though God 'wakes up' to find certain contingent things true—there is an independent source of contingent fact at work 'before' God has a chance to do anything about it. Although Molinists may reject such talk as tendentiously impious, there is an important (and potentially troubling) truth behind it. The Molinist conditionals really are supposed to be contingent truths *discovered* by God, not determined by him; and discovered 'before' he creates—at least, 'before' in the order of explanatory priority. Thus, according to Molinism, if God wants to create free creatures, he does face certain limitations—despite the fact that he never actually 'takes risks.' God might turn out to be incredibly *unlucky* in the CFs with which he is forced to make do; although he does not *take* risks, he is nevertheless *subject to* risk.[485]

This limitation is utterly untenable on its face. I cannot believe God could design human beings in such a way that the factors motivating them to make decisions were out of his control. It may be a feature of Molinism, but it is not a concept found in the CCM. The CCM holds that God, even prior to creation, designed his creatures, and part of that design were the parameters that governed how they would respond to circumstances. Accordingly, despite what Zimmerman said for Molinism, under the CCM the CFs are neither contingent nor deterministic. Accordingly, it would be easy for God to "settle" for what Zimmerman would do in any given circumstances, just as he said in the above quotation. Since God desires us to have freedom, to the maximum extent allowed by other constraints he has imposed, he merely brings us to the point where we can exercise our free choice. God knows (as I described above) what we will freely choose. So Zimmerman's objection to Molinism does not apply to the CCM.

---

[485] Zimmerman, Dean. "Yet Another Anti-Molinist Argument." In *Metaphysics and the Good: Themes From the Philosophy of Robert Merrihew Adams*. eds. Samuel Newlands & Larry M. Jorgensen. 2009. Oxford University Press, Oxford. p. 46.

E. Problem of Differentiating Between God's Perfect Will and His Permissive Will

The CCM puts the question of God's will in a different perspective from the normal view. To explain, we must differentiate between *three* categories of God's will. The first category can be described as God's *sovereign* or *hidden* will. It is "hidden" because we do not know what it is until it comes to pass. Since nothing comes to pass unless God ordains it, we can say that everything that comes to pass is in accord with God's sovereign will.

However, this description is not usually what is meant by his *perfect* will or *permissive* will. By "perfect" will we usually mean that which God prefers or that which gives God pleasure. Part of this preference is what is called God's *preceptive* will, which concerns all that he has commanded. We know his preceptive will because he has told us what to do, but God's mandates are only part of the matter. God also desires all to be saved. We know that is his desire because he said so.[486] His desire for all to be saved is part of his perfect will and could be termed his "revealed" will. Therefore, God's preceptive will together with his revealed will can be considered as comprising his perfect will.

Obviously, some outcomes that he desires are not necessarily decreed in his sovereign will. Again, universal salvation is a fitting example. He wishes all to be saved, but he has not decreed that all will be saved. In fact, we know full well that *not* all will be saved. This unfortunate fact is an example of God's "permissive" will. He permits some things that he does not desire.

With this understanding in mind, does the CCM distinguish between these three categories: sovereign (hidden) will, perfect (prescriptive, revealed) will, and permissive will? Let us consider sovereign will. God's sovereign will concerns all that will ultimately come to pass, which in the CCM consists of the contingency God has actually chosen. Because he has chosen an event to happen, ultimately, it is his will that it happen. God's choice of a specific contingency aptly expresses his sovereign or hidden will.

---

[486] 1 Timothy 2:4

God's perfect will (commands and desires) is known to us in the CCM in the same way that it is known in other models. We know what he commands and desires by his revelation, primarily in the Scriptures. We know his permissive will by observing what actually comes to pass, just as in other models. So the difference obtained by comparing his perfect will with actual events is what cries out for an explanation. Does the CCM shed any light? To reiterate, the CCM accepted as a given that the universe must bring glory to God. This criterion is primary. When considering a contingency, such as whether a person will choose to sin or not, the chosen contingency must bring glory to God. Naturally, God opposes sin. If God must choose between the two, one principle is clear. God will permit sin but only to preserve his glory. Fundamentally, God will not compromise where his glory is concerned:

> Isaiah 42:8 I am Yahweh, that is my name; I will not give my glory to another or my praise to idols.[487]

The chosen contingency will always show God's glory yet at the same time may allow sin if that is the best possible contingency. Some seem to have the idea that God's permissive will consists of everything he did not ordain but merely permitted. For example, consider a classic Reformed confession:

> The Second Helvetic Confession: 1566
> Finally, as often as God in Scripture is said or seems to do something evil, it is not thereby said that man does not do evil, but that God permits it and does not prevent it, according to his just judgment, who could prevent it if he wished, or because he turns man's evil into good. ... St. Augustine writes in his *Enchiridion*: "What happens contrary to his will occurs, in a wonderful and ineffable way, not apart from his will. For it would not happen if he did not allow it. And yet he does not allow it unwillingly but willingly." (Art. VIII)[488]

One gets the impression that these permitted events occur by the natural result of a mechanistic universe set in motion by God, so that

---

[487] (HCSB)

[488] Accessed 22 September 2012, from http://www.creeds.net/helvetic/index.htm.

he foreknows that they will occur. He allows them to occur, but he does not *cause* them to occur. Some say that Reformed theologians account for all of history and our exercise of volition, in two ways—as explained by Zimmerman:

> If determinism is true, God set up a chain of cause-and-effect starting as far back as the Big Bang, including a series of events that led inevitably to this decision. Or, even if he left the decision-making process 'indeterministic' from the point of view of natural laws; nevertheless, he may have determined its outcome, in advance, by divine decree.[489]

This impersonal determinism is not the view of the CCM. Although the CCM does agree that God designed the universe to operate with a definite and logical cause-and-effect which gives us a rational system within which to have our being. Under the CCM, God chose all that occurs. His choices do follow a causal chain of sequential events which may give the impression of an impersonal mechanism. The universe does operate by fixed laws, and God has even given a measure of autonomy to inanimate objects, such as our earth in its orbit around the sun. But nothing could be farther from the truth than the idea that evil might happen due to an impersonal mechanism. There is no impersonal cause. Our intensely personal God always chooses the best contingency and the one most perfectly pleasing to himself. Even if a contingency contains elements that he does not perfectly desire, he nevertheless chose that contingency. It is not correct to say, "he did not prevent it," because a positive choice is always required. Nothing happens because God passively did nothing to prevent it. Nothing happens as a result of some mechanical, impersonal consequence. Nothing happens unless God actively chooses it, or so holds the CCM.

7. IS THE CHOSEN CONTINGENCY MODEL TAUGHT IN SCRIPTURE?

We must recognize that the CCM involves decrees and knowledge possessed by God before the creation of the world, and so we cannot see

---

[489] Zimmerman, Dean. "Yet Another Anti-Molinist Argument." *op. cit.*, p. 36.

the CCM in action in the pages of Scripture when discussing things of this world. All that we can do is compare the model to what is taught in Scripture and see whether or not it is harmonious.

A. ELECTION

One of the difficult teachings of Scripture relates to the doctrine of election or the choice of God to save certain people. Let us consider three:

Acts 13:48. When the Gentiles heard this, they rejoiced and glorified the message of the Lord, and all who had been appointed to eternal life believed.[490]

Ephesians 1:4–6. For he chose us in him, before the foundation of the world, to be holy and blameless in his sight. In love he predestined us to be adopted through Jesus Christ for himself, according to his favor and will, to the praise of his glorious grace that he favored us with in the Beloved.[491]

Romans 8:28–30. And we know that in all things God works for the good of those who love him, who have been called according to his purpose. For those God foreknew he also predestined to be conformed to the image of his Son, that he might be the firstborn among many brothers and sisters. And those he predestined, he also called; those he called, he also justified; those he justified, he also glorified.[492]

There has been a diversity of opinion as to what these verses mean. Nearly everyone agrees there is a sense in which God chooses who will be saved, but there is no agreement as to exactly how it happens. Calvinists say God simply and unconditionally saves whom he wills. Arminians are of two minds on this issue: some say God looks into the future, sees who will accept salvation, and predestines those whom he has foreseen. Other Arminians see these verses as speaking of corporate election rather than

---

[490] (HCSB)

[491] (HCSB)

[492] (NIV)

the election of individuals. What, if anything, does the CCM contribute to this conversation?

First, I should say the idea that these verses are speaking only of corporate election is unpersuasive. That is not to say there is no idea of corporate election present, but there must be individual election in order for corporate election to be realized. Also, Scripture talks about foreknowing *people*, not facts about people. So the ideas of Arminianism seem to have a clear difficulty. On the other hand, though Calvinism does seem to understand these verses in their most natural sense, it is this precise sense that is in the most tension with the idea that salvation is conditioned on belief.

How does the CCM reconcile the idea that God saves those who believe with the idea that he chose them before the foundation of the world? Let us consider John 1: 12–13:

> But to all who did receive him, he gave them the right to be children of God, to those who believe in his name, who were born, not of blood, or of the will of the flesh, or of the will of man, but of God.[493]

Let us be clear. We simply must fairly deal with the idea that salvation comes to those who believe in his name; those who receive him. At the same time, they are born through and by the will of God. God chose them before the foundation of the world. The CCM resolves the matter: not by seeing this election as corporate; not by God seeing who would believe (as if there is only one future); and not by an unconditional election prior to belief. The CCM sees God actively choosing an alternative future where he provides sufficient grace for a person to be able to choose God but he does not compel choice. If a person freely chooses to follow Christ in a contingent future that satisfies the purposes of God, then God will choose that future. Otherwise, not. So it is true to say that a person freely chooses to receive Christ. It is also true that God chose that person before the foundation of the world. It is true that all who are appointed to eternal life will believe. It is also true that all who believe will have eternal life, but it is not true to think of God's choice as passive—it was

[493] (HCSB)

interactive to the highest degree. Corporate election is also true, but corporate election is merely a comprehensive view of what God does in electing individuals.

B. FINAL JUDGMENT

Matthew 25:41 Then he will also say to those on the left, "Depart from me, you who are cursed, into the eternal fire prepared for the devil and his angels."[494]

2 Corinthians 5:10 For we must all appear before the judgment seat of Christ, so that each of us may receive what is due to us for the things done while in the body, whether good or bad.[495]

2 Peter 3:9 The Lord does not delay his promise, as some understand delay, but is patient with you, not wanting any to perish but all to come to repentance.[496]

This teaching on the final judgment is the other side of the coin. How do we account for those who are cast into the lake of fire? Clearly, these are the ones who did not accept Christ as Savior. Yet we also see that God does not want any to perish. The Scriptures are clear that God carefully leads us to repentance:

Romans 2:4 Or do you despise the riches of his kindness, restraint, and patience, not recognizing that God's kindness is intended to lead you to repentance?[497]

The CCM understands that salvation is a process. God leads us to repentance and desires all to repent and be saved, but some do not believe. Why is that? The CCM sees certain contingencies as *forensic*—that is, they have to do with God's justice. Some contingencies may not affect our eternal destiny, as, for example, the brand of toothpaste we choose. Some

---

[494] (HCSB)
[495] (NIV)
[496] (HCSB)
[497] (HCSB)

decisions mold our character and gain us reward in heaven or punishment in hell. What ultimately causes us to choose to become a child of God?

Let us be clear. This is the sticking point between the conflicting models. Arminianism, Calvinism, Molinism view this question differently. Does the CCM have anything to add to the conversation?

Of course, ultimately, we must say that God is the cause of our deciding to choose to believe or not. This conclusion follows because God is the ultimate source of everything and also partly because a person's will is not truly free in a fallen world. As causal agents, we human beings do make choices, and we are held accountable for them. God, of course, makes allowances for the degree to which we can be held accountable for our choices.[498] In the CCM, he brings circumstances into our lives to lead us to repentance. He progressively gives us grace to remove the slavery to sin so that we can choose something other than sin. He brings light into our lives and encourages us to move toward the light. Undergirding these choices is our character, which is due in part to our innate characteristics and in part to the choices that we have made. Some of us are "hard soil people" and have immense difficulty in hearing the Word of God. Some of us have made choices that harden us against the Holy Spirit's leading. He is leading us to repentance, but there are some who will not repent.

God will bring us to the point where we can make a choice. He will chose a contingency that will best demonstrate his mercy, justice and other qualities. Some people, due in part to who they are, will not chose life. If there is no contingency where they choose life without undue compulsion, then they will be lost. God is not willing that any should perish. He is patient, but he is also unwilling to compromise his own perfect character.

It will do no good to say: "Yes, I have a hard heart. But you made me that way, God. So it was your fault that I would not repent." That will not work. Yes, in a sense, God is ultimately responsible for making persons the way they are. Despite that, people will be held accountable for their choices. We know God will not be unjust. When the day of judgment

---

[498] Romans 2: 15–16

comes and all the forensic contingencies are examined, the will of every person will be found to have been either:

- free enough to make a valid choice, so they can be held accountable and fall under judgment or
- not capable of making a valid choice, so they are not accountable.[499]

Under the CCM, God knew who would be saved and who would be lost before the foundation of the world. He wanted to demonstrate his justice and his other attributes. He would give everyone a fair opportunity to be saved. That opportunity would derive from the death of Jesus on the Cross which was also planned from before the foundation of the world.

8. CONCLUSION

The CCM is not complicated. It simply affirms that God chose our universe and the future that would occur, before the foundation of the world. It is a world that best accomplishes God's purposes; the one which best fulfills God's design criteria. We can believe, without any doubt, that no matter what occurs in our life, God chose the future for us that would work out to be the best in the end.[500] This world is, truly, the "best of all possible worlds."

DISCUSSION QUESTIONS

1. How is the chosen contingency model different from Molinism?

2. Does the model resolve the tension between God's sovereignty and a person's freedom?

3. Do you believe God is the ultimate cause of everything in the universe? How, then, do you explain the presence of sin? Does the chosen contingency model help you answer?

4. Do you object to the idea that not all choices in life are completely free?

5. How can a loving God cast human beings into the lake of fire?

---

[499] This would normally include (but not be limited to) children or mentally retarded ("backward") people. See 2 Samuel 12:23.

[500] See Romans 8:28. This promise particularly applies to Christians.

SCRIPTURE INDEX
†

†

INDEX

†

†

IF GOD BE FOR US, WHO CAN BE AGAINST US?

Romans 8:31b

†